MERCOSUR

MERCOSUR

The Common Market of the Southern Cone

Rafael A. Porrata-Doria, Jr.

CAROLINA ACADEMIC PRESS
Durham, North Carolina

Library of Congress Cataloging-in-Publication Data

Porrata-Doria, Rafael A.
MERCOSUR : the common market of the southern cone / By Rafael A.
Porrata-Doria, Jr.
    p. cm. -- (Carolina Academic Press studies on globalization and society)
    ISBN 1-59460-010-4 (alk. paper)
1. MERCOSUR (Organization) 2. Southern Cone of South America--
Economic integration. I. Title. II. Series.

    KH736.M47P67 2005
    337.1'8--dc22

                                     2005001655

Carolina Academic Press
700 Kent Street
Durham, NC 27701
Telephone (919) 489-7486
Fax (919) 493-5668
www.cap-press.com

Printed in the United States of America

*This book is dedicated to my wife, Christie
and my children Rafael and Clara,
whose love and support makes everything possible.*

Contents

Acknowledgments

The author gratefully acknowledges the helpful comments of Marina Angel, Jeffrey Dunoff and Henry Richardson. He also particularly appreciates the outstanding efforts of his principal research assistant, Julie Liebenberg, Temple Law School Class of 2004 and of his current research assistant, Suzette Sanders, Temple Law School Class of 2005.

The information in this book is current as of February of 2004.

MERCOSUR

Introduction

MERCOSUR, the "Common Market of the Southern Cone," was created in March of 1990 by the Treaty of Asunción and was meant to create a common market among its four signatories (Argentina, Brazil, Paraguay and Uruguay) by December 31, 1994.[1] This common market would include the graduated elimination of all customs duties among its signatories,[2] the creation of a common external tariff and the adoption of a common trade policy,[3] and the harmonization of economic policies.[4] The Treaty of Asunción, and its supplementary Ouro Preto Protocol,[5] created a number of institutions to assist in the implementation of these goals.[6]

Since its founding in 1990, MERCOSUR has generated many major achievements, more than its predecessor, the Latin American Free Trade Association ("LAFTA")[7] or any other economic integration organization in Latin America. It has formalized and expanded cooperation and trading relationships among Brazil, Argentina, Paraguay and Uruguay and developed these relationships into a viable and vibrant economic integration organization. For a substantial period of time, its members enjoyed unprecedented expanded trade and greater prosperity. Trade and exports among its member states has increased exponentially.[8] Indeed, intra-MERCOSUR trade increased 314 per-

---

1. Treaty of Asunción Establishing the Common Market of the Southern Cone, March 26, 1991, Arg.-Braz.-Uru.-Para., 30 I.L.M.1041 at Art. 1 (hereinafter, "Asunción").

2. Asunción, *supra* note 1 at Art. 5(a) and Annex I (7).

3. *Id.* at Arts. 1 and 5(c).

4. *Id.* at Art. 2, 5(b).

5. Protocolo Adicional al Tratado de Asunción sobre la Estructura Institucional del MERCOSUR-Protocolo de Ouro Preto (Dec. 17, 1994), *available at* http:www.sice.oas.org/trade/mrcsr/ourop (hereinafter, "Ouro Preto").

6. *See supra* notes 1, 5 and accompanying text.

7. *"Treaty Establishing a Free Trade Area and Instituting the Latin American Free Trade Association"*, February 18, 1960 Inter-American Institute of International Legal Studies, INSTRUMENTS OF ECONOMIC INTEGRATION, (Montevideo, Uruguay), reproduced in LATIN AMERICA AND IN THE CARIBBEAN, VOLUME I (New York, Oceana Publications 1975) at 3 (hereinafter, "1960 Treaty").

8. Rona Cohen and Ian McCluskey, *Keep it in the Neighborhood Forget NAFTA— South America is Busy Building its own Powerful Trading Block, Called MERCOSUR*, TIME

cent, to $17.1 billion, during the period 1990–1996,[9] and reached a high of $20.5 billion in 1997 and 1998.[10] It became the third largest trading block in the world, after NAFTA and the European Union.[11]

Institutionally, MERCOSUR has agreed on a common external tariff covering 85% of imports currently being traded by its members[12] and reached agreement on a substantial number of trade matters. It has adopted many directives and resolutions seeking to eliminate barriers to free trade and to harmonize the legal and regulatory systems of the member states, as well as form the basis of a system of community law.[13] It has generated a substantial amount of excitement among the elites of its members states, who now seem to view the idea of economic integration as both feasible and desirable. It acquired two additional members, Bolivia and Chile, in 1996,[14] and entered into an extensive and substantial cooperative relationship with the European Union, and with a number of other organizations and countries.[15] It has an agenda for the future and is working towards its implementation.[16] Commentators in the member states had been talking about more integration, macroeconomic policy harmonization, and even a single currency.[17]

MAG., Aug. 26, 1996, *available at* 1996 WL 10669619.[hereinafter "Keep it in the Neighborhood"].

9. "International Agreements: US Exports to MERCOSUR Members Tripled in 1990–1996, ITC Paper Says," 15 *International Trade Reporter* (BNA)1432 (August 19, 1998).

10. "International Agreements: MERCOSUR Trade Volume Seen Rebounding in 2000,"17 *International Trade Reporter* (BNA) 1454 (September 21, 2000).

11. *Brazil and Argentina, Long Rivals, Move Closer*, WALL ST. J., Nov. 12, 1998 at A25 (hereinafter, "*Rivals*").

12. Antoni Estevadeordal and Ekaternia Krivonos, NEGOTIATING MARKET ACCESS BETWEEN THE EUROPEAN UNION AND MERCOSUR: ISSUES AND PROSPECTS. Occasional Paper 7 (Dec. 2000) INTAL/ITD at 3 (hereinafter, "Negotiating Market Access").

13. *Directives available at* http://www.mercosur.org.uy/espanol/snor/normativa/directivas/.

14. The agreement with Chile was executed on June 26, 1996 at San Luis, Argentina. *Acuerdo de Complementación Económica Mercosur-Chile, ACE # 35* (6/25/96) (*available at* http://www.sice.oas.org/trade/msch/ACUEDO.asp) (hereinafter, "Chile Agreement"). *Acuerdo de Complementación Económica Mercosur-Bolivia, ACE #36* (12/17/96) (*available at* http://www.sice.oas.org/trade/mrcsbo/MERBO1_S.asp) (hereinafter, "Bolivia Agreement").

15. *See infra* Chptr. 7 notes 5–58, 83–114 and accompanying text.

16. *See* Comunicado del 15 de Diciembre de 2000, Florianópolis *available at* http://www.mercosur.org.uy/espanol/snor/varios/com0200.htm at paragraph 9 (hereinafter, "Comunicado de Florianópolis"); Comunicado del 30 de Junio de 2000, Buenos Aires, (hereinafter, "Comunicado de Buenos Aires"). Comunicado del 8 de Diciembre de 1999, Montevideo, *available at* http://www.mercosur.org.uy/espanol/snor/varios/com 0299.htm at paragraph 11 (hereinafter, "Comunicado de Montevideo").

17. *See* Florianópolis, *supra* note 16; International Agreements: Argentine President Carlos Menem Urges MERCOSUR Work Towards Monetary Union,"15 *International Trade Reporter* (BNA) 1314 (July 29, 1998); "International Agreements: Argentina's

This optimistic environment has changed somewhat since 1999. Severe economic difficulties since 1999, first in Brazil, then in Argentina and the other member states, have had a dramatic effect on MERCOSUR and its development. The severe economic downturn in the region still continues, however, and has had a highly detrimental impact on regional trade.[18]

MERCOSUR now also faces a hemispheric competitor, the United States sponsored Free Trade Area of the Americas ("FTAA"), a multilateral, comprehensive free trade agreement treaty to be entered into among the 34 nations that attended the Miami Summit.[19] Negotiations on a draft FTAA agreement started in June of 1998[20] and are meant to be concluded no later than January of 2005, with the Treaty coming into effect no later than December of 2005.[21]

Recent interactions between Brazil and Argentina indicate renewed vitality in MERCOSUR.[22] The MERCOSUR presidents in July of 2002 reaffirmed their commitment to "the achievement of the objectives of The Treaty of Asunción" despite the member states' current economic difficulties.[23] Furthermore, the new presidents of Argentina and Brazil, meeting in Brasilia on June 11, 2003, again reaffirmed their commitment to the revitalization and expansion of MERCOSUR and, as part of this process, pledged to create a MERCOSUR parliament and a joint monetary institute that would begin the process of achieving a common currency.[24] They have also pledged not to sign any individual

Menem to Propose Single Currency for MERCOSUR," 15 *International Trade Reporter* (BNA) 422 (March 11, 1998).

18. *See* Larry Rohter, *Argentina in Scramble to Bolster Peso, Again,* THE NEW YORK TIMES, July 10, 2002, at W1.

19. *Id.* Summit of the Americas, Fourth Trade Ministerial, San José, Costa Rica (March 19th, 1998), Joint Declaration (hereinafter, "San José Declaration"), *available at* http://www.alca-ftaa.org/ministerials/denver_e.asp at paragraphs 1–2.

20. Second Summit of the Americas, Plan of Action (hereinafter, "Second Plan of Action"), *available at* http.www.sice.oas.org/FTAA/santiago/sapoa_el.asp at par. III.A.1.

21. Free Trade Area of the Americas, Sixth Meeting of Ministers of Trade of the Hemisphere, Ministerial Declaration, Buenos Aires, Argentina (April 7, 2001) *available at* http://www.alca.ftaa.org/ministerials/BAmin_e.asp (hereinafter, "Buenos Aires Declaration") at paragraph 3.

22. Louis Uchitelle, *Argentina's Woes May Strengthen its Ties to Brazil,* THE NEW YORK TIMES, January 10, 2002, at C1.

23. *See* Comunicado July 2002, *infra* Chptr. 7 note 52 at par. 3.

24. Kevin Hall, *Argentina, Brazil put U.S. Bid for Trade Zone on Back Burner,* PHILADELPHIA INQUIRER, June 12, 2003 at A24; Terry Wade, *Latin Trade Block Flexes its Muscle,* THE WALL STREET JOURNAL, June 16, 2003 at A13; Eleonora Gosman, *Kirchner y Lula se Juraron Fidelidad para Negociar Juntos ante el ALCA,* CLARIN (Buenos Aires, Argentina), June 12, 2003, *available at* http://www.clarincom/diario/hoy/p-00601.htm, *Lula y Kirchner Pretenden Ampliar el Bloque,* EL PAIS (Montevideo, Uruguay), June 11, 2003, *available at* http://www.diarioelpais.com/03/06/11/ultimo_44810.asp, *Kirchner y Lula quieren Hacer Realidad la Unión del MERCOSUR,* NOTICIAS (Asunción, Paraguay), *available at* http://www.diarionoticias.com.py/20030612/internacionales-nota1.php; *Kirchner y Lula*

free trade area agreements with the United States and to participate as a group in the forthcoming Free Trade Area of the Americas negotiations[25] and have engaged in trade liberalization negotiations with a number of countries.[26]

Regardless of the region's continuing economic difficulties and potential competition from another organization, MERCOSUR's members apparently remain committed to the concept of regional economic integration in general and to the maintenance and development of MERCOSUR in particular. Indeed, regional trade organizations like MERCOSUR have emerged as a driving force in the global economy.[27] MERCOSUR is here to stay and continues to be a critical factor in Latin American economic and trade policy. Accordingly, knowledge of MERCOSUR and its legal system are still essential to the serious student of international trade law.

This book, relying substantially on primary MERCOSUR materials in Spanish and Portuguese, is the first comprehensive description of MERCOSUR, its history, institutions and legal system, in the English language and seeks to provide its readers with information essential to the understanding of MERCOSUR and its legal system. Accordingly, Chapter I of this work considers some of the history of integration in Latin America and the direct antecedents to MERCOSUR. Chapter II then generally describes the Treaty of Asuncíon and describes and evaluates MERCOSUR's institutions. Chapter III explores MERCOSUR's dispute resolution mechanisms and institutions. Chapter IV addresses the MERCOSUR trade regulation system, including is trade liberation program, common external tariff, rules of origin, and safeguard measures regime clause. Chapter V then considers and evaluates a sample of five of the major types of legal norms through which MERCOSUR intends to implement the common market: its "community law." Chapter VI examines the MERCOSUR's associate member relationships with Bolivia and Chile. Chapter VII considers MERCOSUR's relationship with the European Union and its negotiations and agreements with other entities and countries. Chapter VIII will briefly discuss and evaluate MERCOSUR's recent relaunching attempt. Several appendices will include MERCOSUR's basic treaty documents.

---

llamaron a 'la Integración Regional,' CLARIN (Buenos Aires, Argentina), June 11, 2003, *available at* http://www.elclarin.com/diario/2003/06/11/um/m-5731.33.htm.

25. *Id.*

26. *See infra* Chapter VII.

27. Guy de Jonquieres, *Popular Trend is at Odds with Global Free Trade: Regional Trade Agreements,* THE FINANCIAL TIMES (London), November 30, 2001; Guy de Jonquieres, *Trading Nations Agree Deals Two by Two: Bilateralism and Regionalism,* THE FINANCIAL TIMES (London), October 16, 2001.

Chapter 1

Prolegomenon:
The Road to MERCOSUR

This chapter broadly describes some of MERCOSUR's historical antecedents. It first briefly sketches the spearhead of the modern Latin American integration effort: the import substitution and integration theories and initiatives of the United Nations Commission for Latin America ("ECLA") and its long time director, Argentine economist Raúl Prebisch. It then sets forth the first Latin American effort to implement these theories: the Latin American Free Trade Association ("LAFTA") and analyzes the reasons for the failure of this organization. It then briefly describes LAFTA's successor, the Latin American Integration Association. ("ALADI"), which essentially allows its members to strike their own "integration deals."

The second part of this chapter examines the history of one such deal: the integration efforts of the MERCOSUR four (Argentina, Brazil, Paraguay and Uruguay), which culminated in the creation of MERCOSUR. It starts by examining the premise that, because of the unusually high degree of complementarity, both economic and otherwise, of these countries, some kind of economic integration effort (an integration "marriage") was almost inevitable. It then describes the economic integration initiatives among them that led to the creation of MERCOSUR.

A. ECLA and Import Substitution

In order to place the development of MERCOSUR in context, it is first necessary to understand modern Latin American integration efforts, which derive from the the import substitution and integration theories and initiatives of ECLA and its long time director, Argentine economist Raúl Prebisch. These theories and initiatives led to the creation of LAFTA, the principal predecessor of MERCOSUR.

The consensus seems to be that the modern attempts at Latin American economic integration were spearheaded during the 1950s and 1960s by the United Nation's Economic Commission for Latin America ("ECLA") and its long time director, Argentine economist Raúl Prebisch.[1] To Prebisch, countries which have reached a high degree of industrialization formed the center of the world economy. All countries not in the center were in the periphery. They produced a large number of finished goods, which were then exported to the rest of the world. These countries were also consumers of primary goods (raw materials used in industrial production or food), which formed the principal exports of non-industrialized countries—those in the periphery of the world economy.[2] Increases in technology, development of new products and increases in productivity lowered the production costs and increased the demand for the finished goods produced by the center countries. These goods were exported to the countries of the periphery, which use their scarce capital and foreign exchange to pay for them.[3]

The countries of the periphery found themselves in a difficult position: technological innovation and efficiency did not affect the production of primary goods as it did that of industrial goods. Demand and prices of primary products were far more volatile than those of finished products and technical innovation may eliminate their market completely. Shortages of capital prevented the formation of new industries and competition from the big multinational enterprises destroyed those few industries that have been formed in the periphery.[4] The end result of this process is that the countries of the center stay and become richer and richer, and those countries in the periphery will stay poor.

What, then was the solution? The countries of the periphery must engage in a policy of industrial development managed by the state (the only actor in the countries of the periphery that is powerful, technically competent and "objective" enough to implement such a policy), based on the substitution of imports of finished goods.[5] Such a policy would have a number of characteristics, which would include, first of all, a limitation on the growth or a reduction in imports of finished goods from the countries of the center.[6] Furthermore, this

---

1. Juan Lanus, INTEGRACIÓN ECONÓMICA DE AMÉRICA LATINA (Buenos Aires 1973), at 24–25 (hereinafter, "Lanus"); Milenky, THE POLITICS OF REGIONAL INTEGRATION IN LATIN AMERICA: THE LAFTA (New York 1973) at 11–12 (hereinafter, "Milenky"); F. John Mathis, ECONOMIC INTEGRATION IN LATIN AMERICA: THE PROGRESS AND PROBLEMS OF LAFTA, (Austin, 1969) (hereinafter, "Mathis") at 9–10; Juan Mario Vacchino, INTEGRACION LATINOAMERICANA: DE LA ALALC A LA ALADI (Buenos Aires, Ediciones Depalma 1983) (hereinafter, "Vacchino") at 27.

2. United Nations Economic Commission for Latin America, THE ECONOMIC DEVELOPMENT OF LATIN AMERICA AND ITS PRINCIPAL PROBLEMS, (New York, 1950) (hereinafter, "ECLA Report") at 8.

3. ECLA Report, *supra* note 2, at 16–18.

4. *Id.* at 13–14, 37.

5. *Id.* at 6, 15.

6. *Id.* at 47.

policy must encourage the creation of new industries producing previously imported goods for which there is a local demand. These industries would be financed by savings achieved from the limitation of imports, government expenditures and funds from international organizations.[7] Lastly, this policy must protect these infant industries from foreign competition through the use of foreign investment limitations, subsidies, tariffs and similar devices.[8]

Given the small size of most of the countries in Latin America, however, economic development in Latin America as anticipated by ECLA would require economic integration on a regional scale. This would be necessary in order to attract capital and technology to a larger market, which would enable the producers of these newly manufactured products to be efficient. This process of economic integration should be a gradual one, and should culminate in a common market.[9]

ECLA was highly instrumental (and, indeed, spearheaded the process) in the creation of a Latin American common market. Its studies on interregional trade and regional integration during the 1950's set the stage for discussions regarding the possibility of the establishment of a Latin American common market or another form of regional economic cooperation.[10]

The ECLA Trade Committee was created in 1956 to analyze and recommend solutions to problems arising out of interregional trade. At its economic conference in Buenos Aires in 1959, the possibility of a common market or free trade zone was discussed and its participants agreed on the desirability of a common market. ECLA then established a Working Group on the Latin American Common Market, which first met in Santiago, Chile in 1958. This Working Group presented a proposal for a Latin American Common Market to an ECLA conference in Panama City in May of 1959.[11] At this conference the ECLA draft proposal was extensively discussed and these discussions were followed by intensive negotiations among the governments in the region. These discussions and negotiations resulted in 1960 in the execution of the Treaty of Montevideo, which created LAFTA.[12]

7. *Id.* at 6, 56–57.

8. *Id.* at 53.

9. ECLA Report, *supra* note 2 at 6–7; Vacchino, *supra* note 28, at 34–36; Raúl Prebisch, "*Cinco Etapas de mi Pensamiento sobre el Desarrollo*," L. El Trimestre Economico (Mexico, Fondo de Cultura Económica, Abril–Junio 1983) at 1077, 1084 (hereinafter, "Prebisch"); Robert J. Radway, "*The Next Decade in Latin America: Anticipating the Future from the Past*,"13 Case W. Res.J.Intl.L. 3, 13 (1981) (hereinafter, "Radway"); Michael S. Wionczek, Latin American Economic Integration (New York, Praeger 1966)at 74 (hereinafter, "Wionczek").

10. Wionczek, *supra* note 9, at 74.

11. *Id.* at 75.

12. 1960 Treaty, *supra* Intro. note 7 at Art. 3.

B. LAFTA: The Great Leap Forward

LAFTA was the first effort to implement ECLA's integration recommendations and create a generalized economic integration organization. Study of its mission, structure and failure provided, I believe, critical guidance for MERCOSUR's founders. It was a road map of how *NOT* to create an economic integration organization or a common market.

The Treaty of Montevideo created a Latin American Free Trade Association, which was to be brought into full operation and effect within 12 years of its creation.[13] The goal of the LAFTA was to:

"Gradually eliminate, in respect of substantially all their reciprocal trade, such duties, charges and restrictions as may be applied to imports of goods originating in the territory of any contracting Party."[14]

This gradual elimination was to be achieved through a complex series of negotiations, which included the National Schedules, the Common Schedule, Sectoral Agreements, and Agricultural Agreements.[15] Each member state in LAFTA would enjoy most favored nation treatment, where any benefit given by a member state to any third country was to be automatically and immediately extended to all other member states.[16]

These extensive tariff reductions were subject to two major exceptions. The first allowed member states to, on a provisional basis, impose nondiscriminatory restrictions on imports, if these imports had, or were likely to have, serious repercussions on specific productive activities "of vital importance to the national economy"; or to extend any measures intended to correct an unfavorable balance of payments to trade in the area.[17] The second exception dealt with countries determined to be "at a relatively less advanced state of economic

---

13. 1960 Treaty, *supra* Intro. note 7 at Art. 2.

14. *Id.* at Art. 3

15. In the negotiations involving the National Schedules, each member state, on an annual basis, agreed to grant to the other member states reductions in duties equivalent to at least 8% of the weighted average of the duties and charges it applied to third countries. Similarly, in the Common Schedule negotiations, all the member states would, on a triennial basis, collectively agree to reduce duties on products which constituted no less than 25% of the trade among them. Sectoral agreements would be the product of negotiations by the member states involving individual industrial sectors. The goal of these agreements were the "progressively closer coordination of the corresponding industrialization policies" of each such industrial sector. Lastly, agricultural agreements sought the coordination of member states' agricultural development and agricultural trade policies, with a view to efficient utilization of resources, guaranteeing supplies to consumers and raising the standard of living of the rural population, all without disrupting "the regular productive activities" of each member state.1960 Treaty, *supra* Intro. note 7 at Art. 2-7, 16-17, 27.

16. *Id.* at Art. 14.

17. *Id.* at Art. 23–24.

development" than the other member states. These states would be given advantages not extended to other member states to encourage the introduction or expansion of particular productive activities. These states would also have the ability to implement the treaty's tariff reduction problem under more favorable conditions, to adopt appropriate measures to correct an unfavorable balance of payments, and to establish non discriminatory protective measures to protect products vital to its economies. These member states were also entitled to receive technical or financial support for development from LAFTA and from the other member states.[18]

The Treaty created two institutions to manage LAFTA: The Conference and the Standing Executive Committee.[19] The Conference was the supreme decision making body of the organization, with delegations from all the member states that met yearly. Quorum for meetings of the Conference was 2/3 of the member states and each delegation had one vote. Decisions had to be adopted by a 2/3 majority of all the member state delegations, with no negative votes. In essence, then, decisions of the Conference were by consensus.[20] The Standing Executive Committee (led by an Executive Secretary and with a very small staff) was responsible for supervising the implementation of the Conference's decisions. It was not very effective.[21]

LAFTA was not very successful. One basic problem was that the organization was meant to supervise the integration of trade in the region and there was hardly any trade to integrate.[22] Negotiations for trade concessions (to be in the National and Common Schedules) began, and most of the trade concessions made by the member states were made in the first two to four years of LAFTA's existence. Indeed, 73.4% of *all* trade concessions made by LAFTA member states during its existence were made between 1962 and 1964.[23] Many of these concessions were not used or were given for products not traded among the member states. Accordingly, most of these concessions did not reflect goods *actually* traded among the LAFTA member states.[24]

The first crisis for LAFTA arose in 1963 over the issue of reciprocity.[25] Some member states, chiefly Argentina, Brazil and Mexico, felt that reciprocity sim-

---

18. *Id.* at Art. 32. Bolivia and Paraguay were the two member states given this status. *See* Protocol V.

19. *Id.* at Art. 33.

20. *Id.* at Arts. 34–36.

21. *Id.* at Arts. 39–42; Milenky, *supra* note 1, at 27–28.

22. Mathis, *supra* note 1, at 17–18.

23. Vacchino, *supra* note 1, at 86.

24. *Id.* at 78.

25. Milenky, *supra* note 1, at 72–74. A key concept in the Treaty of Montevideo was that of reciprocity: all concessions and tariff reductions granted by one member state would apply to all other member states. 1960 Treaty, *supra* Intro. note 7, and Arts. 10 and 13.

ply meant that all tariff reductions and concessions given by a member state would apply to all. Other states disagreed with this interpretation.[26] To them, the key concept behind LAFTA was that, if tariffs among the member states were lowered, the flow of trade among those countries would increase.[27] Unfortunately, the experience of the first three years of LAFTA did not agree with this expectation. Some member states, such as Chile, Colombia and Peru, found themselves with trade deficits, rather than increased trade. Others, such as Ecuador and Paraguay,[28] felt that, because they were at a much lower stage of development than other states in the region, they were at a permanent disadvantage and simply could not compete unless they received some compensation and assistance.[29] They demanded exemptions, compensation and assistance so that they could protect their own infant industries from regional competition and build their economic and industrial infrastructure. These demands met with substantial opposition from other member states, and LAFTA did not really resolve the dispute.[30]

The issue behind this dispute was the issue of whether LAFTA should be an organization whose sole purpose is trade liberalization through the elimination of tariffs and trade restrictions, or whether it should also be an "economic development" organization. The solution to this issue was highly problematic. The more LAFTA and its member states "liberalized trade" (by reducing tariffs and trade restrictions) the more the member states with developed economies and export industries would benefit. The smaller and less economically developed member states would keep falling behind, just as Professor Prebisch described. The solution, according to Professor Prebisch, would be substantial protection and economic assistance. The problem was neither LAFTA nor its member states had the economic resources to provide this assistance. Furthermore, many of the wealthier member states balked at the prospect of providing this assistance.[31] Lastly, the more developed states would balk at protection measures which would have the effect of limiting their own exports within the region.

This fundamental difference of opinion on the purpose and mission of the Treaty of Montevideo and LAFTA continued to fester. By 1966–67, the lesser developed member states in LAFTA were still suffering trade deficits and continually complained of unfair treatment. They then refused to cooperate in the negotiations on new trade concessions unless they received more aid and con-

---

26. *Id.* at 73.

27. *Id.* at 72–74; Vacchino, *supra* note 1, at 59.

28. Both these countries had been declared countries at a relatively less advanced stage of economic development in accordance with Article 32 of the Treaty of Montevideo. Wionczek, *supra* note 9 at 113, Vacchino, *supra* note 1, at 77.

29. Vacchino, *supra* note 1, at 72, 73, 75.

30. *Id.* at 79, Milenky, *supra* note 1, at 79.

31. *Id.*

cessions. The more developed countries by now were extremely reluctant to keep pouring scarce resources into other countries' economic development. Cooperation broke down and new negotiations produced few concessions.[32] In 1971, for example, only 38 concessions were granted, compared to 7593 in 1961–1962.[33] The organization floundered. Finally, in August of 1980, a New Treaty of Montevideo[34] abolished LAFTA and replaced it with a new and different organization.[35]

LAFTA was one of the first modern attempts at Latin American economic integration and it appears to have failed miserably. It never met any of its ambitious goals and was essentially disbanded by consensus after twenty years. Why did it fail?

There are several answers to this question, all of which are relevant to any attempt at Latin American economic integration. First, the LAFTA member states did not have a common understanding of the purposes of the treaty they were entering into. There was no consensus on the purpose and mission of LAFTA. The more developed, exporting countries saw the purpose and mission of the facilitation of their exports by means of the liberalization of trade regulation. Others, no doubt influenced by Professor Prebisch's views on economic development, saw "more economic development" as the principal purpose of LAFTA, with the liberalization of trade regulation as only a part of a "package" which would also include the economic aid for infrastructure and industrial development, and protection for these infant industries. These goals are contradictory. On the one hand, preferences, restricted markets and other measures "for the creation and protection of infant industries" form a key concept of "economic development" as understood by ECLA's import substitution theory. Free trade and the elimination of trade restrictions are simply not compatible with the import substitution theory. It was impossible to engage in "import substitution style" economic development and multilateral trade liberalization at the same time. In the end, neither was accomplished.

Secondly, LAFTA could not be successful because it had nothing to build on. Its principal purpose seemed to be to integrate regional trade by trade liberalization. In fact, there was very little regional trade in Latin America to be liberalized. In most cases, trade had to be created, not facilitated. As the lesser developed members of LAFTA argued, tariff reductions alone do not create trade. It

---

32. It did not help that, by 1967, trade reductions on all of the less significant and controversial items had been negotiated. Milenky, *supra* note 1 at 98; Radway, *supra* note 9, at 13.

33. Milenky, *supra* note 1, at 70–71.

34. Treaty of Montevideo establishing the Latin American Integration Association, 20 I.L.M. 672 (1981) (hereinafter, "ALADI Treaty").

35. This organization was named the "Latin American Integration Association", and will hereinafter be referred to as "ALADI" (its acronym in the Spanish language).

was not operating to formalize and harmonize an existing state of affairs but was trying to bring about and regulate a state of affairs that did not exist.

Third, the LAFTA treaty framework was unworkable. It provided for a complicated series of negotiations and agreements in an extremely short period of time. Completing these negotiations in the time set forth for them would have been extremely hard to do in the best of times, with all the parties acting by consensus. As we have seen, this was not the case.[36] Since these negotiations and agreements were interrelated in the treaty, the failure of any of them would affect the others. This framework was set for failure.

Fourth, LAFTA did not have a strong and activist institutional infrastructure. Its executive institution had no funds, no personnel and no real power. Its member states had fundamental disagreements its purpose and mission and could not agree on much. A strong and well organized administrative body, such as the European Commission, could have served as a powerful engine for the process of integration, working with the member states to obtain a consensus on what the mission and purposes of the organization were and preparing plans and mechanisms to achieve them. LAFTA, unfortunately, had no such engines.

C. Let a Hundred Flowers Bloom: ALADI

LAFTA's failure did not destroy the desire for economic integration among its members. ALADI, the organization created to replace LAFTA, seeks to continue the economic integration ideal in a more modest scale. Its specific authorization for its members to reach individual economic integration agreements among themselves provided the legal basis and framework for the MERCOSUR agreement.

ALADI, seems to have had a much more modest general purpose than its predecessor. It was to:

> "develop...the promotion and regulation of reciprocal commerce, economic complementation, and the development of systems of economic cooperation which stimulate the expansion of the markets."[37]

---

36. A more effective process would have been the prior agreement by the parties on certain automatic tariff reductions which would then be included in the treaty and would not require further agreement to implement. Maria Haines-Ferrari, "MERCOSUR: A NEW MODEL OF LATIN AMERICAN ECONOMIC INTEGRATION?" 25 CASE.W. RES. J. INT'L L. 413, 417 (1993). As we shall see below, this is the process adopted by MERCOSUR.

37. ALADI Treaty, *supra* note 34, at Art. 2. Although Art. 3(b) of the ALADI Treaty refers to the concept of "convergence" ("the progressive multilateralization of agreements of partial scope through periodic negotiations among the member countries, as a function of establishing the Latin American Common Market") as one of the principles to be used to achieve ALADI's organizational purpose, the establishment of a Latin American common

The cumbersome system of negotiations, leading to the creation of a common market, found in LAFTA, was gone. Indeed, the ALADI treaty stresses "pluralism," "flexibility," "differential treatment and multiplicity" as equally important principles to apply to the process of Latin American integration.[38]

The objectives of ALADI were to be achieved through the use of three mechanisms: a regional tariff preference,[39] agreements of regional scope (in which all member states participate)[40] and partial scope agreements.[41] Partial scope agreements are those in which all member states do not participate. These agreements could cover commerce, economic complementation, agriculture, scientific and technical cooperation, promotion or tourism and preservation of the environment. These agreements could be entered into between two or more member states, who could negotiate their own norms, which would not apply to the other member states. Other members states, however, must be allowed to enter into negotiations for adherence to any of these agreements.[42] These partial scope agreements allow for the imposition of different norms and rules to smaller groups of countries, eliminating the need to negotiate a broad and all encompassing agreement among all the member states.[43] As was seen with LAFTA, such negotiations among nations with different levels of economic development and different trading relations with each others would be, at best, extremely difficult. Clearly, ALADI was not going to fall into the LAFTA pattern: interminable negotiations with little agreement.

As was the case with LAFTA, ALADI does provide a "system of support for countries with a lesser degree of development" ("LDC's") in the establishment of regional scope and partial scope agreements.[44]

In order to supervise ALADI's work, the Treaty created four institutions, which are composed primarily of representatives of the member states and which act primarily by consensus.[45] These institutions seem to follow the same

---

market or free trade area does not appear to be a main objective or purpose of ALADI, as it was for LAFTA in 1960. *Compare* 1960 Treaty, *supra* Intro. note 7, at Arts. 2–4.

38. Vacchino, *supra* note 1, at 151–155.

39. ALADI Treaty, *supra* note 34, at Art. 5.

40. *Id.* at Art. 6.

41. *Id.* at Art. 7.

42. *Id.* at Arts. 8, 14.

43. Vacchino, *supra* note 1, at 155.

44. ALADI Treaty, *supra* note 34, at Art. 23. For Regional Scope Agreements, this support consists of negotiated list of LDC exports for which all other member states shall agree to, without reciprocity, the elimination of all duties and restrictions. *Id.* at Art. 15. The Treaty encourages LDC's to enter into Partial Scope Agreements (*Id.* at Art. 19) and also mandates that member states negotiate "special programs of cooperation" with LDC's, which may include aid in the form of investments, financing and technology. *Id.* at Arts. 20–21.

45. These institutions include the Council of Ministers, the Conference of Evaluation and Convergence, the Committee of Representatives, and the Secretariat. *Id.* at Art. 28.

model as LAFTA's: institutions dominated by representatives of the member states which generally must act by consensus (or close to it). Similarly, ALADI's Secretariat is no EU Commission: it suffers from a similar lack of funding, personnel and power that hobbled its LAFTA predecessor.[46]

ALADI is, of course, a vastly different creature from LAFTA. The treaty encourages individual member states to "strike their own deals" for tariff liberalization and economic integration. ALADI itself seems to emphasize these partial agreements and is de-emphasizing the multilateral negotiation model created in LAFTA.[47] The ALADI treaty itself makes it clear that, under its framework, competing models of integration, both within and outside Latin America, are meant to coexist and cooperate with each other.[48] This emphasis allows the member states who have successful trading relationships to formalize and improve them, thus building an integration model out of existing trading pattern, and not anticipated future trading relationships. Furthermore, the ability to have more than one integration model existing at the same time creates a healthy competition: more member states will seek to join the more "popular" (or "successful") integration agreement. As shall be argued later in this work, that is precisely what has occurred with MERCOSUR. The "popularity" of such agreements would, of course, depend on how successful they have been in improving trade relationships among its members.

In short, ALADI seems to be primarily a framework within which member states can negotiate and enter into economic integration agreements with each other and a "keeper of the flame" for the ideal of integration in Latin America.

The Council, the highest policymaking body, meets when convoked by the Committee of Representatives. *Id.* at Arts. 30–32. The Conference, apparently an evaluative and analytical body, meets every three years. *Id.* at Arts. 33–34. The Committee consists of the permanent representatives of the member states and seem to have some day to day supervision over the affairs of ALADI. *Id.* at Arts. 35–37. These three bodies act by 2/3 majority vote, except for 10 types of matters enumerated in the ALADI treaty, which require a 2/3 majority vote with no negative votes. The last institution, the Secretariat, is in charge of ALADI's administrative affairs. *Id.* at Art. 38.

46. *Compare* ORIGINS AND DEVELOPMENT OF THE EUROPEAN COMMUNITY (David Weigall and Peter Stirk, eds., Leicester University Press, Leicester and London 1992) at 198; with ALADI Treaty, *supra* note 34 at Art. 38. *See also* LAFTA, *supra* notes 13–33 and accompanying text.

47. Haines-Ferrari, *supra* note 36, at 418; Radway, *supra* note 9, at 12. This is not to say that ALADI has abandoned the concept of an integrated Latin American economy. As noted by one commentator, the route for getting there has changed. The thought is that, eventually, the remaining member states, by negotiation, would eventually join the most attractive Partial Scope Agreement and therefore achieve an economically integrated Latin American system in that fashion. Haines-Ferrari, *supra* note 36, at 418.

48. *See* ALADI Treaty, *supra* note 34, at Arts. 24–26.

D. The MERCOSUR Four: An Inevitable Marriage?

The idea that the nations of Latin America should undertake political and economic integration is not recent. As early as 1797, immediately after independence, and throughout the nineteenth century, a number of conferences and negotiations undertook several attempts to create confederations or similar arrangements among the various states of Central and South America.[49] For a number of reasons, these efforts have tended to be unsuccessful in the past.[50]

Many Latin American countries who have attempted economic or political integration have had little in common with each other.[51] Argentina, Brazil, Chile and Uruguay, on the other hand, seem unusually complementary to each other, politically, economically and historically. They have many things in common, starting with geography: three out of the four (Paraguay, Argentina and Brazil) share extensive common borders,[52] as do Brazil and Uruguay.[53] Uruguay and Argentina were actually once politically united.[54] The political systems of all four countries had undergone recent substantial democratization[55] and had taken part in the process of economic liberalization that took place in the region in the 1970's and 1980's.[56] All four countries actually traded with each other, and had a history of economic cooperation, including joint administration of transnational infrastructure projects.[57]

In spite of prior cooperation between them in the construction of the Corpus and Ytaipú dams in the late 1970's, relations in the early 1980's between Brazil and Argentina were difficult. Argentine military governments tended to

---

49. *Id.* One of the most interesting of these proposals is found in an 1826 document written by Simon Bolivar. In it, he proposes that the nine newly independent nations of South America enter into a political and economic union with the British empire. This proposal was not seriously considered. Lanus, *supra* note 1, at 21.

50. Lanus, *supra* note 1, at 24–25; Milenky, *supra* note 1 at 11–12; Mathis, *supra* note 1 at 9–10.

51. Mathis, *supra* note 1, at 17–18; Vacchino, *supra* note 1 at 59, 72–79, 86; Milenky, *supra* note 1, at 70–74, 79.

52. *See* CIA WORLD FACTBOOK 2002 *available at* http://www.cia.gov/gov/cia/publications/factbook.htm (hereinafter, "CIA Factbook").

53. *Id.*

54. Argentina and Uruguay were part of the United Provinces of the River Plate from 1810 through 1880. Information *available at* http://www.wtove2003/com/ing_argentina.shtml.

55. *See* Peter Coffey, LATIN AMERICA-MERCOSUR (Kluwer Academic Publishers, 1998) at 257–59 (hereinafter, "Coffey").

56. *Id. See also* Paz Millet et.al, CHILE-MERCOSUR: UNA ALIAZA ESTRATEGICA (editorial Los Andes 1997) at 135 (hereinafter, "Chile-Mercosur").

57. Coffey, *supra* note 55 at 29–33, 21–23.

foster rivalry with Brazil and their foreign policy towards that country tended to stress competition rather than cooperation.[58] Brazilian governments, on the other hand, retorted with strong protectionist measures aimed at Argentine exports, whose quantity and value had fallen greatly since 1980.[59]

This situation changed after the military regimes of Argentina and Brazil were replaced by democratic governments in the mid 1980's. Both the Brazilian and Argentine governments began to see the advantages of further cooperation and integration and a series of agreements between them were signed in quick succession.[60]

It can be argued that this turn of events was unavoidable. The relationship between Argentina and Brazil has been described as similar to that of France and Germany at the time of the creation of the European Economic Community: both countries had a long history of (sometimes hostile) interrelationships, and the exports of one (France, or in this case, Argentina) tended to be primarily agricultural, while those of the other (Germany, or in this case, Brazil) tended to be primarily industrial.[61]

This complementarity becomes striking upon examination of certain economic characteristics. To begin with, Brazil and Argentina are the largest countries, in territory and population, in South America[62] and each have large and highly developed consumer markets.[63] Argentina is rich in natural resources, and has a highly developed export-oriented agricultural sector, which produces a variety of products.[64] Although Argentina's industrial sector also produces a variety of products,[65] it is considered to be weaker than other sectors.[66] Argentina also has a very large service sector, which accounted for 66% of GDP in 2001.[67] Its exports, which were estimated at $26.5 billion in 2000, included edible oils, fuels and energy, cereals,

---

58. Coffey, *supra* note 55 at 29–30.

59. Atilio Anibal Alterini and Maia Critina Boldorini, EL SISTEMA JURIDICO EN EL MERCOSUR; 1, ESTRUCTURA GENERAL-INSTRUMENTOS FUNDACIONALES Y COMPLEMENTARIOS (Buenos Aires, Abeledo-Perrot, 1995) (hereinafter, "Alterini") In this time period, however, trade between both countries was significant. In 1983, for example, trade between Argentina and Brazil totaled $1.350 billion in exports from Argentina to Brazil and $654 million in imports. Coffey, *supra* note 82 at 38.

60. Coffey, *supra* note 55, at 4, 6, 30–34, 122–25.

61. Coffey, *supra* note 55, at 122, Alterini, *supra* note 59, at 168.

62. CIA Factbook, *supra* note 52.

63. *Id.*

64. *Id.* These products include sunflower seeds, soybeans, lemons, grapes, corn, tobacco, peanuts, tea, wheat and livestock. This sector was estimated to compose about 6% of GDP in 2001. *Id.*

65. *Id.* These products include processed foods, motor vehicles, consumer durables, textiles, chemicals and petrochemicals and steel. This sector was estimated to compose about 28% of GDP in 2001. *Id.*

66. Daniel Heymann, *Regional Interdependence and Macroeconomic Crises. Notes on MERCOSUR*, UN, ECLAC (Buenos Aires, Nov. 2001) (hereinafter, "Heymann") at 132.

67. *Id.*

feed and motor vehicles.[68] Its imports, which totaled $23.8 billion in 2000, chiefly included machinery and equipment, motor vehicles, chemicals, metal manufactures and plastics. Argentina's principal trading partners in 2000, for both exports and imports, included Brazil, the United States, Chile, Spain, China and Germany with Brazil being both its principal import and export partner.[69] Argentina also exported 3.7 billion kWh and imported 7.5 billion kWh of electricity in 2000.[70]

Brazil, on the other hand, has a much larger economy than Argentina's,[71] and has large and well developed agricultural, mining, manufacturing and service sectors.[72] Its principal agricultural products include coffee, soybeans, wheat, rice, corn, sugarcane, cocoa, citrus and beef.[73] Principal industrial products include textiles, shoes, chemicals, cement, lumber, iron ore, tin, steel, aircraft, motor vehicles, and other machinery and equipment.[74] Its exports, which totaled $57.8 billion in 2001, were principally manufactures, iron ore, soybeans, footwear, coffee and autos.[75] Its imports, which totaled $57.7 billion in 2001, include machinery and equipment, chemical products, oil, electricity, autos and auto parts. Brazil's principal trading partners in 2001, for both exports and imports, included the United States, Argentina, Germany, Japan, Italy and the Netherlands.[76] The United States and Argentina were Brazil's principal trading partners.[77] Brazil also imported 42.3 billion kWh of electricity from Paraguay in 2000.[78]

Uruguay, with a much smaller land mass[79] and population[80] than either Brazil or Argentina, has as the largest sector of its economy a well developed services

---

68. CIA Factbook, *supra* note 52. Argentina's principal export trading partners in 2000 were Brazil (26.5%), the United States (11.8%), Chile (10.6%) and Spain (3.5%).

69. *Id.*

70. *See Id.* (Noting that imported electricity chiefly came from Paraguay. Electricity exports were destined for Argentina.)

71. Brazil had an estimated GDP (purchasing power parity) of $1.34 trillion in 2001.*Id.* Argentina, on the other hand, had an estimated GDP (purchasing power parity) of $453 billion in that year. *Id.*

72. In 2001, the agricultural sector composed 9% of GDP, the industrial sector 32% and the services sector 59%. *Id.*

73. *Id.*

74. *Id.*

75. *Id.* Brazil's principal export trading partners in 2001 included the United States (24.4%), Argentina (11.2%), Germany (8.7%), Japan (5/5%) and Italy (3.9%).

76. *Id.*

77. *Id.* The United States accounted for approximately 24% of Brazil's exports and 23% of its imports on that year. *Id.* Argentina accounted for approximately 11% of Brazil's imports and exports during that period.

78. *Id.*

79. Uruguay has a total area of approximately 176,000 square kilometers compared with a total area of approximately 8,500,000 square kilometers for Brazil and approximately 2,766,000 square kilometers for Argentina. CIA Factbook *supra* note 52.

80. Uruguay had an approximate total population of 3,386,000 in 2002, compared with an approximate total population of 176,000,000 for Brazil and approximately 37,800,000

industry.[81] Its agricultural sector, which principally produces rice, wheat, corn, barley, livestock and fish, is extensive and export-oriented[82] Uruguay's industrial sector involves food processing, electrical machinery, transportation equipment, petroleum products, textiles, chemicals and beverages.[83] Its exports, which totaled $2.24 billion in 2001, included meat, rice, leather products, wool, vehicles and dairy products.[84] Its imports, which totaled $2.9 billion in 2001, chiefly included machinery, chemicals, road vehicles and crude petroleum.[85] Its principal trading partners in 2001, for both exports and imports, were the MERCOSUR countries, the European Union and the United States, with the former representing Uruguay's primary trading partner.[86]

Paraguay, on the other hand, has a very different economy from the others. Its informal sector, which includes both re-export of imported consumer goods to neighboring countries and the activities of thousands of micro-enterprises and urban street vendors, is extremely large and important.[87] A large percentage of the population derives their living from agricultural activity, often on a subsistence basis.[88] Paraguay grows cotton, sugarcane, soy beans, corn, wheat, tobacco, tapioca, fruits, vegetables, beef, pork, eggs, milk and timber.[89] It has an industrial sector which produces cement, textiles, beverages and processed food products.[90] A principal export industry is that of electricity generation, which accounted for substantial exports in 2000.[91] Its principal exports, which totaled $2.2 billion in 2001, include electricity, soybeans, feed, cotton, meat and edible

---

for Argentina. CIA Factbook *supra* note, 52.

81. This sector represented 65% of Uruguay's GDP (purchasing power parity) of $31 billion in 2001. Seventy percent of the Uruguayan labor force were employed in this sector. *Id.*

82. This agricultural sector composed 29% of Uruguay's GDP for 2001 and employed 14% of its labor force.

83. *Id.* Uruguay also produced 7.5 billion kWh in 2000. Of this production, approximately 950 million kWh were exported, and the importation of approximately 1.3 billion kWh was necessary in order to meet local demand.

84. *Id.*

85. *Id.*

86. *Id.* The MERCOSUR countries accounted for approximately 40% of Uruguay's exports and 44% of its imports. *Id.*

87. *Id.* These activities take part informally, with its participants not reporting their activities or their profits to any authorities. CIA Factbook, *supra* note 52. For this reason, accurate economic data on Paraguay is very difficult to obtain. *Id.*

88. *Id.* The estimate is that approximately 45% of the labor force is employed in agriculture. *Id.*

89. *Id.*

90. *Id.*

91. In that year, the Paraguayan electrical generation industry generated approximately 56 billion kWh of electricity, of which approximately 47.3 billion kWh were exported. *Id.*

oils.[92] Its principal imports included road vehicles, consumer goods, tobacco, petroleum products and electrical machinery.[93] Paraguay's principal trading partners included Argentina, Brazil and Uruguay.[94]

Although there are a few areas of competition among them (such as the automotive industry)[95], a number of natural economic connections among them surface from the brief descriptions set forth above. Thus, Brazil's extensive manufacturing sector has a natural market among Argentina's, Uruguay's and Paraguay's populations.[96] Argentina's (and to a lesser degree Paraguay's) extensive natural resources and agricultural sectors also have ready made markets in Brazil. Uruguay has had extensive economic connections with Argentina for many years. Its services industry (especially its financial services sector) also has many potential customers across the Rio de la Plata in Argentina. Lastly, Paraguay's electrical generation industry very profitably supplements Argentina's and Brazil's massive energy needs.

These economic connections and long history of interaction among Brazil, Argentina, Uruguay and Paraguay make successful integration efforts among them more likely to happen. Thus, MERCOSUR is a consummation of a likely, if not inevitable economic marriage.

---

92. *Id.*

93. *Id.*

94. *Id.*

95. *See* Stephen P. Sorensen, *"Open regionalism or Old Fashioned Protectionism? A Look at the Performance of MERCOSUR's Auto Industry,* 30 U. Miami Inter-Am. L. Rev. 371 (Winter 1998).

96. Indeed, a point of contention between Brazil and Argentina during the recent economic crisis was that Brazil was flooding its market with cheap imports. *See, e.g.,* Peter Fritsch, *Brazil and Argentina at Breaking Point,* WALL ST.J. 7/28/99 at A20; *Sour MERCOSUR,* The Economist, Aug. 14, 1999 at 13.

Chapter 2

MERCOSUR
and Its Institutions

This chapter describes MERCOSUR and its institutions. It starts with a sketch of its principal terms and concepts derived from its basic documents. As we learned in the case of LAFTA, the design and operating principles of an economic integration organization like MERCOSUR are critical for its successful operations and the fulfillment of its mission. Accordingly, this chapter then describes and evaluates MERCOSUR's institutions.

A. Formalizing the Relationship

The first step on to the path of greater cooperation between Brazil and Argentina was taken in the Iguazú Declaration, signed by Presidents Alfonsin of Argentina and Sarney of Brazil, on November 29, 1985.[1] In this declaration, both presidents indicated joint positions on a number of economic and foreign policy issues.[2] The most important part of this Declaration, however, was the agreement that cooperation, harmonization and integration of a number of sectors of the economy was desirable and the creation of an implementation mechanism.[3] The Presidents then announced the creation of a Joint Commission that would explore and make recommendations for bilateral cooperation and integration.[4]

---

1. Iguazú Declaration, reproduced in, Todo el Mercosur: Desde sus Primeros Antecedentes a la Union Aduanera (Instituto de Relaciones Internacionales, Universidad Nacional de la Plata, Buenos Aires, 1995) (hereinafter, "IRI") at 51–57.

2. *Id. See, e.g.,* sections 9 (foreign debt), 12 (support for the Contadora Group), 13, (cooperation on issues relating to the Plate River basin), 14 (joint position on the Falklands Islands dispute), and 15, (drug policy).

3. *Id.* Some of these sections included: energy, transport and communications (sections 22–27); scientific and technical cooperation (sections 28–29) and general economic and commercial cooperation (section 30).

4. *Id.* at sections 18–20.

Eight months later, the negotiations started by the Iguazú Declaration resulted in an Agreement on Argentine-Brazilian Integration.[5] The Integration Agreement created an Integration and Economic Cooperation Program between Brazil and Argentina. This program would involve a number of economic sectors and would seek to achieve economic cooperation and integration in a flexible and gradual fashion.[6] Specific guidelines for individual economic areas were set forth in 12 protocols. Between 1986 and 1988, Argentina and Brazil signed 12 more protocols covering other economic sectors.[7] This program was to be established and implemented by an Implementation Commission which would meet every six months and whose membership would consist of senior cabinet ministers from both countries.[8]

During this time period, Uruguay was also involved with economic integration efforts with Brazil and Argentina. It had signed economic cooperation agreements with Argentina (known as CAUCE agreements for their Spanish acronym) in 1974 and 1985[9] and commercial expansion treaties (known as PEC agreements for their Spanish acronym) in 1975 and 1986.[10] These bilateral agreements gave Uruguay substantial tariff concessions for exports to Argentina and Brazil, effectively granting it preferential access to their markets. Not surprisingly, trade between Uruguay and Brazil and Argentina increased substantially.[11]

Further negotiations between Argentina and Brazil resulted in the Act of Buenos Aires, where both countries agreed in principle to establish a common market between them. This common market would be implemented by December 31, 1994.[12]

---

5. Agreement on Argentine-Brazilian Integration, 1988, Arg.-Braz., 27 I.L.M. 901 (hereinafter, "Integration Agreement").

6. *Id.* at Arts. 1–2.

7. *See* Coffey, *supra* Chptr. 1 note 55, at 34. The first twelve protocols included, capital goods, wheat, complementarity of the food supply, expansion of trade, joint companies, financial matters, investment funds, energy, biotechnology, economic studies, nuclear accidents and radiological emergencies, and aeronautical cooperation. Integration Agreement, *supra* note 5 at 902–904.

8. *Id.* at Arts. 3–5.

9. Alterini, *supra* note Chptr. 1 note 59, at 166.

10. *Id.* at 168.

11. Coffey, *supra* Chptr. 1 note 55, at 166–170.

12. Act of Buenos Aires reproduced at IRI, *supra* note 1 at 63–64.

B. Creating a Common Market: Partial Scope Agreement 14

This agreement in principle was fleshed out in Partial Scope Agreement 14 ("PSA 14") signed in Montevideo on December 20, 1990.[13]

PSA 14 sets forth a number of concepts that will later be incorporated in the Treaty of Asunción, which created MERCOSUR. First, the parties agreed to eliminate all customs duties, tariffs and restrictions between them by December 31, 1994.[14] During the transition period before this date, all previously agreed tariff preferences between both countries would be maintained.[15] This elimination of customs duties applied to all products, with the exception of those excepted by the parties in Annexes III and IV to the Agreement. Tariffs on these products were to be eliminated at the rates of 20% a year.[16]

Second, the parties agreed, as a necessary adjunct to the elimination of all tariffs, on the harmonization of all macroeconomic policies, especially those linked to the flow of commerce.[17]

The parties also agreed on rules of origin for products originating in their territory. These rules of origin were also included in the treaty as an Annex.[18]

During the transition period (until December 31, 1994), each country could request the application of safeguard clauses against the importation of goods from the other.[19] When an importing nation felt that the increase in imports of a particular good would cause great damage to its markets, it could solicit consultations on how to minimize this damage.[20] These consultations could result in agreement on the imposition of a "safeguard clause," which would limit or otherwise place restrictions on imports of that good into the other country for a period of up to one year.[21] The parties also agreed to promote and adopt more measures to integrate their economies and correct any temporary distortions in their markets caused by increased trade.[22]

---

13. Acuerdo de Complementacion Eonomica ("PSA 14") reproduced at IRI, *supra* note 1 at 65–73. This agreement was filed with ALADI as a partial scope agreement under the Treaty of Montevideo Establishing the Latin American Integration Association, 20 I.L.M. 672 (1981) (hereinafter, "ALADI Treaty"), at Arts. 7–145, hence its name.

14. PSA 14, *supra* note 13, at section 3.

15. *Id.* at Arts. 5, 6, 13–14.

16. *Id.* at Art. 8.

17. *Id.* at Art. 10.

18. *Id.* at Art. 15.

19. *Id.* at Art. 16.

20. *Id.* at Arts. 17–18.

21. *Id.* at Arts. 18–20.

22. *Id.* at Art. 22.

The agreement would be administered and implemented by the Argentina-Brazil Common Market Group, which had been created by the Act of Buenos Aires.[23]

After the signature of the Act of Buenos Aires, Paraguay and Uruguay expressed a strong interest in joining the Argentina-Brazil common market and negotiations began on an agreement to create a common market among all four countries.[24] For Uruguay, this represented a natural "next step" from its prior negotiations and agreements with Brazil and Argentina.[25] For Paraguay, which saw itself as a supplier of energy to its large neighbors,[26] this too represented a natural progression from its prior cooperation on hydroelectric matters with Argentina and Brazil.

Three months after the signature of PSA 14, on March 20, 1990, the negotiations among Argentina, Brazil, Paraguay and Uruguay resulted in the signing of the Treaty of Asunción, which created MERCOSUR. As shall be seen below, a whole new era of Latin American integration had begun.

C. The Treaty of Asunción and Its Protocols

An analysis of MERCOSUR's legal and institutional foundation must begin with four key documents, the Treaty of Asunción and its five Annexes,[27] the Ouro Preto Protocol on the Institutional Structure of MERCOSUR,[28] the Brasilia Protocol on the Resolution of Controversies and the Olivos Protocol for the Resolution of Controversies.[29] These documents form the backbone of the MERCOSUR legal system.[30]

1. The Common Market

The Treaty of Asunción borrows a large number of concepts from PSA 14 and looks very similar to that agreement.[31] Its purpose is to create a common market among its four signatories (Argentina, Brazil, Paraguay and Uruguay) by Decem-

---

23. *Id.* at Arts. 23–24; Act of Buenos Aires, *supra* note 12, at Art. 2.

24. Alterini, *supra* Chptr. 1 note 59, at 73–75.

25. *Id.*

26. Coffey, *supra* Chptr. 1 note 55, at 9.

27. Asunción, Intro. *supra* note 1.

28. Ouro Preto, Intro. *supra* note 5.

29. Protocol of Brasilia for the Solution of Controversies. MERCOSUR/CMC/Dec No.1/91(I), *available at* http://www.mercosur.org.uy/espanol/snor/varios/protocolo_brasilia.htm (hereinafter, "Brasilia"). Protocolo de Olivos Para La Solucion de Controversias en el MERCOSUR. MERCOSUR/GANPSSC/Acta No. 5/01 (Feb. 18, 2002) (hereinafter, "Olivos") *available at* http://www.mercosur.org.uy/espanol/snor/varios/protocolo_olivos_2002.htm.

30. These documents are reproduced in the Appendices.

31. *See supra* notes 13–26, and accompanying text.

ber 31, 1994.[32] This is the same date that PSA 14 sets for the elimination of all tariff barriers among its signatories.[33] Like PSA 14, the Treaty of Asunción calls for the graduated elimination of customs duties among its signatories at the rate of 20% a year (with certain exceptions for Paraguay and Uruguay),[34] the exception of certain mutually agreed upon areas from these tariff reductions,[35] the harmonization of economic policies,[36] the creation of rules of origin very similar to those of PSA 14,[37] and the continuation of the safeguard clause system.[38] Unlike PSA 14, the Treaty of Asunción calls for a common external tariff and for the adoption of a common trade policy.[39] The Ouro Preto Protocol creates a number of additional MERCOSUR institutions and further enumerates and expands the roles of all of these institutions. The Brasilia Protocol and the Olivos Protocol augment the perfunctory provisions set forth in the Treaty of Asunción and the Ouro Preto Protocol[40] for the resolution of disputes among member states and individuals. The major provisions of the latter documents will be discussed in some detail below.

D. The MERCOSUR Institutions

Under the Treaty, the Ouro Preto Protocol, and the Olivos Protocol seven institutions are charged with implementing MERCOSUR's principles and purposes. They include the Council of the Common Market ("Council"), the Common Market Group ("the Group"), the MERCOSUR Commerce Commission ("MCC"), the Joint Parliamentary Commission, the Economic and Social Consultative Forum ("Forum"), the Administrative Secretariat ("Secretariat"), the Permanent Appellate Tribunal ("the Tribunal") and the Committee of Permanent Representatives ("CPR").

1. The Council

The Council consists of the Foreign Relations and Economics Ministers of the four member states.[41] Its presidency rotates among the member states, in alpha-

---

32. Asunción, *supra* Intro. note 1, at Art. 1.
33. *See supra* note 17, and accompanying text.
34. Asunción, *supra* note 1, at Art. 5(a) and Annex I (7).
35. *Id.* at Annex I.
36. *Id.* at Arts. 2, 5(b).
37. *Id.* at Annex II.
38. *Id.* at Annex II. *See supra* notes 13–21, and accompanying text.
39. *Id.* at Arts. 1, 5(c).
40. *Id.* at Annex III. Ouro Preto, *supra* Intro. note 5, at Arts. 43–44.
41. Asunción, *supra* Intro. note 1, at Art. 11, Ouro Preto, *supra* Intro. note 5, at Art. 4. The rotating president is known as the "President Pro Tem."

betical order, every six months.[42] The Council is responsible for the political leadership of the integration process and for taking decisions to ensure the implementation of the objectives of the Treaty of Asunción.[43] In addition, the Council is the legal representative of MERCOSUR, entitled to sign agreements with third party countries, groups of countries, or international organizations.[44] It supervises the other MERCOSUR institutions, and can modify or eliminate them.[45] It also acts on policy proposals sent to it by the Group[46] and has the power to designate the Director of the Secretariat.[47] The Council acts by means of "Decisions," which, according to the Ouro Preto Protocol, are "obligatory for the member states."[48] The Council is the most important and powerful MERCOSUR institution.

2. The Group

The Group has four alternate representatives from each member state designated by their governments.[49] Representatives from the economics and foreign ministries and central bank must be included in each member state's delegation, which is coordinated by the Ministers of Foreign Relations of the member states.[50] Its principal responsibilities include monitoring compliance with the Treaty of Asunción, proposing policy for consideration by the Council and ensuring compliance with Council decisions.[51] Analysis and recommendations on proposals or recommendations submitted by other MERCOSUR institutions are also part of the Group's responsibilities.[52] It may, if authorized by the Council, become MERCOSUR's representative in negotiating agreements with non-member countries, groups of countries or international organizations.[53] Administratively, the Group approves the MERCOSUR budget, the Secretariat's annual expenditures, and supervises the Secretariat staff and Council meetings.[54] The Group has its own internal regulations[55] and can create "work-

---

42. Asunción, *supra* Intro. note 1, at Art. 12, Ouro Preto, *supra* Intro. note 5, at Art. 5.
43. Ouro Preto, *supra* Intro. note 5, at Art. 3.
44. Ouro Preto, *supra* Intro. note 5, at Art. 8(III-V).
45. *Id.* at Art. 8(VII).
46. *Id.* at Art. 8(V).
47. *Id.* at Art. 8(IX).
48. *Id.* at Art. 9.
49. *Id.* at Art. 11.
50. *Id.*
51. *Id.* at Art. 14(II-III).
52. *Id.* at Art. 14(VI).
53. *Id.* at Art.14(VII).
54. *Id.* at Art. 14(VIII-XIV).
55. Reglamento Interno del Grupo Mercado Común. MERCOSUR/CMC/DEC No. 04/1991, *available at* http://www.mercosur.org.uy/espanol/snor/normativa/decisiones/1991/04-91.htm.

ing subgroups" to assist it in its work.[56] The Group's "Resolutions" are "binding on the member states."[57]

The Council and the Group bear a superficial resemblance to the European Union's Council and Commission. In both organizations, the Council is controlled by the member states and has the power to create policy or "community law"[58] while the other institutions, the Commission in the EU and the Group in MERCOSUR, represent the proposer and implementer of policy.[59] The European Commission and the Group are, however, very different institutions. The former is a supranational institution whose members are independent of the member states and which controls a substantial permanent staff. They have a substantial independent power base.[60] The latter is controlled by the member states whose senior civil servants serve as its members, has no staff, and no independent power base. Its role seems to be primarily administrative, rather than that of a planning and policy making entity.[61]

3. The MCC

The MCC, a creature of the Ouro Preto Protocol, has four representatives and four alternates from each member state.[62] It monitors the application of and implements the common commercial policy agreed to by the member states. Decisions regarding the administration and application of the common external tariff, and proposals relating to changes to the common external tariff and the common commercial policy are also part of its responsibilities. The MCC also provides information to the Group on the evolution and application

---

56. The Group currently has 12 working groups (Communications, Mines, Technical Regulations and Evaluation, Financial Affairs, Transport and Infrastructure, Environment, Industry, Agriculture, Energy, Labor, Employment and Social Security, Health and Investments), seven ad hoc groups (Institutional Aspects, Sugar, External Relations, Administrative Secretariat Budget, Treatment of Public Policies that Distort Competition, Public Contracts, and Followup of Economic and Commercial Linkages) five Specialized Meetings (Science and Technology, Tourism, Social Communication, Women, Drugs and Drug Addicts), a Service Group and three Commissions (Sociolaboral, Administrative/ Mercosur-Bolivia and Administrative/Mercosur-Chile), *available at* http://www.mercosur.org.uy/gmc.

57. Ouro Preto, *supra* Intro. note 5, at Art. 15.

58. Malcom Rowat, Michele Lubrano and Rafael Porrata-Doria, COMPETITION POLICY AND MERCOSUR, WORLD BANK TECHNICAL PAPER NO 385 at 14, 15 (hereinafter, "RL+P"). *See, e.g.,* Consolidated Version of the Treaty Establishing the European Community, *available at* http://europa.eu.int/eur-lex/en/treaties/dat/EC_consol.pdf, at Art. 189 (hereinafter, "Treaty of Rome") at Arts. 145–146.

59. *See, e.g., Id.* at Art. 155.

60. *See, e.g., Id.* at Arts. 156–159.

61. *See* Ouro Preto, *supra* Intro. note 5.

62. Ouro Preto, *supra* Intro. note 5 at Art. 17.

of the common commercial policy.[63] The MCC also considers and decides applications submitted to it by the member states regarding the administration of MERCOSUR's common external tariff and common commercial policies and monitors matters dealing with common commercial policies, intra-MERCOSUR trade and trade relations between MERCOSUR and non member states.[64] The MCC also has internal regulations which regulate its proceedings.[65] Furthermore, it also has the power to create Sub-Working Groups to examine and make proposals regarding different specific areas related to the common external tariff and the common commercial policy.[66] It also has under the Olivos Protocol, the power to consider claims by individuals relating to member state violations of the Treaty and community law.[67] The MCC issues either "Directives" or "Proposals," with the former being "binding on the member states."[68] The MCC, with its specialized personnel is a technical body whose principal task involves the analysis of areas of policy and the preparation of proposals relating thereto. In December of 2003, the Council instructed the MCC to schedule additional follow-up meetings. These meetings are to undertake whatever preparatory work is necessary to prepare agenda issues for consideration at the next regularly scheduled MCC meeting and whatever other tasks the MCC may assign it.[69]

4. The Joint Parliamentary Commission

The Joint Parliamentary Commission, another Ouro Preto creation, serves as a representative of the legislatures of the member states.[70] Each member state has equal number of members who are designated by their par-

---

63. *Id.* at Art. 19.

64. Asunción, *supra* Intro. note 1, at Art. 16. Ouro Preto, *supra* Intro. note 5, at Art. 19.

65. "Reglamento Interno de la Comisión de Comercio del Mercosur." MERCOSUR/CMC/Res 61/96, *available at* http://www.mercosur.og.uy/espanol/snor/normativa/resoluciones/1996/res9661.htm (hereinafter, "Internal Regulations").

66. Ouro Preto, *supra* Intro. note 5, at Art. 19(IX), Internal Regulations, *supra* note 65, at Art. 6(IX). The MCC currently has ten Technical Committees (Tariffs, Nomenclature and Classification of Goods; Customs Matters, Commercial Disciplines and Norms, Competition, Consumer Protection, Automobile Sector and Textile Sector). It also has a Commercial Defense and Safeguard Measures Committee, *available at* http://www.mercosur.org.uy/CCM.

67. Olivos, *supra* note 29 at Arts. 39–43.

68. Ouro Preto, *supra* Intro. note 5, at Art. 20.

69. MERCOSUR/CMC/Dec. No. 30/03 "Funcionamiento de la Comisión de Comercio de MERCOSUR," *available at* http://www/mercosur.org.uy/espanol/snor/normativa/decisiones/2003/Dec_030_003.htm at Arts. 1–2. These follow up meetings will be coordinated by the member state holding the MERCOSUR Presidency Pro Tem and will be staffed by individuals designated by the member states. *Id.* at Arts. 1–3.

70. Ouro Preto, *supra* Intro. note 5, at Art. 22.

liaments.[71] One of its principal missions is to engage in planning and set the stage to create a future MERCOSUR parliament.[72] It is also meant to be an institution which will assist MERCOSUR in the implementation of its policies and in the harmonization of national legislation therewith.[73] It has an advisory function at this point. However, as shall be discussed in chapter 7, there are current plans to strengthen this institution and evolve it into a MERCOSUR Parliament.

5. The Forum

Under the Ouro Preto Protocol, the Forum's members represent the various sectors of economic and social life such as merchants, consumers and workers.[74] Its functions are purely advisory and this advice takes the form of "Recommendations" to the Group and other MERCOSUR institutions.[75] It is meant to "cooperate actively" to promote economic and social progress within MERCOSUR, analyze and evaluate the social and economic impact of the various integration policies and their implementation, recommend economic and social norms and policies relating to integration, and perform studies and research on economic and social matters that are relevant to MERCOSUR.[76]

6. The Secretariat

The Secretariat is the only institution within MERCOSUR to have a permanent staff. It is permanently headquartered in Montevideo, Uruguay[77] and, at present, its staff consists of approximately 27 persons.[78] Its proposed 2002 budget was approximately $980,000.[79] The Secretariat's responsibilities include translation of documents, logistical support for all of the other institutions, editing the MER-

---

71. *Id.* at Arts. 23–24.

72. Reglamento de la Comisión Parlamentaria Conjunta del MERCOSUR, MERCO-SUR/CPC/Res. No. 2/1997, at Art. 3, *available at* http://www.mercosur.org.uy/espanol/snor/normativa/resoluciones/RES297.htm.

73. *Id.* at Art. 25.

74. Ouro Preto, *supra* Intro. note 5, at Art. 28.

75. *Id.* at Art. 29.

76. Reglamento Interno del Foro Consultivo Economico Social, MERCOSUR/CMC/Res. No. 68/96 at Art. 2 (I–VI), *available at* http://www.mercosur.org.uy/espanol/snor/normativa/resoluciones/1996/RES9668.htm.

77. Ouro Preto, *supra* Intro. note 5, at Art. 31.

78. Estructura y Manual de Cargos y Funciones de la Secretaria Administrativa del MERCOSUR. MERCOSUR/CMC/RES no. 15/02 *available at* http://www.mercosur.org.uy/espanol/snor/normativa/resoluciones/2002/RES0215.htm (hereinafter, "Res 15/02").

79. Presupuesto de la SAM para el Ejercicio 2002. MERCOSUR/CMC/Res No. 01/02 *available at* http://www.mercosur.org.uy/espanol/snor/normativa/resoluciones/2002/RES0201.htm (hereinafter, "Res. 01/02").

COSUR Official Gazette, information gathering for the other institutions and communications with the member states.[80] The Secretariat also has the task of monitoring and reporting on the implementation of all the MERCOSUR norms by each of the member states into its national legal system.[81] Furthermore, the Secretariat manages the panel of Arbitrators established by the Brasilia and Olivos Protocols to resolve disputes arising out of the Treaty of Asunción and its implementation.[82] The Secretariat appears to have no substantive decision making power. Again, the member states of MERCOSUR have clearly sought to ensure that control over the integration process remains in the hands of the member states, and not in a group of independent international civil servants. The Secretariat is headed by a Director which is appointed by the Group.[83] The MERCOSUR Secretariat is divided into four major sections: Documents and Communications, Norms, Administration and Information Technology.[84]

In December 2002, as part of an effort to transform the Secretariat from an "Administrative Secretariat" to a "Technical Secretariat," the Council added a Technical Assessment section to the Secretariat.[85] This Technical Assessment section is to provide technical assistance to the other MERCOSUR institutions, follow up and evaluate the implementation of the integration process, undertake studies regarding the integration process and monitor the legal consistency of the actions and norms enacted by the various MERCOSUR institutions.[86] The Technical Assessment section is staffed with four individuals, two of whom are to be lawyers and two of whom are to be economists.[87]

This Directive did, however, recognize that a larger and stronger Secretariat is necessary to the consolidation and progress of the MERCOSUR integration process and instructed the Group to consider future changes to make it a more effective institution.[88]

---

80. *Id.* at Art. 32.
81. *Id.* at Art. 32(IV).
82. *Id.* at Art. 32(V). *See infra* Chptr. 3 notes 13–27, and accompanying text.
83. *Id.* at Art. 33.
84. Res No. 15/02, *supra* note 78 at Art. 3 (01).
85. MERCOSUR/CMC/DEC No. 30/02, "Transformación de la Secretaría Administrativa del MERCOSUR en Secretaría Técnica," *available at* http://www.mercosur.org.uy/espanol/snor/normativa/decisiones/2002/Dec_030_002_Transformacion htm, at Art. 1.
86. *Id.* at Annex I, Art. 2.
87. *Id.* at Art. 1 and Annex II, Art. 1.
88. *Id.* at Arts. 4–7.

7. The CPR

The CPR was created by the Council, using its powers under the Ouro Preto Protocol,[89] in October of 2003.[90] Its mandate includes assisting the Council and its President Pro Tem, in those matters where the former request their assistance; presenting initiatives to the Council regarding matters relating to the MERCOSUR integration process, external negotiations and implementation of the common market; and strengthening the economic, social and parliamentary relationships in MERCOSUR, by establishing links with the Joint Parliamentary Commission, the Economic and Social Consultative Forum, and the MERCOSUR specialized meetings.[91]

The CPR is to be composed of the Permanent Representatives from each member state to MERCOSUR and a President.

The President is to be a "distinguished political personality" who is a national of one of the member states. He is to be nominated by the presidents of member states, elected by the Council,[92] and will serve for a two year period, which can be extended for an additional year.[93] He is to preside over meetings of the CPR and attend all Council meetings and meetings of MERCOSUR ministers.[94] He may also, as appointed by the Council, represent MERCOSUR in its relations with third countries, groups of countries and international organizations[95] And must present a report on the activities of the CPR meetings at meetings of the Council.[96] Eduardo Duhalde, former president of Argentina, was named as the first president of the CPR in October of 2003.[97]

The CPR is to be permanently based in Montevideo and is to be assisted and supported by the Secretariat.[98] The member state whose national serves as

---

89. Ouro Preto, *supra* Intro. note 5 at Arts. 1, 8 (VII). These articles grant the Council authority to create any new institutions that are "are necessary for the implementation of the objectives of the integration process." *See* MERCOSUR/CMC EXT/Dec No. 11/03, "MERCOSUR Comisión de Representantes Permanentes" (hereinafter, "Decision 11/03") *available at* http://www.mercosur.org.uy/espanol/snor/normativa/decisiones/2003/Dec_011_003.htm.

90. *Id.* at Art. 1.

91. *Id.* at Art. 4.

92. *Id.* at Art. 2.

93. *Id.* at Art. 3.

94. *Id.* at Arts. 5–6.

95. *Id.* at Art. 5.

96. *Id.* at Art. 7.

97. MERCOSUR/IV CMC EXT/DEC No. 14/03, "Designación del Presidente de la Comsión de Representantes Permanentes del MERCOSUR", *available at* http://www.mercosur.org.uy/espanol/snor/normativa/decisiones/2003/Dec_014_003.htm at Art. 1.

98. Decision 11/03, *supra* note 89, at Art. 8.

president of the CPR will be responsible for the financing necessary for the expenses of the CPR presidency.[99]

The CPR seems to resemble the European Union's Committee of Permanent Representatives ("COREPER") which is a committee composed the the permanent representatives of the EU member states. It is divided into two parts, one composed of the permanent representatives and the other of its deputies. COREPER's role and responsibility is the preparation of the European Council's proceeding, with the exception of European issues. In order to complete this mission, COREPER has a large number of working parties, which are composed of national delegates and experts, who specialize in particular areas.[100] The main difference between the CPR and COREPER is that the former, unlike the latter, does not seem at this time to have any staff to assist it other than the Secretariat. As has been seen above, the Secretariat is rather small and overworked and its assistance to the CPR is bound to be relatively small.[101] Furthermore, CPR's mission and mandate does not seem to be as expressly delineated as that of COREPER. CPR's future importance is, accordingly, unclear at this time.

MERCOSUR's quasi judicial institution, the Appellate Tribunal, is discussed in the next chapter.

---

99. MERCOSUR/IV CMC EXT/DEC No. 54/03, "Presupuesto de la Presidencia de la Comsión de Representantes Permanentes del MERCOSUR", *available at* http://www.mercosur.org.uy/espanol/snor/normativa/decisiones/2003/Dec_014_003.htm at Art. 1.

100. *See* "European Union Institutions and other Bodies: The Council of the European Union," *available at* http://europa.eu.int/institutions/council/index_en.htm, *Information Handbook of the Council of the European Union* (February 2002), *available at* http://ue.eu.int/librarie.pdf/item_239_123014.pdf at p. 9.

101. *See supra* notes 79–88 and accompanying text.

Chapter 3

Dispute Resolution Procedures and Institutions

A. Introduction

This chapter describes and evaluates MERCOSUR's dispute resolution procedures and institutions, as set forth in the Brasilia Protocol, the Olivos Protocol[1] and the newly enacted Regulations to the Olivos Protocol.[2] The latter, enacted in December of 2003, provide detailed procedural rules for some of the dispute resolution mechanisms described below and should be consulted by the parties involved therewith.

B. Member State Disputes

The Brasilia and Olivos Protocols provide that controversies between member states regarding the interpretation, application or failure to comply with the Treaty of Asunción or any of its Protocols, Council Decisions and Group Resolutions ("controversy")[3] are subject to the dispute resolution procedures set forth therein. The Olivos Protocol also allows a controversy to be submitted either by the complainant or by mutual agreement of the parties, to the dispute resolution systems of the World Trade Organization, or of any other IEO in

---

1. Brasilia Protocol, *supra* Chptr. 2 note 29. The Protocol entered into effect 30 days after the deposit of the fourth ratification thereto. Olivos, *Id.* at Art. 52. At that point, its provisions expressly repeal the Brasilia Protocol and its regulations. Olivos, *Id.* at Art. 55. As shall be seen below, the Olivos Protocol continues a substantial number of the provisions of the Brasilia Protocol.

2. MERCOSUR/CMC/Dec. No. 37/03, "Reglamento del Protocolo de Olivos para la Solucion de Controversias en el MERCOSUR," *available at* http://www.mercosure.org/uy/espanol/snor/normativa/decisiones/2003/Dec_037_003.htm (hereinafter, "Olivos Regulations").

3. Brasilia, *supra* Chptr. 2 note 29, at Art. 1. Olivos, *supra* Chptr. 2 note 29 at Art. 1.

which the individual may participate.[4] The parties to a controversy should first engage in direct negotiations to resolve the controversy and inform the Secretariat of their progress and the results thereof.[5] If the controversy is not resolved, or partially resolved by these negotiations, any member state involved therein may submit it to the Group for resolution.[6] Each party to the controversy will then present its position to the Group, will consult experts, and analyze and evaluate each party's claim.[7] The Group will then present a recommended resolution of the controversy to the parties.[8]

If the Group's recommendation is rejected by one of the parties, or, under the Olivos Protocol, if the Complainant chooses to do so at the conclusion of negotiations, then any party to the controversy is free to seek arbitration before an ad hoc arbitral panel of three arbitrators (from a list kept by the Secretariat).[9] Under the Olivos Protocol, the parties to a controversy which has not been resolved by negotiations may agree to submit the controversy to the Permanent Appellate Tribunal (the "Tribunal") rather than to the Group or an ad hoc arbitration tribunal, for resolution. In such a situation, the Tribunal acts as an arbitration panel and its decision is final.[10] The arbitral panel is free to apply "community law" and "applicable principles of international law" to resolve the controversy and must render its award within a maximum period of 90 days.[11]

Member states refusing to comply with such an arbitral award may be subject to the imposition of "temporary compensatory measures."[12]

---

4. Olivos, *Id.* at Art. 1(2).

5. Brasilia, *Id.* at Arts. 2–3. Olivos, *Id.* at Arts. 4–5. Under the Olivos Protocol, these negotiations must be concluded within 15 days. *Id.*

6. Brasilia, *Id.* at Art. 4(I). Olivos, *Id.* at Art. 6.

7. Brasilia, *Id.* at Art. 4(2). Olivos, *Id.* at Art. 6.

8. Brasilia, *Id.* at Art. 5. Olivos, *Id.* at Art. 6. Under the Olivos Protocol, the Group must do so within 30 days. Olivos, *Id.* at Art. 8.

9. Brasilia, *Id.* at Art. 9. Olivos, *Id.* at Art. 10.

10. Olivos, *Id.* at Art. 23.

11. Brasilia, *Id.* at Arts. 19–20. Olivos, *Id.* at Arts. 16, 34.

12. Brasilia, *Id.* at Art. 23. Olivos, *Id.* at 31–2. The Olivos Protocol substantially expands the concept of "compensatory measures". They are described as measures such as "the suspension of concession or equivalent obligations." Olivos, *Id.* at Art. 31 (1). These compensatory measures should involve, to the degree possible, the suspension of concessions or obligations in the same economic sector or sectors as the controversy. *Id.* at Art. 31(2). Disputes regarding the question of whether compensatory measures in particular are necessary or appropriate, may be submitted to an arbitration panel or the Tribunal. *Id.* at Art. 32.

C. Appealing the Award

The Olivos Protocol dramatically changes MERCOSUR's dispute resolution mechanism by making arbitration awards appealable to the Tribunal created therein.[13] The Tribunal is to be composed of five arbitrators four of whom are appointed by each member state for two year terms (renewable twice)[14] and one of whom shall be unanimously appointed by all the member states for a three year nonrenewable term.[15] The Olivos Regulations establish that the Tribunal shall have a Secretariat, which is charged *inter alia*, with serving as a repository for the filing, transmission and storage of documents, assisting the Tribunal in its functions, and enforcing orders issued by the Tribunal's arbitrators.[16] The appeal will be limited to legal issues dealt with in the award or to legal interpretations of community law set forth in the award[17] and will be considered, depending on the number of member states involved in the controversy, by three or five arbitrators.[18] The Tribunal must render an award within thirty days after the filing of a response to the appeal[19] and in its own award may confirm, modify, or revoke the legal reasoning and the decision of the award of the original arbitration panel.[20] It shall prevail over the arbitration panel's award.[21]

Awards of the Tribunal and arbitration panels are to be adopted by majority vote and signed by all of its members.[22] The former are firm, final and unappealable and obligatory to all member states involved in the controversy.[23] The latter are firm, final, unappealable and obligatory to the parties involved therein unless they have been appealed to the Tribunal.[24] They must be complied with in accordance with their terms within the time period set forth therein.[25]

---

13. Olivos, *Id.* at Art. 17(1).

14. Olivos, *Id.* at Art. 18 (1)-(2).

15. Olivos, *Id.* at Art. 18(3). The member states may unanimously agree to extend the fifth arbitrators term. *Id.*

16. Olivos Regulations, *supra* note 2 at Art. 35.

17. Olivos, *Id.* at Art. 17 (2).

18. Olivos, *Id.* at Art. 20. When the controversy involves two member states, the Tribunal will consist of three arbitrators, one from each member state and one chosen by the Administrative Secretariat. *Id.* at Art. 20(1). When the dispute involves more than two member states, the Tribunal will consist of five arbitrators. *Id.* at Art. 20 (2).

19. Olivos, *Id.* at Art. 21.

20. Olivos, *Id.* at Art. 22(1).

21. Olivos, *Id.* at Art. 22(2).

22. Olivos, *Id.* at Art. 25.

23. Olivos, *Id.* at Art. 26(2).

24. Olivos, *Id.* at Art. 26(1).

25. Olivos, *Id.* at Art. 29(1).

Any of the parties to a controversy may request clarification of the award from the Tribunal or arbitration panel.[26] A beneficiary of an award who feels that the measures taken thereunder do not comply with its provisions may bring this matter to the Tribunal or arbitration panel, which will determine within thirty days whether the award has been complied with.[27]

D. Advisory Opinions

The Olivos Regulations provide that all the member states, the Council, the Group or the MCC may request an advisory opinion on any legal issue arising out of the Treaty of Asunción, the Ouro Preto Protocol, other protocols and agreements, Council Decisions, Group Resolutions or MCC Directives from the Tribunal.[28] The Tribunal is also authorized to issue advisory opinions on the legal issues described above at the request of any Superior Court of Justice (with national jurisdiction) located in any of the member states.[29]

Member states requesting an advisory opinion from the Tribunal must file a draft request therefor with the other member states. If there is a consensus among the member states that the advisory opinion should be requested, the President Pro Tem of the Council will finalize the request and submit it to the Tribunal through its Secretariat.[30] MERCOSUR institutions wishing to request an advisory opinion must submit it to the President Pro Tem of the Council, which will then transmit it to the Tribunal, again through its Secretariat.

The Tribunal must issue its written advisory opinion within forty-five days from its receipt of the request therefor.[31]

This procedure somewhat resembles that set forth in Article 234 of the Treaty of Rome, which grants the European Court of Justice the right to issue preliminary rulings on the interpretation of the Treaty of Rome or the validity and interpretation of acts of institutions of the Union. These preliminary rulings may be given, however, only where the issue has been raised in a court of tribunal of a member state and that court considers a ruling thereon necessary

---

26. Olivos, *Id.* at Art. 28.

27. Olivos, *Id.* at Art. 30.

28. Olivos Regulations, *supra* note 2, at Art. 3(1).

29. *Id.* at art. 4(1). The procedure by means of which these courts will request an advisory opinion from the Tribunal will be created after consultation with the courts of the member states. *Id.* at Art. 4(2).

30. *Id.* at Art. 3(2).

31. *Id.* at Art. 7.

for its resolution of the matter.[32] It is not available, however, at the request of a member state or a community institution.

E. Claims by Individuals

Individuals with a claim against a member state based on the sanction or application by that state, in violation of the Treaty, its Protocols, Council Decisions or Group Resolutions, of legal or administrative measures which have a restrictive, discriminatory or disloyally competitive effect on that individual ("individual controversy")[33] may file a claim before the National Section of the Group where the claimant resides.[34] The National Section of the Group which receives the claim will either a) negotiate with the National Section of the Group to which the member state against whom the claim has been brought to resolve it, or b) send the claim to the Group without any further proceeding or recommendation.[35] The Group will then evaluate the claim and may dismiss it or convoke a panel of experts on the subject matter of the controversy for an opinion on its merits.[36] The panel of experts consists of at least three members appointed by the Group[37] and will render a decision regarding the individual controversy to the Group.[38] If the decision agrees with the claimant, then any member state may request from the defendant member state the annulment of the challenged actions or corrective measures ("relief"). If the defendant member state refuses to provide such relief, then the member state requesting relief may commence an arbitration proceeding against the defendant member state under the process described above.[39]

F. An Evaluation

This MERCOSUR dispute resolution system, even as strengthened by the addition of the Tribunal in the Olivos Protocol, is simply not adequate and leaves much to be desired. The system is chiefly designed to be used where two or more member states submit a dispute arising out of the MERCOSUR norms to an ad hoc panel of arbitrators appointed for that particular case. There is no

---

32. Treaty of Rome, *supra* Chptr. 2 note 58, at Art. 234.
33. Brasilia, *Id.* at Art. 25.Olivos, *Id.* at Art. 39.
34. Brasilia, *Id.* at Art. 26. Olivos, *Id.* at Art. 40
35. Brasilia, *Id.* at Art. 27–28. Olivos, *Id.* at Art. 41.
36. Brasilia, *Id.* at Art. 29. Olivos, *Id.* at Art. 42.
37. Brasilia, *Id.* at Art. 30. Olivos, *Id.* at Art. 43.
38. Brasilia, *Id.* at Art. 32. Olivos, *Id.* at 44.
39. *Id.*

effective mechanism to protect the rights under community law of individual entities or persons. Furthermore, the Tribunal's Secretariat notwithstanding, there is no effective mechanism by means of which the institution *itself* can enforce compliance with its norms. It is cumbersome and complicated to use, and its three part process is guaranteed to ensure a lengthy wait prior to any resolution of the dispute. Justice delayed is often justice denied, especially if one of the parties to the dispute feels that this lack of resolution is harmful to its interests.[40] Furthermore, this system is inadequate to deal with what is likely to be a major component of the majority of disputes: the interpretation of the meaning or intent of a particular MERCOSUR norm. There is no court that can issue interpretations of these norms in a consistent fashion, creating a body of knowledge that parties in the future can rely upon in planning their actions. These arbitrators, depending on their identity or nationality, may not necessarily be objective. The arbitrators are selected from a list of arbitrators compiled and kept by MERCOSUR. They serve for the individual case, and there is no guarantee that they will be reappointed to another case.[41] They are not obligated to follow (or even take into account) any other arbitrators' reasoning or interpretations. They create their own rules of procedure and have a great discretion about what law they will apply and how they will do so.[42] Although the arbitration awards entered into pursuant to this system are published, the process itself is private among the parties only. Participation by others such as *amici curiae* is not contemplated.

The addition of a "permanent" appellate arbitration panel to hear appeals under the Olivos Protocol does not really solve this problem. The Tribunal is simply a "super arbitration panel" which operates as such and which is empowered to resolve issues of law and policy interpretation dealt with by another, more ad hoc panel. Again, there is no procedure for intervention by other interested parties. It is true that its members, by virtue of their appointment for a period of years, will have the opportunity to develop a consistent set of interpretations of community law. This is not, however, the equivalent of a panel of permanently appointed, objective, professional judges, sitting in open court in transparent proceedings, and whose opinions will be perceived as fair by virtue

---

40. *See, e.g.,* Brasilia, *supra* Chptr. 2 note 29 at Art. 19(1). Olivos, *supra* Chptr. 2 note 29 at Art. 34.

41. There are only three arbitrators from the list who have served more than once. *See* Lista de Arbitros *available at* http://www.mercosur.org.uy/espanol/snor/varios/lista_de_arbitros.htm.

42. Even though the Brasilia Protocol authorizes an arbitral tribunal to adopt provisional remedies to prevent "irreparable harm to one of the parties," the important question to ask is: who will enforce these provisional remedies? There is no real enforcement provision in the Protocol for these remedies. Who is to prevent the malefactor from simply ignoring the arbitral tribunal's order? *See* Brasilia, *supra* Chptr. 2 note 29, at Art. 18. Olivos, *supra* Chptr. 2 note 29 at Art. 15.

of this transparency and the opportunity to participate therein of all persons or entities who might have an interest in the controversy, whether they are a direct litigant or not. This perception of fairness ensures that its rulings will be followed (or at least acquiesced to) by all participants.[43] The process is not transparent even though they are kept by the Secretariat in a publicly available compilation.[44]

To date, the process has been used a limited number of times.[45] These awards are not likely to form an intelligible body of jurisprudence providing parties with reliable and consistent interpretations of community norms.

Finally and most important, the enforcement mechanism for these arbitral awards is extremely weak.[46] Given the fact that all decisions by MERCOSUR institutions are required to be taken by consensus and in the presence of all the member states,[47] it is unlikely that such a unanimous decision to sanction a member state will ever be taken. Furthermore, a boycott of the proceedings by a member state would prevent the Council from taking such a decision in the first place. This system is clearly not designed to be a mechanism which MERCOSUR itself can use to enforce compliance with the norms it enacts. Clearly, a better system is needed.

---

43. Indeed, there are some ECJ cases where the court has actually "created" new legal principles out of provisions of the Treaty of Rome. *See, e.g.*, Van Gend en Loos v. Nederlande Administratie der Belastingen, 26/62 [1963] ECR1, [1963] CMLR 105. The Court's high standing among the member states makes it certain that decisions such as this will be accepted.

44. Ouro Preto, *supra* Intro. note 5, at Art. 32.

45. There have been 9 Arbitration Awards: Laudos Arbitrales: I) Comunicados DECEX (Arg./Bras.); II) Carne de cerdo (Arg./Bras.); III) Productos textiles (Bras./Arg.); IV) Pollos (Bras./Arg.); V) Bicicletas (Uru./Arg.); VI) Neumaticos (Uru./Bras.); VII) Fitoanitarios (Arg./Bras.) VIII) IMESI (Para./Uru.) IX Lana (Arg/Uru.) *available at* http://www.mercosur.org.uy/espanol/normativa/laudos.htm.

46. Article 23 of the Brasilia Protocol and Articles 31 and 32 of the Olivos Protocol provide for "temporary compensatory measures"(such as the suspension of concessions "or other equivalents") awarded by the other member states as the sole enforcement remedy for a successful party in a dispute. Brasilia, *supra* Chptr. 2 note 29 at Art. 23. Olivos, *supra* Chptr. 2 note 29 at Arts. 31, 32.

47. Ouro Preto, *supra* Intro. note 5, at Art. 37.

Chapter 4

The MERCOSUR
Trade Regulation System

A. Introduction

This chapter describes and discusses the MERCOSUR trade liberation program. This discussion will trace the development of and describe the MERCOSUR trade liberation program, including its tariff reduction program, common external tariff and nomenclature, its rules of origin regime, and its safeguard clauses procedure.

B. The MERCOSUR Trade Liberation Program

1. PSA 14

As has been noted above, PSA 14, which was executed by Argentina and Brazil on December 20, 1990, is the direct predecessor to the Treaty of Asuncion, in that it sets forth a number of concepts that were later incorporated into the latter document.[1]

In PSA 14, Argentina and Brazil first agreed to eliminate all duties, charges and other restrictions that applied to their reciprocal trade no later than December 31, 1994.[2] The terms "duties" and "charges" meant all customs duties and other charges having an equivalent effect, whether they were related to fiscal, monetary, exchange or other sectors levied on foreign trade.[3]

A "restriction" was any administrative, financial, exchange or other measure through which one of the parties unilaterally impeded or hindered reciprocal trade.[4]

---

1. *See supra* Chptr. 2 notes 13–26 and accompanying text.
2. PSA 14, *supra* Chptr. 2 note 136, at Art. 3.
3. *Id.* at Art. 4(a).
4. *Id.* at Art. 4(b).

The agreement was meant to cover the total tariff universe of goods, as classified by the ALADI Tariff Nomenclature.[5] It first preserved and listed all preferences (consisting of a percentage reduction of the most favorable import tariffs applicable to non ALADI member states) previously agreed upon by the parties.[6]

The principal trade liberalization measure set forth in PSA 14 is the agreement by Brazil and Argentina to a program, starting on January 1, 1991 of gradual, linear and automatic tariff reductions on all products in the ALADI tariff nomenclature in accordance with a set timetable. This program would be implemented through a series of preferences (tariff reductions set forth as percentages of the appropriate tariff) applied in accordance with the timetable to the tariffs in effect at that particular time.[7]

The timetable for the application of preferences started on January 1, 1991 and was implemented every six months. It was meant to be completed by December 31, 1994. Some goods seemed to have a relatively short preference period. For goods classified in chapters 96–100 of the ALADI Nomenclature (diverse objects and merchandise and objets d'art and antiques), the preference would consist of a 100% reduction in tariffs effective January 1, 1991.[8] Goods classified in chapters 91–95 (optical, photographic, electronic and precision tools and equipment and weapons and ammunition), would have a 95% preference apply on January 1, 1991 and a 100% preference apply on June 30, 1991.[9] Goods described in chapters 86–90 (transport materials) would enjoy 90%, 95% and 100% preferences on January 1, 1991, June 30, 1991 and December 31, 1991 respectively.[10] Common metals and their manufactures, electronic, sound and television equipment and their accessories (Chapters 81 through 85) would enjoy preferences of 85%, 89% 93%, 97% and 100% every six months through December 31, 1992.[11] Preferences of 80%, 85%, 90%, 95% and 100%, on January 1, 1991 through December 31, 1992 would apply to goods described in chapters 76 through 80 (Common metals and their manufactures).[12] Similarly, goods described on chapters 71–75 (pearls, precious stones and common metals and their manufactures) enjoyed preferences of 75%, 80%, 85%, 90%, 95% and 100% through June 30, 1993.[13]

---

5. *Id.* at Art. 2. The ALADI Tariff Nomenclature (hereinafter, "ALADI Nomenclature") *available at* http://www.aladi.org/nsfaladi/naladi02.nsf/naladisaweb.

6. *Id.* at Arts. 5–6, and Annexes I and II.

7. *Id.* at Art. 7.

8. *Id.* ALADI Nomenclature, *supra* note 276, at Sections XX and XXI.

9. *Id.* ALADI Nomenclature, *Id.* at Sections XVIII and XIX.

10. *Id.* ALADI Nomenclature, *Id.* at Section XVII.

11. *Id.* ALADI Nomenclature, *Id.* at Section XV and XVI.

12. *Id.* ALADI Nomenclature, *Id.* at Section XVI.

13. *Id.* ALADI Nomenclature, *Id.* at Section XIV and XV.

Three categories of goods had longer preference periods, ending in December 31, 1993. For example, shoes, hats, clothing articles, feather products, artificial flowers and hair products (chapters 66–70) had preferences of 70%, 75%, 80%, 85%, 90%, 95% and 100% through that time period.[14] Similarly goods described in chapters 61 through 65 (textile products and manufactures, shoes and hats) had preferences of 65%, 71%, 77%, 83%, 89%, 96% and 100%[15] and goods described in chapters 56 through 60 (textile products and manufactures) had preferences of 60%, 67%, 74%, 81%, 88%, 95% and 100%, respectively.[16] Two categories of goods had preference periods ending on June 30, 1994. These included goods described in chapters 51–55 (silk, cotton, wool, artificial filaments or fibers), which had preferences of 55%, 61%, 67%, 73%, 79%, 86%, 93% and 100%.[17] Secondly, goods included in chapters 46–50 (straw products, wood paste products, paper and cardboard products and books) had preferences of 50%, 57%, 64%, 71%, 78%, 85%, 92% and 100% respectively.[18]

Two other categories of goods, setting forth almost half of the ALADI tariff nomenclature, had preference periods ending on December 31, 1994. These included goods described in chapters 41–45 (furs, leather goods and manufactures, wood products and cork products), with preferences of 45%, 52%, 59%, 66%, 73%, 80%, 87%, 94% and 100%.[19] Lastly, goods described in chapters 1 through 40 (live animals and animal kingdom products, products of the animal kingdom, animal or vegetable fats and oils, food industry products, alcoholic beverages, tobacco, mineral products, products of chemical industries, plastic and rubber and their manufactures) had preferences of 40%, 47%, 54%, 61%, 68%, 75%, 82%, 89% and 100% respectively.[20]

These preferences would be applied over the tariff in force at the time of their application. In case either party to the agreement increased their tariff on importations from third countries, the preference would apply to the tariff in effect on January 1, 1991. If these tariffs were to be lowered, the preferences would apply to the new, lower tariff on the date in which they go into effect.[21]

These preferences would not apply to any products that Brazil and Argentina chose to exclude from the program.[22] These exclusions were listed in two Addenda to the agreement and the parties agreed to reduce the list by 20%

---

14. *Id.* ALADI Nomenclature, *Id.* at Sections XIII and XIV.
15. *Id.* ALADI Nomenclature, *Id.* at Sections XI and XII.
16. *Id.* ALADI Nomenclature, *Id.* at Sections XI.
17. *Id.* ALADI Nomenclature, *Id.* at Section XI.
18. *Id.* ALADI Nomenclature, *Id.* at Sections IX–XI.
19. *Id.* ALADI Nomenclature, *Id.* at Sections VIII–IX.
20. *Id.* ALADI Nomenclature, *Id.* at Sections I–VII.
21. PSA 14, *supra* Chptr. 2 note 13, at Art. 7.
22. *Id.* at Art. 8.

on a yearly basis.[23] The products that were removed from the exclusion lists would then be subject to the schedule of preferences described above.[24] Both parties agreed to maintain these preferences, against each other, and to maintain an agreed upon tariff preference with regard to third parties. They also agreed to consultations prior to any tariff reduction toward third parties that would invalidate the previously agreed upon tariff preferences.[25]

Three other concepts are also part of the PSA 14 trade liberation program. First, the agreement provided that both parties would harmonize their macroeconomic policies, as set forth in the Cooperation, Integration and Development agreement, which they had previously agreed to.[26] This harmonization would start with the macroeconomic policies which are connected with the flow of commerce and with the configuration of the industrial sector in both countries.[27] Secondly, the parties agreed on a process of industrial sector harmonization, which would be incorporated as additional addenda to the agreement.[28] Lastly, a party to the agreement finding itself in an emergency supply situation regarding a certain import would first consult with the other party regarding the possibility of having the latter provide the product under normal market conditions. If the second party did not reply or agree to provide the product, and if the first party then lowered its tariff on that product on a temporary basis in order to meet the emergency, the modified tariff would not be taken into account in the tariff reduction program discussed above.[29]

2. *Treaty of Asunción*

As noted previously,[30] the Treaty of Asunción provides that its signatory states will create a common market among themselves by December 31, 1994.[31] This common market was to be characterized by the free movement of goods, services and factors of production through the elimination of customs duties and non-tariff restrictions, the establishment of a common external tar-

---

23. *Id.* The addenda were set forth in Addendums III and IV of PSA. They are currently unavailable electronically.

24. *Id.* at Art. 9.

25. *Id.* at Art. 13.

26. *Id.* at Art. 10.

27. *Id.*

28. *Id.* No Sectoral Harmonization Agreements appear to have been negotiated thus far.

29. *Id.* at Art. 14.

30. *See supra* Chptr. 2 note 32.

31. Asunción, *supra* Intro. note 1, at Art. 1.

iff and the adoption of a common trade policy, and the co-ordination of macroeconomic and sectoral policies in several areas.[32]

During the transition period before December 31, 1994, a trade liberalization program, consisting of progressive, linear and automatic tariff reductions accompanied by the elimination of non-tariff restrictions or equivalent measures, as well as any other restrictions on trade between the member states, was to be implemented.[33] The purpose of this program was to arrive at a zero tariff and non-tariff restrictions environment for the area of member states by December 31, 1994.[34]

The term "duties and charges" was defined as customs duties and other charges of equivalent effect, whether related to fiscal, monetary, foreign exchange or other matters, levied on foreign trade. This concept did not cover fees and other similar charges corresponding to the approximate cost of services rendered.[35] The term "restrictions" was defined as any administrative, financial, foreign exchange or other measures by means of which a member state unilaterally hinders or impedes reciprocal trade.[36]

As was the case in PSA 14, the principal concept surrounding the Treaty of Asuncion's trade liberation program was a program of gradual, linear, and automatic tariff reductions, which was to benefit products classified according to the ALADI tariff nomenclature.[37] These reductions were to be made according to a timetable ending on December 31, 1994.[38] According to this timetable, tariffs on ALL products in the ALADI tariff nomenclature were to be reduced 47% by June 30, 1991; 54% by December 31, 1991; 61% by June 30, 1992; 75% by June 30, 1993; 82% by December 31, 1993, 89% by June 30, 1994 and 100% by December 31, 1994.[39]

These tariff reductions, or preferences, were to apply to the tariff in force at the time of their application and consisted or the specified percentage reductions in the most favorable duties and charges applied to imports of products coming from third countries not members of ALADI. If one of the member states increased any tariff for imports for third countries, the established tariff reduction timetable continued to apply at the tariff level in force on January 1, 1991. If, on the other hand, tariffs were reduced, the corresponding preference

---

32. *Id.* These areas included foreign trade, agriculture, industry, fiscal and monetary matters, foreign exchange and capital, services, customs, transport and communications, and any further areas that may be agreed upon. *Id.*

33. *Id.* at Art. 5(a).

34. *Id.*

35. *Id.* at Annex I, Art. 2(a).

36. *Id.* at Annex I, Section 2(b).

37. *Id.* at Annex I, Art. 3.

38. *Id.*

39. *Id.*

would apply automatically to the new tariff on the date on which that new tariff entered into force.[40]

Preferences agreed to in partial scope agreements concluded by the member states in the framework of ALADI (such as PSA 14) were to be expanded, under the tariff reduction program, according to a timetable described below. These reductions were to apply only in the context of the corresponding partial scope agreement and was not to benefit other member states or apply to products included in their respective exceptions schedules.[41]

The timetable is virtually identical to the tariff reduction schedule set forth in PSA 14.[42] The timetable for the application of preferences started on January 1, 1991 and was implemented every six months. It was meant to be completed by December 31, 1994. Goods classified in chapters 91–95 would have a 100% preference on June 30, 1991.[43] Goods described in chapters 86–90 were subject to 95% and 100% preferences on June 30, 1991 and December 31, 1991 respectively.[44] Chapters 81 through 85 goods would enjoy preferences of 89% 93%, 97% and 100% every six months through December 31, 1992.[45] Preferences of 85%, 90%, 95% and 100%, on January 1, 1991 through December 31, 1992 were to be imposed to goods described in chapters 76 through 80.[46] Similarly, goods described on chapters 71–75 had preferences of 80%, 85%, 90%, 95% and 100% through June 30, 1993.[47]

Three categories of goods had longer preference periods, ending in December 31, 1993. For example, chapters 66–70 goods had preferences of 75%, 80% 85%, 90%, 95% and 100% through that time period.[48] Similarly goods described in chapters 61 through 65 had preferences of 71%, 77%, 83%, 89%, 96% and 100%[49] and goods described in chapters 56 through 60 had preferences of 67%, 74%, 81%, 88%, 95% and 100%, respectively.[50]

Two categories of goods had preference periods ending on June 30, 1994. These included goods described in chapters 51–55 with preferences of 61%, 67%, 73%, 79%, 86%, 93% and 100%.[51] Secondly, goods included in chap-

---

40. *Id.* The Treaty also required all member states to exchange among themselves and transmit to ALADI an updated copy of their customs tariff and copies of those in force on January 1, 1994.
41. *Id.* at Annex I, Art. 4.
42. *See supra* notes 7–20 and accompanying text.
43. *Id. See* ALADI Nomenclature, *supra* note 5 at Sections XVIII and XIX.
44. *Id.* ALADI Nomenclature, *Id.* at Section XVII.
45. *Id.* ALADI Nomenclature, *Id.* at Section XV and XVI.
46. *Id.* ALADI Nomenclature, *Id.* at Section XVI.
47. *Id.* ALADI Nomenclature, *Id.* at Section XIV and XV.
48. *Id.* ALADI Nomenclature, *Id.* at Sections XIII and XIV.
49. *Id.* ALADI Nomenclature, *Id.* at Sections XI and XII.
50. *Id.* ALADI Nomenclature, *Id.* at Sections XI.
51. *Id.* ALADI Nomenclature, *Id.* at Section XI.

ters 46–50 had preferences of 57%, 64%, 71%, 78%, 85%, 92% and 100% respectively.[52]

Two remaining categories of goods, again setting forth almost half of the ALADI tariff nomenclature, had preference periods ending on December 31, 1994. These included goods described in chapters 41–45 with preferences of 52%, 59%, 66%, 73%, 80%, 87%, 94% and 100%[53] and goods described in chapters 1 through 40 with preferences of 47%, 54%, 61%, 68%, 75%, 82%, 89% and 100% respectively.[54]

The tariff reduction timetable described above did not apply to products included in the schedules of exceptions submitted by each of the member states. Argentina's exception list included 394 items set forth in the ALADI Nomenclature items. Brazil's list of exceptions included 324 items, while Paraguay's list included 439 items. The largest list of exceptions was Uruguay's with 960 items.[55] These exception lists were set forth in Appendices I–IV of the Treaty.[56]

Argentina and Brazil pledged to remove 20% of the items in these exception lists yearly through December 31, 1994.[57] Paraguay and Uruguay, on the other hand, had a longer time to whittle down their exception lists. Their schedule of reductions was to be 10% on the date of entry into force of the Treaty, 10% on December 31, 1991, 20% on December 31, 1992, 20% on December 31, 1993, 20% on December 31, 1994 and 20% on December 31, 1995.[58] Products removed from the exception lists would have the preferences resulting from the tariff reduction program apply to them automatically on the date on which they are removed therefrom.[59]

Member states were allowed to apply up to December 31, 1994 only the non-tariff restrictions expressly mentioned in the notes supplementing the complementary agreement to be concluded by the member states in the framework of the ALADI treaty.[60] All non-tariff restrictions were to be eliminated from the common market area as of December 31, 1994.[61]

As was the case in PSA 14, the member states were expected to coordinate any macroeconomic and sectoral policies which may be agreed upon and

---

52. *Id.* ALADI Nomenclature, *Id.* at Sections IX–XI.
53. *Id.* ALADI Nomenclature, *Id.* at Sections VIII–IX.
54. *Id.* ALADI Nomenclature, *Id.* at Sections I–VII.
55. *Id.* at Annex I, Art. 6.
56. *See Id.* at Appendices I through IV.
57. *Id.*, Annex I, Art. 7(a).
57. *Id.* at Annex I, Art. 7(b).
59. *Id.* at Annex I, Art. 9.
60. *Id.* at Annex I, Art. 10. This agreement is Partial Scope Agreement 18, Acuerdo de Complementación Económica No. 18 (AAP.CE No. 18) Argentina, Brazil, Paraguay y Uruguay, *available at* http://www.ALADI.org/nsfALADI/textacdos.nsf.
61. *Id.*

specifically referred to in the Treaty,[62] beginning with those connected with trade flows and the composition of the productive sectors of the member states.[63]

3. The Common External Tariff

a. Background

The Treaty of Asunción provided that MERCOSUR would adopt a common external tariff ("CET") applicable to all imports from non-member states into MERCOSUR territory.[64] The MERCOSUR CET, together with a tariff nomenclature was adopted by Council Decision 22/94 in 1994.[65] Decision 22/94 also delegated to the Group the power to approve modifications to the CET.[66]

b. Increases to the CET

In 1997, the Council approved a three percent temporary across the board increase to the CET, applicable to all but a limited number of products.[67] This increase was not to be extended beyond December 31, 2000.[68] At that time, it was extended for a maximum period of two years from January 1, 2001 and was reduced to two and a half percent.[69] This increase was reduced to one and a half percent effective January 1, 2002[70] and further extended through December 31, 2003.[71] These temporary increases apply to the current CET.[72]

---

62. *See Id.* at Art. 1.

63. *Id.* at Annex I, Art. 11.

64. Asunción, Intro. *supra* note 1, at Art. 1.

65. MERCOSUR/CMC/Dec. No. 22/94, (hereinafter, "Decision 22/94") *available at* http://www.mercosur.org.uy/espanol/snor/normativa/decisiones/Dec2294.htm at Art. 1.

66. *Id.* at Art. 8.

67. MERCOSUR/CMC/Dec. No. 15/97, (hereinafter, "Decision 15/97") *available at* http://www.mercosur.org.uy/espanol/snor/normativa/decisiones/1997/9715.htm at Art. 1; "International Agreements: MERCOSUR Nations Agree to Implement 3 Percent CET Hike," 15, International Trade Reporter (BNA) 22 (January 7, 1998).

68. *Id.* at Art. 5.

69. MERCOSUR/CMC/Dec. No. 67/00, (hereinafter, "Decision 67/00") *available at* http://www.mercosur.org.uy/espanol/snor/normativa/decisiones/2000/6700.htm at Art. 1.

70. MERCOSUR/CMC/Dec. No. 06/01, (hereinafter, "Decision 06/01") *available at* http://www.mercosur.org.uy/espanol/snor/normativa/decisiones/2001/dec06-01.htm   at Art. 1.

71. MERCOSUR/CMC/Dec. No. 21/02, (hereinafter, "Decision 21/02") *available at* http://www.mercosur.org.uy/espanol/snor/normativa/decisiones/2002/dec_021_002_.htm at Art. 1.

72. MERCOSUR/GMC/RES No. 65/01, (hereinafter, "Resolution 65/01), *available at* http://www.mercosur.org.uy/espanol/snor/normativa/resoluciones/2001/0165.htm at Art. 2.

c. The Current CET

The current MERCOSUR CET and tariff nomenclature was adopted by the Group in 2001.[73] The tariff nomenclature is extremely similar to the ALADI tariff nomenclature. It consists of 99 chapters arranged in twenty one sections, with a wide ranging variety of tariffs ranging from zero to twenty percent.[74] They shall be briefly described below.

4. *The CET by Sections*

The first four sections of the CET cover agricultural goods. Section one, "live animals and products of the animal kingdom," includes chapters 1 through 5, with tariffs ranging from 0 to 16%.[75] Section two, "products of the vegetable kingdom," includes chapters 6 through 14, with tariffs ranging from zero to fourteen percent.[76] Section three, "animal or vegetable greases and oils" includes chapter 15, with tariffs ranging from four to twelve percent.[77] Section four, "food industry products," includes chapters 16 through 24, with tariffs ranging from 6 through 20%.[78]

The next three sections of the CET cover minerals, chemical and plastic products. Section 5, "mineral products," includes chapters 25 through 27, with tariffs ranging from 0 through 4%.[79] Section 6, "products of the chemical industry," includes chapters 28 through 38, with tariffs ranging from two to eighteen percent.[80] Section 7, "plastic and its manufactures," includes chapters 39 and 40, with tariffs ranging from two to eighteen percent.[81]

The next five sections cover a variety of products. Section 8, "leathers and leather products," includes chapters 41 through 43, with tariffs ranging from two to 20 percent.[82] Section 9, "wood, vegetable charcoal, wood manufactures

---

73. *Id.* at Art. 1.

74. The CET and tariff nomenclature are *available at* http://www.mercosur.org.uy/espanol/snor/aec/anexo_por_seccion_tabla.htm.

75. *Id.* at Chapters 1–5. The highest tariff (16%) is found in chapter 4, "milk and milk products."

76. *Id.* at Chapters 6–14. The highest tariff (14%) are found in chapters 11, "products of the milling industry," and chapter 13, "gum, resins and other vegetable extracts."

77. *Id.* at Chapter 15.

78. *Id.* at Chapters 16–24. The highest tariff (20%) are found in chapters 22, "drinks and alcoholic beverages," and chapter 24, "tobacco and tobacco products."

79. *Id.* at Chapters 25–27. The highest tariff (4%) is found in all three chapters.

80. *Id.* at Chapters 28–38. The highest tariff 18%) are found in chapters 33, "essential and resinoid oils," and chapter 34, "soap and lubricants."

81. *Id.* at Chapters 39–40. The highest tariff (18%) is found in chapter 39, "plastic and its manufactures."

82. *Id.* at Chapters 41–43. The highest tariff (20%) is found in chapter 42, "leather manufactures" and 43, "furs and fur products."

and cork and its manufactures," covers chapters 44 through 46, with tariffs ranging from two to twelve percent.[83] The tariff range of Section 10, "wood paste, other fibrous celluloids, paper and cardboard," (covering chapters 47–49) is from 2 to 16%.[84] "Textiles and their manufactures" are the subject matter of section 11 (chapters 50–63), with tariffs ranging from two to twenty percent.[85] Finally, section 12 covers "shoes, hats, umbrellas, canes and feather and hair products" in four chapters (64 through 67) and lists tariffs ranging from sixteen through twenty percent.[86]

Section 13 (chapters 68–70) covers "plaster, stone, cement, asbestos, ceramic and glass products" and its tariffs range from two to eighteen percent.[87] Section 14 includes one chapter (71), which includes "pearls, precious stones, precious metals, jewelry and coins" and whose tariffs range from zero to eighteen percent.[88] Its antithesis is Section 15 (chapters 72–83), which covers "base metals and their products," with the CET in this section ranging from zero through eighteen percent.[89]

The next three sections cover sophisticated manufactured goods. "Electrical, sound, television and recording equipment" are the subject of section 16 (chapters 84–85). Their CET rates range from zero to twenty percent.[90] Section 17 (chapters 86–89), "transport materials," includes motor vehicles, automobiles, aircraft, spaceships and ships and their tariffs range from zero to twenty percent.[91] Lastly, section 18 includes "optical, photography, medicochirurgical instruments and musical instruments." It covers chapters 90 through 92 and its tariffs range from zero to twenty percent.[92]

Section 19 (chapter 93) covers "arms and ammunition" and these goods are subject to a twenty percent tariff.[93]

---

83. *Id.* at Chapters 44–46. The highest tariff (12%) is found in chapter 46, "straw and straw products."

84. *Id.* at Chapters 47–49. The highest tariff (16%) is found in chapters 48, "paper and cardboard" and 49, "books and newspapers."

85. *Id.* at Chapters 50–63. The highest tariff (20%) is found in chapters 57, "rugs and other floor coverings," 61, "stitched dress accessories," and 63 "other ready made textile articles."

86. *Id.* at Chapters 64–67. The highest tariff (20%) is found all but one chapter (chapter 67 "feathers and feather products").

87. *Id.* at Chapters 68–70 The highest tariff (18%) is found all but one chapter (chapter 68 "stone, plaster, cement and asbestos manufactures").

88. *Id.* at Chapter 71.

89. *Id.* at Chapters 72–83. The highest tariff (18%) is found in chapter 82, "tools, knives and cutlery."

90. *Id.* at Chapters 84–85. The highest tariff (20%) is found in all both chapters.

91. *Id.* at Chapters 86–89. The highest tariff (20%) is found in chapter 89 "ships and other floating structures."

92. *Id.* at Chapters 90–92 The highest tariff (20%) is found all but one chapter (chapter 92 "musical instruments").

93. *Id.* at Chapter 93.

"Miscellaneous merchandise and products" are the subject matter of section 20, which includes chapters 94 through 96. The CET rates applicable to these goods range from fourteen to twenty percent.[94] The last section of the CET (section 21, chapters 97–99) covers "art objects and antiquities," which have a tariff rate of four percent.[95]

C. The MERCOSUR Rules of Origin

1. Applicability of the Rules of Origin

PSA 14 and the Treaty of Asunción provide that the preferences negotiated in accordance with the Trade Liberalization Program described above would apply only to those products originating from its member states, as set forth in the rules of origin set forth therein.[96]

The rules of origin, were originally set forth in Annex V to PSA 14 and Annex II to Asunción,[97] They were protocolized with ALADI in Partial Scope Agreement 18, which was entered into by Argentina, Brazil, Paraguay and Uruguay on November 29, 1991[98] They were amended and restated by the Council Decision 6/94[99] and were further amended by Decisions 3/00[100] and 04/02.[101] These Decisions were repealed by Decison 18/03, which restated and codified the rules of origin.[102]

Under Decision 18/03, the rules of origin are to apply to goods that are in the process of convergence toward the common external tariff, goods subject to the common external tariff but whose inputs, parts, pieces and components

---

94. *Id.* at Chapters 94–96. The highest tariff (20%) is found in chapter 95 "toys and sports equipment").

95. *Id.* at Arts. 97–99.

96. PSA 14, *supra* Chptr. 2 note 13, at Art. 15, Asunción, *supra* Intro. note 1 at Art. 3.

97. PSA 14, *Id.* at Annex V, Asunción, *Id.* at Annex II.

98. PSA 18, *supra* note 60, at Annex I, Additional Protocol VIII.

99. MERCOSUR/CMC/Dec. No. 6/94, Règimen de Origen MERCOSUR, *available at* http://www.mercosur.org.uy/espanol/snor/normativa/decisiones/Dec6/94.htm (hereinafter, "Decision 6/94").

100. MERCOSUR/CMC/Dec. No. 03/00, Règimen de Origen MERCOSUR, *available at* http://www.mercosur.org.uy/espanol/snor/normativa/decisiones/2000/03-000.htm (hereinafter, "Decision 03/00").

101. MERCOSUR/CMC/Dec. No. 04/02, Règimen de Origen MERCOSUR, *available at* http://www.mercosur.org.uy/espanol/snor/normativa/decisiones/2002/0204.htm (hereinafter, "Decision 02/04").

102. MERCOSUR/CMC/Dec.No. 18/03. Règimen de Origen MERCOSUR, *available at* http://www.mercosur.org.uy/espanol/snor/normativa/decisiones/2003/Dec_018_003.htm (hereinafter, "Decision 18/03").

are in the process of convergence, except in the case where the value of the non member state inputs does not exceed 40% of the total FOB value of the final product, different commercial policies applied by one or more member states, or exceptional cases, as decided by the MCC.[103]

2. *General Rules of Origin*

Several principal categories of products will be considered to have been produced in a member state. First, products completely elaborated in the territory of one of the member states with materials exclusively originating therein are considered to originate in those states ("domestic products").[104] Second, all mineral, vegetable and animal products, including the fruits of the hunt and fishing, that have been extracted, cultivated, picked, born and raised in their territory or jurisdictional waters are also domestic products.[105] These include all products of the sea extracted outside their territorial waters or economic zones by ships bearing their flag or chartered by enterprises established within their territory.[106] The third category includes products resulting from operations or processes by which the products acquire their final form and which are carried out in the territory of a member state as products of a member state.[107] Products that acquire their final form simply as a result of assembly, packaging, division into lots or volumes, selection, classification, marking or other equivalent operations or processes, however, are not considered to have been produced in the territory of a member state.[108]

Furthermore, all products in whose manufacture materials not originating in the member states are used, when the manufacture results in a transformation that confers upon them a different form, as shown by a different classification in the MERCOSUR Tariff Nomenclature ("MTN") than those of its inputs, will also be considered domestic products.[109] These products will not be considered as domestic products, however, when the operations or processes consist only of simple assembly, packaging, division into lots or volumes, selection, classification, marking, bundling or similar operations.[110] In cases

---

103. Decision 18/03, *supra* note 60 at Art. 2.

104. PSA 14, *Id.* at Annex V, Art. 1 (a), Asunción, *Id.* at Annex II, Art. 1(a), Decision 18/03, *Id.* at Art. 3(b).

105. PSA 14, *Id.* at Annex V, Art. 1 (a)(I), Asunción, *Id.* at Annex II, Art. 1(b)(I), Decision 18/03, *Id.* at Art. 3(a).

106. PSA 14, *Id.* at Annex V. Art. 1. (A)(ii), Asunción, *Id.* at Annex II, Art. 1(b)(ii), Decision 18/03, *Id.* at Art. 3(a)(vii-viii).

107. Asunción, *Id.* at Annex II, Art. 1(b)(iii) Decision 6/94, *Id.* at Art. 3(c).

108. *Id.*

109. PSA 14 *Id.* at Annex V, Art. 1 (b)(iii). Asunción, *Id.* at Annex II, Art. 1(c), Decision 18/03 *Id.* at Art. 3(c).

110. PSA 14 *Id.* at Annex V., Art. 1(c), Asunción, *Id.*, Decision 18/03. *Id.* at Art. 4.

where the transformation does not result in a classification change in the MTN, goods where the CIF port of destination or maritime port value of the non-member state inputs does not exceed 40% of the FOB value of the final product will also be considered as domestic products.[111]

Products resulting from assembly operations realized in a member state which utilize non member state inputs whose cif port of destination or maritime port value does not exceed 40% of the FOB value of the finished product will also be considered as domestic products.[112] Asunción also included as member state products those products which, in addition to being produced in the territory of a member state, met the specific requirements of Annex 2 of ALADI Resolution 78.[113]

Products which acquire their final form in a member state, but whose classification in the tariff nomenclature does not change as a result of the processing they undergo therein, will also be considered to be domestic products if the CIF (destination port or maritime port) value of the materials originating in non member states do not exceed 40% of the FOB export value of the final product.[114]

The MCC has been given the right, in exceptional and justified cases, to establish future specific origin requirements for particular categories of goods.[115] It may not do so in cases involving goods manufactured exclusively in the territory of a member state with exclusive member state raw materials or parts.[116]

PSA 14 specifically incorporated the rules of origin previously negotiated which were applicable to the import of capital goods,[117] to industrialized food products[118] and to the automotive sector[119] Capital goods were required to have a MERCOSUR origin requirement of 80% of their aggregate value.[120] This requirement was changed to 60% by Decision 23/94 and currently remains at that level.[121]

---

111. *Id.* at Art. 3(d), Decision 18/03 *Id.* at Art. 3(d).

112. Decision 18/03. *Id.* at Art. 3(e).

113. Asunción, *Id.* at Annex II, Art. 1(e). These requirements are set forth at ALADI/CR/Resolución 252 (4 August 1999), Texto Consolidado y Ordenado del Règimen General de Origen de la ALADI, Annex 2.

114. PSA 14 *Id.* at Annex V., Art. 2, Asunción, *Id.* at Annex II, Art. 2. The percentage set forth in these two documents (50%) was changed to 40% in Decision 6/94. Decision 6/94. *Id.* at Art. 3(d).

115. Decision 18/03, *Id.* at Art. 5.

116. Decision 03/00, *supra* note 100, at Art. 2., Decision 18/03. *Id.* at Art. 5.

117. PSA 14 *Id.* at Annex V., Art. 3 and Annex VI.

118. PSA 14 *Id.* at Annex V., Art. 3 and Annex VII.

119. PSA 14 *Id.* at Annex V., Art. 3 and Annex VIII.

120. Decision 6/94. *Id.* at Art. 3.

121. MERCOSUR/CMC/Dec. No. 23/94, Regimen de Origen, at Art. 4, *available at* http://www.mercosur.org.uy/espanol/snor/normativa/decisiones/Dec2394.htm (hereinafter, "Decision 23/94"). Decision 18/03, *Id.* at Art. 3(f).

Finally, the rules apply to products subject to the specific rules of origin requirements set forth in Annex I to Decision 18/03. The specific rules set forth therein will prevail over the general criteria described above, as long as they are not covered by section 3(a) (animal, vegetable and mineral products) or Article 3(b) (products made exclusively in the territory of any of the member states from exclusively domestic materials).[122]

3. Rules of Origin for Specific Goods

The first, rather extensive rules of origin for specific goods were set forth in 1991 at Annex II to the Eighth Additional Protocol to PSA 18.[123] They were amended in 1994 by Decision 23/94[124] and were replaced in 1997 by the specific requirements set forth in Decision 16/97.[125] This decision specifically repealed the list of specific origin requirements set forth in PSA 18.[126] Further changes to the list of specific origin requirements for particular products were set forth in CMC Resolution 27/01[127] in Council Decision 24/02.[128] These specific rules of origin requirements have been replaced by the Annexes to Decision 18/03. Parties considering the importation or exportation of a particular product should check the latter document (and any further amendments) for any specific origin requirements that may be applicable thereto.

4. Application of the Rules of Origin

The member states are to take the elements set forth below, individually or collectively, as a base in order to determine whether or not a particular product meets the rules of origin described above. These elements include:

I.   Materials and other inputs employed in production:

    a)   Raw Materials:
        i)   Primary raw material which gives the product its essential characteristics;

---

122. Decision 18/03, *supra* note 102, at Art. 3(g).
123. PSA 18, *supra* note 60, at Annex II, Additional Protocol VIII.
124. Decision 23/94, *supra,* note 121, *supra* at Annex I.
125. MERCOSUR/CMC/Dec. No. 16/97, Règimen de Origen, *available at* http://www.mercosur.org.uy/espanol/snor/normativa/decisiones/1997/9716.htm.
126. *Id.* at Art. 3.
127. MERCOSUR/GMC/RES No. 27/21, Requisitos de Origen, *available at* http://www.mercosur.org.uy/espanol/snor/normativa/resoluciones/2001/0127.htm. This document was protocolized at PSA 18, *supra* note 60, XXXVAdditional Protocol (2001).
128. MERCOSUR/CMC/DEC No. 24/02, Règimen de Origen del MERCOSUR, *available at* http://www.mercosur.org.uy/espanol/snor/normativa/decisiones/dec2402.htm. *See* Decision 18/03, *supra* note 102.

      ii)   Principal raw materials.

  b) Parts or pieces:

      i)   Parts or principal pieces; and

      ii)   Percentage of the parts or pieces in relation to the total weight.

  c) Other inputs.

II. Process of transformation or elaboration used.

III. Maximum proportion of the value of the materials imported from non member states in relation with the total value of the product, which results from the valuation procedure agreed in each case.[129]

For purposes of determining the requirements of these rules of origin, the materials and other inputs originating out of a member state and used in another member state for the production of a particular product shall be considered to have originated in a member state.[130] "Materials" are defined as raw materials, inputs, intermediate products and pieces or parts utilized in the manufacture of a product.[131] "Territory" is also defined as the territory of the MERCOSUR member states, including their territorial and patrimonial waters located within their geographic limits.[132]

In exceptional cases, where specific origin requirements cannot be met because of supply, availability, technical specifications, delivery, delay and price problems, non member state materials may be used.[133] In this situation, the national certifying agencies that issue a certificate of origin for the goods in question must attach thereto a declaration of need issued by a competent governmental authority, which notifies the importing member state and the MCC of the circumstances and the facts that justify the issuance thereof.[134]

Goods originating in one of the member states will not benefit from the preferential tariffs established in PSA 14 unless they have been shipped directly from the exporting country to the importing country.[135] Goods are considered to have been "shipped directly" when they are transported without passing through the territory of a non member state.[136] Goods shipped in transit (with or without temporary transshipment or storage) under customs custody

---

129. PSA 14 *Id.* at Annex V., Art. 4, Asunción, *Id.* at Annex II, Art. 4, Decision 18/03. *Id.* at Art. 1.

130. PSA 14 *Id.* at Annex V., Art. 6, Asunción, *Id.* at Annex II, Art. 7, Decision 18/03. *Id.* at Art. 7.

131. Decision 18/03. *Id.* at Art. 8.

132. Decision 18/03. *Id.* at Art. 9.

133. Decision 18/03. *Id.* at Art. 6.

134. *Id.*

135. PSA 14 *Id.* at Annex V., Art. 8, Asunción, *Id.* at Annex II, Art.9, Decision 18/03. *Id.* at Art. 10.

136. PSA 14 *Id.* at Art. 8(a), Asunción, *Id.* at Annex II, Art. 9(a),Decision 18/03. *Id.* at Art. 10(a). Goods that are located in a duty free zone within one of the member states are deemed to be within the territory of a member state. Asunción, *Id.* at Art. 9(b).

through a non member state will still be considered to have been "shipped directly" under certain circumstances.[137] These circumstances are that i) the transit through the non-member state justified by geographical or transport related reasons; ii) that the goods are not destined to commerce, trade or use in the transit country; and that iii) they do not undergo, during its transport and deposit, any operation unrelated to its loading, unloading or handling to maintain them in good condition or to ensure their conservation.[138] Third party operators (not including the original shipper or transporter) may intervene in the shipment as long as the requirements set forth above are met and the intervening operator issues its own commercial invoice for the goods, which must be accompanied by a certificate of origin issued by the authorities of the exporting member state.[139]

Lastly any of the member states may propose a revision of the rules of origin. This proposal must explain and justify these changes.[140]

5. *Certificates of Origin*

In order for the importation of a product to benefit from tariff reductions, the goods must be accompanied by a certificate of origin which states that the product has meet the requirements set forth in the rules of origin.[141] The certificate of origin is the document that must accompany the goods being exported and must be issued by an authorized certifying agency, identify the goods to which it refers, and clearly indicate that the merchandise has originated in a member state by meeting the requirements set forth in the rules of origin.[142] An application for a certificate of origin must be accompanied by a sworn statement or other equivalent juridical instrument, taken by the final producer of the goods, which indicates the characteristics and components of the product and of its manufacturing process.[143] The product description in-

---

137. PSA 14 *Id.* at Art. 8(b), Asunción, *Id.* at Annex II, Art. 9(b). Decision 18/03. *Id.* at Art. 10(b).

138. PSA 14 *Id.* at Art. 8(b)(i-iii), Asunción, *Id.* at Annex II, Art. 9(b)(i-ii), Decision 6/94. *Id.* at Art. 9(b)(i-ii).

139. Decision 18/03, *Id.*, at Art. 10(c).

140. PSA 14 *Id.* at Annex V., Art. 5, Asunción, *Id.* at Annex II, Art. 6.

141. PSA 14 *Id.* at Annex V., Art.10, Asunción, *Id.* at Annex II, Art. 11.

142. Decision 18/03 *Id.* at Art. 14.

143. Decision 18/03 *Id.* at Art. 15. These will include, at a minimum:
  a) name of the firm;
  b) legal domicile and plant domicile of the firm;
  c) MTN denomination of the material to be exported;
  d) fob value;
  e) description of the production process
  f) demonstrative elements of the product components indicating:

cluded in the sworn statement must match that corresponding to the MTN classification and that set forth in the commercial invoice for the goods.[144] This certificate will be issued by an official or unofficial entity (such as a chamber of commerce) with juridical personality which has been authorized to do so by the government of the exporting member state.[145] These certificates shall be valid for a period of 180 days from their date of issue[146] and must match the sample certificate set forth in the rules.[147] Their period of validity may be extended by the time period during which the goods covered by the certificate find itself under an import suspension regime which does not permit any alteration to the goods.[148]

Certificates of origin must have a serial number and must be kept in an archive by the issuing entity for a period of two years. This archive must also include the backup documents that were filed with the application for the certificate itself.[149] Certificates of origin may not be issued until the date of issue of the commercial invoice for goods to which they refer or for sixty consecutive days thereafter.[150] They must be presented to the customs authorities of the importing member state at the moment of importation of the goods.[151]

---

i)   national materials, components and/or parts;
ii) member state materials components and/or parts, indicating their origin:
     MTN codes
     cif value in US dollars
     percentage of parts in the final product
iii) non member state materials:
     MTN codes
     cif value in US dollars
     percentage of parts in the final product

144. *Id.*

145. PSA 14 *Id.* at Annex V., Art. 11, Asunción, *Id.* at Annex II, Art. 12, Decision 18/03, *Id.* at Art. 1. When authorizing unofficial entities to issue certificates of origin, the member state should ensure that these entities have national jurisdiction. These entities may delegate some of their responsibilities to local or regional organizations, as long as the former remains directly responsible for the truth and accuracy of the certificates that are issued. *Id.* The government of the member states, before authorizing an unofficial entity to issue certificates of origin, must take into consideration its technical capacity, representativeness and trustworthiness. Decision 18/03 *Id.* at Art. 12.

146. PSA 14 *Id.* at Annex V., Art.12, Asunción, *Id.* at Annex II, Art.13, Decision 18/03, *Id.* at Art. 16.

147. PSA 14 *Id.* at Annex V., Art.13 Decision 6/94, *Id.* at Art. 14. The sample Certificate of Origin is currently set forth at Annex II to Decision 18/03, *Id.*

148. Decision 18/03, *Id.* at 10 Art. 16.

149. *Id.*

150. Decision 18/03, *Id.*, at Art. 7.

151. *Id.*

6. Certificate of Origin Forms

Decision 23/94 set forth the first certificate of origin form meant to be used to certify compliance with the rules of origin.[152] This form was replaced by the form set forth in the VIII Additional Protocol of PSA 18, which was agreed to 1994.[153] A new form was agreed to in the XIV Additional Protocol to PSA 18, which was crafted in 1996.[154] Detailed instructions for the completion of the certificate of origin form were enacted by the MCC in 1996.[155] Additional changes were made to the form by Council Decision 3/00.[156] Additional instructions for the completion of the form were set forth in MCC Directive 4/00.[157] The MCC indicated in 2001 that a new form was to be introduced, and noted that certificates of the form with the changes set forth in Decision 3/00 were to be accepted until June 30, 2001.[158] This deadline was later extended to September 30, 2001[159] and December 31, 2001.[160] The new form appears at Annex II to Decision 18/03 and its Instructions are set forth at Annex III and IV thereof.[161]

7. Certificate of Origin Rules

a. Verification of Certificates of Origin

The appropriate authorities may, in cases of justified doubt regarding the authenticity or veracity of a certificate of origin, request additional informa-

---

152. Decision 23/94, *supra* note 121, at Article 7, Annex.

153. PSA 18, *supra* note 60, at VIII Additional Protocol (1994), Annex III.

154. PSA 18, *supra* note 60, at XIV Additional Protocol (1995), Annex.

155. MERCOSUR/CCM/Dir. No. 12/96 (1996) Régimen de Origen, Annex I *available at* http://www.mercosur.org.uy/espanol/snor/normativa/directivas/1996/dir1296.htm.

156. Decision 3/00, *supra* note 100, at Arts. 6–8. This decision was protocolized with ALADI as the XXIV Additional Protocol to PSA 18. PSA 18, *supra* note 60, at XXIV Additional Protocol (2000).

157. MERCOSUR/CCM/DIR No. 04/00, Texto Consolidado y Ordenado del 'Instructivo para el Control de Certificados de Origen del MERCOSUR por parte de las Administraciones Aduaneras' y del 'Instructivo para las Entidades Habilitadas para la Emisión de Certificados de Origen' *available at* http://www.mercosur.org.uy/espanol/snor/normataiva/directivas/2000/0004.htm, protocolized with ALADI at PSA 18, *supra* note 60 at XXXIX Additional Protocol (2001).

158. MERCOSUR/CCM/Dir. No. 04/01 Régimen de Origen, Mercosur, at Art.1, *available at* http://www.mercosur.org.uy/espanol/snor/normativa/directivas/2001/0104.htm. This decision was protocolized as the XXXII Additional Protocol to PSA 18. PSA 18, *supra* note 369, at XXIV Additional Protocol (2001).

159. PSA 18, *supra* note 60 at XXXIII Additional Protocol (2001).

160. PSA 18, *Id.* at XXXVIII Additional Protocol (2001).

161. Decision 18/03, *supra* note 102 at Annexes II–IV.

tion from the entity that is responsible for the issuance of the certificate so that these doubts may be resolved.[162] Any request for information must be limited to the registries and documents available to official authorities or issuing entities. The request for information may also seek copies of all documentation required for the issuance of a certificate of origin. These requests will indicate in clear and concrete form the reasons that have given rise to doubts regarding the authenticity or veracity of the certificate. These consultations will take place only through one dependency of the appropriate official entity designated for this purpose by each member state.[163]

The appropriate authorities of the importing member state will not stop the importation proceedings of the merchandise subject to the certificate or origin subject to this process but, in order to protect that state's interests, may impose a bond as a condition precedent to the release of the goods from customs. The amount of such a bond may not exceed a value equivalent to the charges, in accordance with the importing state's law, imposed on such merchandise imported from non member states.[164]

This consultation procedure is used without prejudice to any other MERCOSUR norms or national statutes regarding illicit imports. It also does not limit any information exchanges provided for in any customs cooperation agreements entered into by the member states.[165]

The competent authority of the exporting member state must provide the information sought in this consultation procedure within thirty days from the date of receipt of the information request.[166]

The information obtain through this consultation procedure will be confidential and will be used exclusively for the clearing up of the doubts regarding the certificate of origin in question by the competent authority of the importing member state.[167]

b. Investigations

In cases where the information requested under the consultation procedure described in Article 18 of Decision 18/03 is not submitted within the time period provided in Article 19, or where the information is insufficient to clarify the regarding the origin of the merchandise, the competent authority of the importing member state may commence an investigation regarding the matter within

162. Decision 18/03, *Id.* at Art. 18.
163. *Id.*
164. *Id.*
165. *Id.*
166. *Id.* at Art. 19.
167. *Id.* at Art. 20.

40 days from the receipt of the request of information. If not, it must release any bonds imposed on the goods within thirty days from receipt of the request.[168]

An investigation on the origin of merchandise may also be requested by a member state against another member state when there are justified reasons to suspect that the former is suffering competition from merchandise imported with preferential treatment that do not comply with the rules of origin.[169] In this case the competent authority of the member state requesting the investigation will provide the importing authority with the information regarding the matter within 30 days from the request. This investigation will also be undertaken as described below.[170]

Once an investigation is started, the competent authority of the importing member state will not stop the process of new imports of identical merchandise from the same exporter or producer. It may, however, impose a bond as a condition precedent to the release of these new imports from customs. The amount of this bond, if it is imposed, many not exceed the amounts set forth in Article 18 of Decision 18/03.[171]

The competent authority of the importing member state must immediately notify the importer and the competent authority of the exporting member state of the commencement of the investigation.[172]

c. Investigation Process

During the course of the investigation, the competent authority of the importing member state ("the importing authority") may request new information and copies of documents in possession of the issuer of the certificate of origin.[173] It may also send to the competent authority in the exporting member state ("the exporting authority") a written questionnaire, indicating the certificate of origin being investigated, to be submitted to the exporter or producer.[174] Thirdly, the importing authority may request the exporting authority to arrange a visit to the producer s installations, for the purpose of ex-

---

168. *Id.* at Art. 21.
169. *Id.* at Art. 33.
170. *Id.*
171. *Id.* at Art. 22.
172. *Id.* at Art. 23.
173. *Id.* at Art. 24 (a). When the content of the aggregate local or regional aggregate value of a good is sought to be verified, the producer or exporter must facilitate access to information and documentation that permit verification of the import CIF value of the inputs originating out of the member states used in the merchandise being investigated. *Id.*

Similarly, when verifying the characteristics of certain production processes required as specific origin requirements, the exporter or producer must facilitate the access to information and documents that permit said verification. *Id.*

174. *Id.* at Art. 24(b).

amining the productive processes and installations used in the production of the merchandise in question.[175] The importing authority may also request the participation or consultation in the investigation of experts on the subject matter in question[176] or carry out any other proceedings agreed upon by the member states involved in the case under investigation.[177]

The exporting authority must produce the information and documentation requested within thirty days from the date of the receipt of the request.[178] If the information and documents are not produced, if the information and documents produced do not contain sufficient information for a determination of the authenticity or veracity of the certificate of origin to be made, or if the producers of the goods refuse an inspection visit, the importing authority can then conclude the investigation, determine that the goods being investigated do not meet the origin requirements and can thereafter deny them preferential tariff treatment.[179]

The importing authority will use its best efforts to conclude the investigation within a period of 45 days from the receipt of the information and documents previously requested. If new information or proceedings are needed, the importing authority must communicate this fact to the exporting authority and must conclude these proceedings within 75 days from the initial receipt of information. If the investigation is not completed within 90 days of its commencement, any bond posted on the merchandise will be released, without prejudice to the continuation of the investigation.[180]

At the conclusion of the investigation, the importing authority will notify the importer and the exporting authority of the conclusion of the investiga-

---

175. *Id.* at Art. 24 (c). A representative of the exporting authority will accompany the visit of the importing authority, which may include the participation of experts acting as observers. These experts must be previously identified, neutral and have no interest in the investigation. The importing member state may bar from participation experts who represent the interests of the firms or entities involved in the investigation. *Id.*

At the conclusion of the visit, the participants will sign a formal statement ("acta") which will state that the visit took place in accordance with the previously described conditions. The statement must also include the date and location of the visit, an identification of the certificates of origin which required the investigation, an identification of the specific goods being question, a listing of the participants and their affiliations, and a narrative of the visit. *Id.*

The exporting authority may request the postponement of a verification visit for a period not to exceed 30 days. *Id.*

176. *Id.* at Art. 26.

177. *Id.* at Art. 24(d).

178. *Id.* at Art. 25. During the course of the investigation, eventual modifications of the production conditions of the firms being investigated will be taken into account. *Id.* at Art. 30.

179. *Id.* at Art. 27.

180. *Id.* at Art. 28.

tion, the measures adopted regarding the origin of the merchandise, and the reasons for the decision.[181]

If the investigation concludes with an acceptance of the determination of the origin of the merchandise and the validation of the criteria used to determine this origin in the certificate of origin, any bonds will be released no later than 30 days from the conclusion of the investigation.[182] If, on the other hand, the investigation concludes with a rejection of the origin or of the criteria used to determine the origin of the merchandise, then all tariffs will be assessed against the merchandise as if it were imported from a non-member state and all sanctions set forth in the MERCOSUR rules or in the current legislation in each member state shall be imposed thereon.[183] In this case, the importing authority may deny preferential treatment of new imports of identical merchandise from the same producer, until it can be shown that the conditions of productions were modified to comply with the MERCOSUR rules of origin.[184]

d. Appeals from Investigations

If, in a case involving the modification of conditions of production, the importing and exporting authorities cannot agree on the question of whether the merchandises' conditions of production have been modified to meet with the rules of origin, then they may request a consultation from the MCC in accordance with Directive CCM 17/99,[185] request a technical evaluation to determine if the goods meet with the rules of origin,[186] or submit the matter to the MERCOSUR dispute resolution system.[187]

The exporting authority may also request an MCC consultation or a technical evaluation,[188] or submit the matter to the MERCOSUR dispute resolution system, within 60 days of receipt of the notice of conclusion of the investigation.[189] All costs shall be borne by the petitioner.[190]

---

181. *Id.* at Art. 29.
182. *Id.* at Art. 31.
183. *Id.* at Art. 32.
184. *Id.* Once the exporting authority has submitted information demonstrating that these conditions of production were modified, the importing authority shall have 30 days from the date of receipt of this information to make a decision regarding the compliance of this merchandise with the MERCOSUR rules of origin. This time period may be expanded to 60 days if a new verification visit to the producer's facilities is needed. *Id.*
185. *Id.* at Art. 35(a). This consultation will set forth the technical motives and normative foundations for the conclusion by the importing authority that the merchandise does not comply with the rules of origin. *Id.*
186. *Id.* at Art. 35 (b).
187. *Id.* at Art. 32.
188. *Id.* at Art. 36.
189. *Id.* at Art. 42.
190. *Id.* at Art. 37.

The request for a technical evaluation will be submitted to the Pro Tempore President of the Council at least 10 days prior to the next meeting of the MCC and will be accompanied by the dossier of the case.[191] The technical evaluation will be conducted by an expert on the subject matter who is designated by agreement of the parties involved in the MCC meeting described above from a list of four experts chosen prior to the meeting by the member states not involved in the dispute.[192]

The expert(s) will decide the case in accordance with the MERCOSUR rules of origin for the product involved. They may give the member states involved in the dispute the opportunity to make a presentation of their positions. They may also request from the competent authorities of the member states involved in the dispute all information they consider necessary.[193]

The expert's decision will be submitted through the President Pro Tempore of the Council to the MCC for its consideration within 30 days after the appointment of the expert.[194] The report will be considered at the next MCC meeting after its submission to the presidency. Unless the MCC rejects the report by a consensus, it will be considered accepted.[195]

As decided by the MCC, the measures adopted in accordance with Article 32 regarding the origin of the merchandise will be confirmed or revised; the bonds imposed under Articles 18 and 22 will be kept or returned; and the import fees charged in accordance with Article 28 will be confirmed or returned, within 30 days from the date of the MCC meeting in which the technical report was accepted.[196]

---

191. *Id.* at Art. 36.

192. *Id.* at Art. 37. In the absence of an agreement on the appointment of such expert, the Administrative Secretariat will chose the expert by lot from among those set forth in the list described above. If the member states involved in the dispute cannot agree to the decision of a single expert, a panel of three members may be chosen. Each of the member states involved in the dispute will chose an expert and the MCC will choose the third expert from the list of four experts described in Article 36. In the absence of agreement on the third expert, the Administrative Secretariat will choose the third expert by lot as described above.

The experts will act in their individual capacities and not as representatives of a government, and may not have any specific interests in the case under consideration. The member states shall abstain from seeking to influence their actions in any fashion. *Id.* at Art. 38.

193. *Id.* at Art. 39. The failure by an involved member state to provide requested information shall give rise to a presumption in favor of the other party. *Id.*

194. *Id.* at Art. 40. If the matter is being reviewed by three experts, their decision must be made by a majority. *Id.*

195. *Id.*

196. *Id.* at Art. 41.

D. Safeguard Clauses or Measures

1. Safeguard Clauses against Member States

The Treaty of Asunción provided, during the transition period for the common market, for the application by each of the member states of so called "safeguard clauses," if imports from other member states of a particular product included in the trade liberalization program damaged or threatened serious damage to their market as a result of a significant increase in imports of that product from the other member states over a short period of time.[197] These safeguard clauses would be imposed by the affected member state after its determination of the existence of damage or threat of damage, consultations with the other member states affected through the Common Market Group, and final approval of that member state s national delegation in the Common Market Group.[198]

Safeguard clauses were required to include an import quota and were to apply for a year, with a possible extension of an extra year if the damage or threat of serious damage continued. A safeguard clause could only be adopted once for each product.[199]

The safeguard clauses provided for in the Treaty of Asunción were eliminated after December 31, 1994[200] and are currently only of historical interest.

2. Safeguard Clauses against Non-Member State Imports

In 1997, however, the Council adopted new regulations authorizing the imposition of safeguard clauses or measures to imports from states which were not MERCOSUR members.[201]

197. Asunción, *supra* Intro. note 1, at Art. 3 and Annex IV, Arts. 1–2.
198. *Id.* at Arts. 2–3.
199. *Id.* at Arts. 4–5.
200. *Id.* at Art. 5.
201. The Portuguese version of these regulations is located at MERCOSUR/CMC/Dec. No. 17/96. (1997), *available at* http://www.sice.oas.org/trade/mrcsrs/decisiones/DEC 1796P.asp. The Spanish version appears at MERCOSUR/CMC/Dec. No. 4/97 (1997) (hereinafter, "Decision 4/97"), *available at* http://www.mercosur.org.uy/espanol/normativa/decisiones/1997/9704.htm. These regulations were incorporated into PSA 18 as the Nineteenth Additional Protocol (December 17, 1997), *available at* http://www.ALADI.org/textacdos.nsf.

a. Application of Safeguard Measures in General

Safeguard measures are first defined in the Regulation as those provided for in Article XIX of the GATT 1994 (Emergency Measures over the Importation of Determined Products).[202] MERCOSUR may impose safeguard measures, either by itself or in the name of one of its member states, if an investigation[203] determines that imports of this product into the MERCOSUR territory as a whole, or into the territory of one of its member states, have increased in such quantities (either in absolute terms or in relation to the domestic production or MERCOSUR or one of its member states[204]) and have caused or threaten to cause grave damage[205] to the domestic production of MERCOSUR or one of its member states.[206] Safeguard measures will be applied to the imported prod-

---

202. Decision 4/97, *supra* note 201, at Art. 1. Article XIX of the GATT can be found at http://www.wto.org/english/docs_e/legal_e/gatt47_02_e.htm.

203. The investigation will evaluate the relevant objective and quantifiable factors that are related to the the domestic production situation, in particular: the rhythm and amount of the increase in import of the product in absolute and relative terms; the part of the MERCOSUR of member state market where the increased imports are being absorbed, and the changes in the level of sales, production, productivity, capacity utilization, profits and losses and employment. *Id.* at Art. 5. Other factors may also be considered, such as the prices of the imports, (especially to determine if there was a significant undervaluation in relation to the price of a similar product in the domestic market) and the evolution of domestic prices of similar or directly competing products, to determine if there was a fall or no increases in prices which would otherwise would have occurred. *Id.* at Art. 6. When the threat of great damage is being alleged, an additional factor to be considered is whether the particular situation is likely to be effectively transformed into great damage. To that end, factors such as the rate of increase of exports to MERCOSUR or one of its member states, the export capacity (actual or potential) in the near future of the country of origin or export and the probability that this capacity will be used to export to MERCOSUR or one of its member states will also be considered. *Id.* at Art. 7.

204. "Domestic production" of MERCOSUR or one of its member states is defined as the group of producers of similar or directly competing products that operate in MERCOSUR or one of its member states, or those whose joint production of similar or directly competing products constitute an important proportion of the total production of these products in MERCOSUR or in one of its member states. *Id.* at Art. 3

205. "Grave damage" is defined as a significant general reduction of the situation of a particular domestic production of MERCOSUR or one of its member states. *Id.* at Art. 4(I). The term "threat of grave damage" is defined as the clear imminence of a grave damage. *Id.* at Art. 4(II).

206. *Id.* at Art. 2. When safeguard measures are imposed by MERCOSUR on its own behalf, the requirements for the determination of the existence of grave damage or the threat or grave damage will be based on conditions existing in the MERCOSUR as a whole. *Id.* at Art. 2.1. When safeguard measures are imposed by MERCOSUR on behalf of one of its member states, the requirements for the determination of the existence of grave damage or the threat of great damage will be based on conditions existing in that member state and the safeguard measure will be limited to that member state. *Id.* at Art. 2.2.

ucts, with the exception of textile or agricultural products, regardless of its origin.[207]

b. Adoption of Safeguard Measures by MERCOSUR on Its Own Behalf

1. The Process

Two entities are critical in the adoption of safeguard measures by MERCOSUR on its own behalf, the Safeguards and Commercial Defense Committee ("Committee") and the MCC. The former is in charge of conducting an investigation to determine the existence of increased exports, grave harm or threat of great harm to the MERCOSUR domestic production of similar or directly competing goods, and the causal relationship between the increase of imports of the product and the great harm or threat of great harm[208]. The MCC decides on the opening of an investigation, the adoption of provisional or final safeguard measures, the closing of an investigation without the adoption of safeguard measures, and their revocation, acceleration or liberalization.[209]

The process begins by a producer or other entity filing a written complaint with the national sections of the Committee.[210] The national sections of the Committee will then jointly examine the application to determine whether it is acceptable.[211] Once the Committee decides to accept the application, its national sections will jointly prepare a report about the advisability of opening an investigation regarding the existence of great harm of the threat of great harm to the MERCOSUR domestic production by the increased imports and will submit this report to the MCC.[212]

The MCC, in its first meeting after the receipt of the report, will, by means of a Directive, decide whether to open an investigation.[213] The President Pro

---

207. *Id.* at Art. 2.3. Textile and agricultural products will be subject to the Agreement on Agriculture and the Agreement on Textiles and Clothing of the World Trade Organization. *Id.* at Art. 82.

208. *Id.* at Art. 9.

209. *Id.* at Art. 10.

210. *Id.* at Art. 12. This application must be accompanied by evidence of the increase in imports, the grave harm or threat of great harm, and the causal relationship between the two. They must also be accompanied by an adjustment plan that places the MERCOSUR domestic production in better competitive conditions regarding those imports. *Id.*

211. *Id.* at Art. 12.2.

212. This report will contain a preliminary determination regarding the existence of great harm or threat of great harm and will also set forth a preliminary analysis of the adjustment plan submitted by the applicant. *Id.* at Art. 13.

213. *Id.* at Art. 14. The Directive will also indicate the time periods within which submissions may be made to the Committee by any interested parties. *Id.* at Art. 14.2.

Tem of the MERCOSUR Council will then notify the Safeguards Committee of the World Trade Organization of the opening of the investigation.

The Committee is responsible for the supervision of the investigation, while its national sections will collect information and data therefor.[214] The Committee's national sections will jointly draft the report regarding the existence of grave harm or the threat of great harm to the MERCOSUR domestic production caused by the increased exports of the product in question and the viability of the MERCOSUR domestic production adjustment plan. The report is then submitted to the MCC, who will consider it at its next meeting and will make the final decision regarding the adoption of safeguard measures.[215]

2. Consultations

Before the MCC imposes any safeguard measures, the President Pro Tem of the MERCOSUR Council must notify the Safeguards Committee of the World Trade Organization of its intentions. This notification must indicate the member state's willingness to engage in consultations regarding the matter.[216] The MCC must then give adequate opportunity for consultations with the governments of the countries that may have a substantial interest in the matter as exporters of the product involved.[217] The Committee will coordinate the consultation proceedings and will draft and send to the MCC a report regarding the consultations and their effects on the proposed adoption of the safeguard measure.[218]

---

214. *Id.* at Art. 15. The national sections may send questionnaires to any interested parties, may consult other sources of information, and may make site visits. *Id.* at Art. 16. They may also conduct hearings to hear any interested parties that demonstrate that they may be affected by the results of the investigation and who have special reasons to be heard. *Id.* at Art. 18. They will also evaluate the proposed actions set forth in the adjustment plan presented by the MERCOSUR domestic production, to determine if it is appropriate for its proposed goals. *Id.* at Art. 19.

Neither the Committee of its national sections will disclose any confidential information submitted to it as part of the investigation. *Id.* at Art. 21.

215. *Id.* at Arts. 20, 22. If the Committee s report does not find the existence of great harm or the threat of great harm to the MERCOSUR domestic production caused by the increased imports, or finds that the adjustment plan is not viable or adequate, it will close the investigation without the adoption of any safeguard measures. *Id.* at Art. 22.

216. *Id.* at Art. 22.2.

217. *Id.* at Art. 22.3.

218. *Id.* at Art. 22.4-22.5. The President Pro Tem of the MERCOSUR Council will notify the Safeguards Committee of the WTO of the results of the consultations. *Id.* at Art. 23.

3. Provisional Safeguard Measures

In a critical situation where any delay would create a harm that would be difficult to repair and where there is clear evidence that an increase in imports of a particular product has caused or threatens to cause great harm to the MERCOSUR domestic production, preliminary safeguard measures may be imposed.[219]

Provisional measures may not exceed 200 days. During that period, the investigation and consultation processes set forth in Articles 12 through 23 must be followed.[220] Provisional safeguard measures will take the form of increases in import tariffs in addition to the Common External Tariff.[221] The duration of these provisional measures will be included in the period of any final safeguard measures that may be imposed later.[222]

4. Final Safeguard Measures

Final safeguard measures will be determined by the MCC only if the measure is necessary to prevent or repair great harm and to facilitate the adjustment of the MERCOSUR domestic production[223] and will be imposed by a Directive.[224]

Safeguard measures may be imposed as increases to import tariffs above the Common External Tariff[225] or quantitative restrictions.[226] They will be im-

---

219. *Id.* at Art. 24. The process would involve, first a joint report by the Committee's national sections making a preliminary determination regarding the existence of great harm or the threat of great harm caused by increased imports and the existence of critical circumstances justifying immediate action. *Id.* at 24.1. This report would be submitted to the MCC, who would decide whether to impose provisional safeguard measures. These provisional safeguard measures would be imposed by a Directive, which will contain a summary of the preliminary determination of great harm or threat of great harm and the existence of critical circumstances. *Id.* at Art. 24.2-24.3. The President Pro Tem of the MERCOSUR Council would notify the World Trade Organization of the imposition of the provisional safeguard measures and would indicate the member states readiness to engage in consultations with any country that, as exporters of the goods involved, have a substantial interest in the matter. *Id.* at Art. 24.6. These consultations would be coordinated by the Committee. *Id.* at Art. 24.7.

220. *Id.* at Art. 25.

221. These may be ad valorem tariffs, specific tariffs, or a combination thereof. *Id.* at Art. 26. If the subsequent investigation finds that the increased imports did not cause or threaten to cause great harm to the MERCOSUR domestic market, any tariffs collected as part of provisional safeguard measures will be immediately refunded. *Id.* at Art. 27.

222. *Id.* at Art. 28.

223. *Id.* at Arts. 29–30.

224. *Id.* at Art. 29. The Directive will describe the conclusions regarding all matters of fact and law considered, including a detailed analysis of the matter under investigation and a demonstration of the relevance of all of the factors that were considered. *Id.* at Art. 29.1.

225. These may take the form of ad valorem tariffs, specific tariffs, or a combination of the two. *Id.* at Art. 31.I.

226. These quantitative restrictions may not reduce the quantity of imports below

posed only for the period of time necessary to prevent or repair the grave damage and facilitate the adjustment of the MERCOSUR domestic production, but may not exceed four years, unless extended.[227] The total period of a safeguard measure, including the period of provisional measures and all extensions, shall not exceed eight years.[228] In order to facilitate the adjustment of the MERCOSUR domestic production, a safeguard measure expected to be in place for a period of more than a year shall be progressively liberalized, at regular intervals, during the period it is in effect. In measures whose duration exceeds three years, the Committee will examine its concrete effects no later than the average of the duration period and the MCC may, if appropriate, revoke the measure or accelerate its liberalization. An extended measures may not be more restrictive than that in place at the end of its initial term and must be liberalized at regular intervals.[229] New safeguard measures may not be imposed on products

---

the level of the average of the imports during the last three representative years for which statistics are available, unless there is a clear indication of the necessity of fixing a different level to prevent or repair great harm. *Id.* at Art. 31.ii. In cases involving a quota assigned to a group of exporting states, the Committee may try to come to an agreement regarding the distribution of parts of the quota with the governments of the countries that have a substantial interest in the supply of the product involved. In cases where this method is not viable, the Commission, on the basis of a report by the Committee, will assign quotas to the countries that have a substantial interest in the supply of the product, based on the relative participation of each one, the values or quantities, or the imports of the product, considering a prior representative period and taking into account any special factors that may have affected or be affecting the trade on this product. *Id.* at Art. 32. The Commission may adopt other criteria for the assignment of quotas in cases of a determination of grave harm, as long as consultations with the governments of the interested countries are held under the sponsorship of the WTO Safeguards Committee and it is demonstrated that imports originating from certain countries have increased by a disproportionate percentage in relation to the total increase of imports of the product considered in the representative period. *Id.* at Art. 33.

227. *Id.* at Art. 34. The period of the safeguard measures may be extended if the MCC determines, after following the procedure set forth in articles 2–33, that the safeguard measures are still necessary to prevent or repair great harm and that there is sufficient evidence to determine that the affected production is in the process of adjustment. *Id.* at Art. 35. Before the period of the safeguard measure is extended, the Safeguards Committee of the World Trade Organization shall be notified and the Committee shall coordinate consultations with the governments of the countries with a substantial interest in the matter, as exporters of the goods in question and report thereon to the MCC. *Id.* at Arts. 35.2–35.4. The MCC shall, if it decides to impose the extension, do so in the form of a Directive, which will set forth the justifications therefor. *Id.* at Arts. 35.5–35.6. The extension shall be notified to the Safeguards Committee of the WTO. *Id.* at Art. 35.8.

228. *Id.* at Art. 36. This period may be extended in accordance with Article 9 of the WTO Agreement on Safeguards for an additional period of two years. *Id.*

229. *Id.* at art. 37,. The MCC may, at any time, revoke or alter a safeguard measure to reflect changed circumstances. *Id.* at Art. 38.

previously subject to a safeguard measure until the passage of a period no less than two years or more than half of the term of the previous measure.[230]

3. Adoption of Safeguard Measures by MERCOSUR on Behalf of a Member State

a. The Process

As noted above, the regulations provide that MERCOSUR may impose safeguard measures on behalf of one of its member states.[231] The process is very similar, but the entities involved are different.

The process begins by a producer or other entity filing a written complaint with a competent governmental "technical entity" in the member state.[232] The technical entity decides if the application is acceptable and will so notify the other member states and the President Pro Tem of the MERCOSUR Council.[233] The technical entity will make a preliminary determination regarding the advisability of opening an investigation regarding the existence or great harm of the threat of great harm to the domestic production of a member state caused by the increase of imports of a particular good, as well as a preliminary analysis of the adjustment plan submitted by the applicant, which will then be submitted to the other member states.[234]

The appropriate entities of the member states will then decide on the opening of an investigation and will prepare a document so ordering.[235]

The investigation is then conducted by the technical organs of the government of the member states and will be conducted in an almost identical manner to the investigations conducted in MERCOSUR cases.[236] At the conclusion of the investigation, the technical organs will jointly draft a report regarding the existence or great harm of the threat of great harm to the member state domestic production caused by the increased imports of the products in question and the viability of the adjustment plan for domestic production, which will be submitted to the member states through the President Pro Tem of the MERCOSUR Council.[237]

---

230. *Id.* at Art. 39.

231. *See supra* note 203 and accompanying text.

232. *Id.* at Art. 41. The application is almost identical to that used in safeguard measures imposed on behalf of MERCOSUR. *Id.* at Art. 41.1. *See supra* note 203 and accompanying text.

233. *Id.* at Art. 41.2.

234. *Id.* at Arts. 42–43.

235. *Id.* at Art. 44. This document is essentially identical to the Directive issued by the MCC which starts the investigation in MERCOSUR cases. *Id.* at Art. 44.1-5. *See supra* note 23 and accompanying text.

236. *Id.* at Art. 45-50. *See supra* note 214 and accompanying text.

237. *Id.* at Arts. 51–52. The report is essentially identical to that prepared by the Committee in MERCOSUR cases. *See supra* notes 214–215 and accompanying text.

b. Consultations

Prior to the imposition of safeguard measures, the technical authorities of the member states will engage in a consultation procedure identical to that used in MERCOSUR cases.[238]

c. Provisional Safeguard Measures

In a critical situation where any delay would create a harm that would be difficult to repair and where there is clear evidence that an increase in imports of a particular product has caused or threatens to cause great harm to the member state[239] domestic production, preliminary safeguard measures may be imposed. The nature of the provisional safeguard measures, as well as their substantive content, are identical to those in MERCOSUR cases, with the difference that the decision to impose the sanctions is made by the technical authorities of the member states.[240]

d. Final Safeguard Measures

Final safeguard measures will be determined by the technical authorities of the member states only if the measure is necessary to prevent or repair great harm and to facilitate the adjustment of the member state domestic production in question and will be imposed by a document whose contents are virtually identical to those of a Directive imposing final safeguard measures in a MERCOSUR case.[241] The substantive measures that may be imposed are identical to those that may be imposed in a MERCOSUR case.[242] The period of time for during which they may be imposed, and the conditions under which they may be extended or otherwise reviewed and revised are identical to those in MERCOSUR cases, except for the fact that the entities involved in the extension, review or revision process are the technical authorities of the member states.[243]

---

238. *Id.* at Art. 54. The only principal difference is that the consultations will be held with the attendance and participation of all the member states. *Id.* at Art. 54.5. The report on the consultations is then jointly prepared by the technical authorities of the member states. *Id.* at Art. 54.8 *See supra* notes 216–219 and accompanying text.

239. *Id.* at Art. 55.

240. *Id.* at Arts. 56–61. *See supra* notes 220–223 and accompanying text.

241. *Id.* at Arts. 62–63. *See supra* notes 224–225 and accompanying text.

242. *Id.* at Arts. 64–66. *See supra* notes 226–227 and accompanying text.

243. *Id.* at Arts. 67–74. *See supra* notes 228–231 and accompanying text.

4. Concession Levels and Other MERCOSUR Obligations under GATT 1994

In adopting safeguard measures, MERCOSUR will seek to maintain a level of concessions and other obligations substantially equivalent to those assumed by the member states in the context of the General Agreement on Tariffs and Trade, 1994. ("GATT 1994") In order to do this, MERCOSUR and its member states may enter into agreements regarding any adequate method of commercial compensation for the unfavorable effects of the safeguard measure on trade.[244]

Before the introduction of a safeguard measure, it shall be kept in mind that, if the consultations described above[245] fail to reach an agreement on adequate measures of commercial compensation, the affected exporting states may, in accordance with the World Trade Organization Agreement on Safeguards, suspend the application to MERCOSUR commerce of concessions and other substantially equivalent obligations resulting from the GATT 1994 whose suspension is not disapproved by the WTO Council on Trade in Goods. This right to suspend concessions and other substantially equivalent obligations will not be exercised during the first three years of the term of a safeguard measure, if the measure has been adopted as a result of an increase in absolute terms of imports and if it conforms to the provisions of the Agreement on Safeguards of the WTO.[246]

5. Differential Treatment for Developing Countries

No safeguard measures shall be applied against a product originating in a developing country when the portion of the imports into MERCOSUR of the product in question that is attributable to that developing country does not exceed 3%, if the developing countries whose participation in the exports is less than 3% do not together represent more than 9% of the total imports of the product in question.[247]

6. Dispute Resolution

Any disputes regarding the application, interpretation or failure to comply with the provisions of the Safeguard Measures Regulation will be resolved in

---

244. *Id.* at Art. 75.
245. *See supra* notes 216–219 and 231 and accompanying text.
246. *Id.* at Art. 76.
247. *Id.* at Art. 78.

accordance with the Brasilia Protocol and the General Procedures for Claims before the MCC set forth in the Annex to the Ouro Preto Protocol.[248]

7. Imposition of Safeguard Measures

Safeguard measures on third party imports appear to have been imposed twice by the Council. The first safeguard measure was imposed by the Council on behalf of Argentina in April 2001.[249] The second measure was imposed by the Council on behalf of Argentina and covers capital goods.[250] Both measures have also been widely discussed elsewhere.[251] They are apparently still in effect.

---

248. *Id.* at. Art. 87

249. *See* MERCOSUR/CMC/Dec No. 01/01, Medidas Excepionales en el Ambito Arancelario, *available at* http://www.mercosur.org.uy/espanol/snor/normativa/decsiones/2001/0101.htm.

250. MERCOSUR/CMC/Dec No. 25/02, Medidas Excepionales en el Ambito Arancelario, *available at* http://www.mercosur.org.uy/espanol/snor/normativa/decsiones/2002/Dec_025)002.htm.

251. For a description of these measures and of the process by means of which they were imposed *See* International Agreements: Brazil Agrees to let Argentina Alter Common External Tariff, 18 *International Trade Reporter* (BNA) 513 (March 29, 2001); International Agreements: Argentina s MERCOSUR Tariff Waiver called Necessary to Pre-Summit Unity, 18 *International Trade Reporter* (BNA) 547 (April 5, 2001); International Agreements: Argentina s MERCOSUR Tariff Waiver Continues to Generate Concern, 18 *International Trade Reporter* (BNA) 586 (April 12, 2001); International Agreements: Brazil to Hold Talks on Argentine Safeguards; Argentina Agrees to Maintain MERCOSUR CET, 18 *International Trade Reporter* (BNA) 1661 (October 18, 2001); International Agreements: Brazil may Suspend some Concessions Provided to Argentina through MERCOSUR, 19 *International Trade Reporter* (BNA) 127 (January 24, 2002)

Chapter 5

The MERCOSUR Legal System

A. The MERCOSUR Legal System

The "Common Market" envisioned by Article 1 of the Treaty of Asunción was to be "in place" by December 31, 1994.[1] It was to have a number of major characteristics: freedom of movement of goods, services and factors of production, the establishment of a common external tariff and the adoption of a common commercial policy with regard to third party states, the coordination of macroeconomic and sectoral policies among the member states and the harmonization of member state legislation in all areas relevant to these subjects.[2] The principal tools to be used in its creation were a trade liberalization program,[3] the gradual coordination of macroeconomic policies,[4] the creation of a common external tariff[5] and the adoption of sectoral agreements.[6] These tools are clearly meant to be used, and the policies designed to create the common market are meant to be designed, by and substantially through the actions of the Council.[7]

The Council has indeed been extremely active in the formulation of policy meant to implement the common market. In addition to the common external tariff approved in 1993[8] the Council has approved, through June 30, 2000, 208

---

1. Asunción, *supra* Intro. note 1, at Art. 1.
2. *Id.*
3. This "trade liberalization program" is defined as one of "progressive, linear and automatic tariff reductions, accompanied by the elimination of all non tariff restrictions or equivalent measures." *Id.* at Art. 5(a).
4. *Id.* at Art. 5(b).
5. *Id.* at Art. 5(c).
6. These agreements are are meant to "optimize the use and mobility of factors of production and to achieve efficient scales of operation." *Id.* at Art. 5(d).
7. As noted in the Ouro Preto Protocol, the Council is meant to "formulate the policies and promote the measures necessary to build the common market."Ouro Preto, *supra* Intro. note 5, at Art. 8 III.
8. *See supra* Chptr. 4 notes 62–95 and accompanying text.

other "Decisions" meant to create common market policy.[9] These Decisions cover a large number of policy matters, and constitute the beginning of a "MERCOSUR legal system."

These policies are meant to form a system of MERCOSUR community law, based first on the Treaty and its Protocols and secondly on the administrative law created by Council Decisions, Group Resolutions and MCC Directives adopted since the effective date of the Treaty of Asuncion.[10] In order to become effective, MERCOSUR law must be incorporated into each member state's legal system by means of the procedures set forth in their individual national legislation. The Ouro Preto Protocol makes this incorporation obligatory. Member states first enact legislation incorporating a particular community law provision into the domestic legal system. The norm becomes effective thirty days after the Administrative Secretariat notifies the member states that the norm has been incorporated by all.[11] Thus, MERCOSUR does not have the equivalent of an EU Regulation which, under Article 189 of the Treaty of Rome is directly applicable to the member states without the need for incorporation into the national legal system.[12] Unlike the European Union, MERCOSUR is not a "new legal order...comprising not only the Members but also their nationals."[13] It also appears that the familiar EU law principle of the supremacy of community law over national law is not applicable in the MERCOSUR legal system.[14] Furthermore, the EU principle of "direct effect," whereby certain provisions of community law were enforceable within (and by) the member states' legal system without the need for any incorporation action, is also not applicable in the MERCOSUR legal system.[15] To the contrary, it appears clear that the legal norms of the MERCOSUR legal system become part of national law only if the member states choose to make it so.

Several concerns become apparent about the current status of the MERCOSUR legal system. First, it is not a separate legal system. The MERCOSUR norms are meant to be incorporated into the legal systems of the member states and, indeed, are not valid and binding until this happens. Secondly, because each member state follows its own adoption process in accordance with its own constitutional norms, there is a substantial risk that these norms will not be adopted in a uniform manner. Indeed, in some member states, their own status within the national legal hierarchy may be unclear. This means that,

---

9. A listing which includes all of the Council's Decisions since 1991 is *available at* http://www.mercosur.org.uy/espanol/snor/normativa/decisiones.htm.

10. Ouro Preto, *supra* Intro. note 5, at Art. 41.

11. *Id.* at Art. 40.

12. Treaty of Rome, *supra* Chptr. 2 note 58, at Art. 189.

13. Van Gend En Loos, *supra* Chptr. 3 note 43.

14. Flamino Costa v. E.N.E.L., Case 6/64 [1964] ECR 585.

15. Van Gend En Loos, *supra* Chptr. 3 note 43, at 29.

as long as there is absolute consensus among (and *in*) the member states about the desirability of a particular MERCOSUR norm, its adoption into their legal systems would not be problematic. The moment this consensus does not occur, however, paralysis will occur. Furthermore, even if the norms have been adopted, there will be no guarantee that all member states will interpret or apply the norm in the same way (or even in a consistent fashion). Given the fact that the creation and management of the common market depends on these norms (as is the case with the European Union), these problems may delay (or even inhibit) the creation of the common market.

B. A Sampler of MERCOSUR Law

This section will consider five different areas of MERCOSUR legislation: harmonization of judicial assistance and jurisdiction rules, the creation of minimum rules for the regulation of securities markets, competition policy, the regulation of commerce in services, and the regulation of foreign investment. These areas involve the harmonization of procedural rules, the establishment of minimal rules of substantive norms, and the harmonization of macroeconomic policies. This examination will enable us to determine the methodology through which MERCOSUR intends to achieve the common market and gauge its effectiveness.

C. Harmonization of Procedural Rules

The Council has adopted six major protocols and agreements dealing with the harmonization of rules relating to judicial and other proceedings. These include the Protocol on Jurisdictional Assistance and Cooperation in Civil, Commercial, Labor and Administrative Matters ("Cooperation Protocol");[16] the Protocol on Extraordinary Measures["Medidas Cautelares"] ("Extraordinary Measures Protocol");[17] the Buenos Aires Protocol on International Jurisdiction in Contract Matters ("Buenos Aires Protocol")[18] the Protocol on Mutual Judicial Assistance in Penal Affairs ("the Penal Matters Protocol");[19] the

---

16. Cooperation Protocol, MERCOSUR/CMD/Dec. No. 5/92 (1992) *available at* http://www.mercosur.org.uy.espanol/snor/normativa/decisiones/1992/9205.htm.
17. Extraordinary Measures Protocol, MERCOSUR/CMC/Dec. No. 27/94 (1994) *available at* http://www.mercosur.org.uy.espanol/snor/normativa/decisiones/Dec2794.htm.
18. Buenos Aires Protocol, MERCOSUR/CMC/Dec. No. 1/94 (1994) *available at* http://www.mercosur.org.uy.espanol/snor/normativa/decisiones/Dec194.htm.
19. Penal Matters Protocol, MERCOSUR/CMC/Dec. No. 2/96 (1996) *available at* http://www.mercosur.org.uy.espanol/snor/normativa/decisiones/1996/9602.htm.

Santa María Protocol on International Jurisdiction in Consumer Relations Matters ("Santa María Protocol")[20] and the Agreement on MERCOSUR International Commercial Arbitration ("International Arbitration Agreement").[21] They shall each be discussed in turn.

1. The Cooperation Protocol

The main concept of Cooperation Protocol is the mutual assistance and extensive jurisdictional cooperation among the court systems of the member states in civil, commercial, labor and administrative matters.[22] Closely related to this concept is the concept of national treatment, whereby the member states agree that all nationals and permanent residents of any member state will have equal access to the court systems of any other member state.[23] The three major types of judicial assistance and cooperation agreed to by the member states involve essentially three categories of matters: assistance in transmission of documents and other procedural matters,[24] recognition and execution of judgments and arbitral awards[25] and recognition of public documents.[26]

a. Assistance in Procedural Matters

The assistance in procedural matters contemplated in the Protocol covers two types of matters: the transmittal of purely procedural documents such as those relating to the service of process or other administrative notifications and discovery requests. For each of these, the requesting party or court ("the requesting authority") files a Request ("Exhorto") with its Central Authority, which then transmits it to the Central Authority of the receiving state. The Central Authority of the receiving state may either implement the Request itself or submit it to the court or administrative entity having appropriate jurisdiction in this matter within the receiving state ("the receiving authority"). Each request must contain certain information regarding the requesting authority, the case, the parties, the party who or parties who are to be served in the receiving state, and nature and timing of the assistance request of the judicial authorities of the

---

20. Santa Maria Protocol, MERCOSUR/CMC/Dec. No. 10/96 (1996) *available at* http://www.mercosur.org.uy.espanol/snor/normativa/decisiones/1996/9610.htm.

21. International Arbitration Agreement, MERCOSUR/CMC/Dec. No. 3/98 (1998) *available at* http://www.mercosur.org.uy.espanol/snor/normativa/decisiones/1998/9803.htm.

22. Cooperation Protocol, *supra* note 16, at Art. 1. This agreement in the protocol is limited, however, only to those administrative matters include recourse to the courts.

23. *Id.* at Art .3.

24. *Id.* at Arts. 5–17.

25. *Id.* at Arts. 18–24.

26. *Id.* at Arts. 25–30.

receiving state. The appropriate authorities within the receiving state *must* then fulfill the Request without delay, unless the nature of the Request constitutes a violation of the pubic policy or public order of the receiving state.

The requesting authority may request to be notified of the time and place of any proceedings which may be held to implement the Request, and it, and any interested parties in the matter or their representatives have the right to appear and participate in any such proceedings to the extent local law allows them to do so. The receiving state's domestic law will apply to any such proceedings.[27]

b. Recognition of Judgments and Arbitral Awards

The Protocol also provides for the recognition of enforcement of all judgments and arbitral awards rendered in the member states in civil, commercial, labor and administrative matters, including judgments in criminal matters providing for restitution or payment of damages ("judgments").

The procedure to follow in enforcing these judgments is very similar to that involved in assistance in procedural matters. A party wishing to have a judgment rendered in a member state recognized or enforced must file a Request with its own state's Central Authority, which is then transmitted to the Receiving State's Central Authority. The judgment will be recognized and enforced as long as it meets certain conditions. As in the case of assistance in procedural matters, any enforcement proceedings for the judgment will be held in accordance with the local law. In short, under this procedure, any such final judgment or arbitral award rendered in a member state is easily recognizable and enforceable, with one exception in any other member state.[28]

c. Recognition of Public Documents

The Protocol also provides that all public documents (including all documents issued by a state judicial or administrative entity, as well as deeds and other documents prepared by or filed by a Notary Public), prepared in a member state will have full faith and credit in all other member states. Copies of public documents certified by the Central Authority of a member state will not require any apostille or other formality in order to be valid in any other member state and shall have the same legal effect as any similar domestic public documents in any other member state.

The member states also agreed to continue to consult with each other regarding implementation of the provisions of the Protocol. They also agreed to

---

27. *Id.* at Arts. 5–17.
28. *Id.* at Arts. 18–24.

submit any disputes that could arise regarding the application of the Protocol in accordance with the Brasilia Protocol.

In order to facilitate the implementation of the Protocol, each member state is to designate a Central Authority charged with the receipt and processing of any requests for assistance under the Protocol. This Central Authority has the power to transfer any request received under the Protocol to the appropriate judicial or administrative authority within its judicial system.[29]

The Protocol became effective March 17, 1996, after its ratification by the member states and the Council has approved forms for use by the member state Central Authorities in its implementation.[30]

2. The Extraordinary Measures Protocol

·The Extraordinary Measures Protocol is meant to regulate among the member states the enforcement of judicial extraordinary measures.[31] These extraordinary measures are judicial measures destined to stop the occurrence of an irreparable harms to persons, goods or obligations.[32] They can be used in any kind of civil, commercial or labor judicial proceeding, and can be utilized before the start of judicial proceedings, incidental to an ongoing judicial proceeding, or in order to guarantee the execution of a judgment.[33]

a. Enforcement of Extraordinary Measures

The Protocol first asserts that the appropriate of any member state shall enforce all extraordinary measures decreed by courts or judges of the other member states. Whether and under what terms an extraordinary measure may be entered in a particular proceeding is decided by the courts of the state in which the proceeding is pending, in accordance with their local law. Any matters related to the enforcement of these measures is to be decided by the courts of the state in which enforcement is requested, again in accordance with their local law.[34]

b. Enforcement Process

The enforcement process under the Extraordinary Measures Protocol is similar to that set forth in the Cooperation Protocol. Specifically, a letter rogatory requesting enforcement of a particular extraordinary measure if filed with the Central Authority of the member state where enforcement is sought, together with

---

29. *Id.* at Art. 2.
30. *Id.* at Arts. 25–30.
31. Extraordinary Measures Protocol, *supra* note 17.
32. *Id.* at Art. 1.
33. *Id.* at Arts. 2–3.
34. *Id.* at Arts. 4–7.

certain documentation. If a party against whom the extraordinary measure is to be enforced, or any interested third party, opposes the enforcement of the measure before the appropriate court in the enforcing state, the court in the enforcing state will return the record to the judge who issued the measure for a ruling on the objection. This letter rogatory will generally be enforced unless fundamental documents, or requirements of information which render it inadmissable are missing. The enforcing court will then notify the requesting court when the requested extraordinary measure was enforced or, if it was not, why not.[35] If the extraordinary measure is entered to preserve the status quo prior to the commencement of a litigation, its effectiveness will terminate upon the filing of the complaint in the matter.[36] With certain exceptions, the party requesting the enforcement of an extraordinary remedy is responsible for the payment of all enforcement costs.[37]

As was the case with the Cooperation Protocol, the member states also agreed in the Extraordinary Remedies Protocol to continue to consult with each other regarding implementation of its provisions and any disputes arising thereunder would be resolved in accordance with the dispute resolution procedures in the Brasilia Protocol. This Protocol became effective April 19, 1997, after its ratification by member states. As was the case with the Cooperation Protocol, the Council has also approved forms for use by the member state Central Authorities in its implementation.[38]

3. The Buenos Aires Protocol

The Buenos Aires Protocol determines jurisdiction in international contracts.[39] International contracts (with certain exceptions)[40] are those civil or commercial agreements celebrated between physical or legal persons who are domiciled (or have their registered office) in different MERCOSUR member states or, where at least one of the parties is domiciled in a MERCOSUR member state, there is a forum election agreement in favor of a court in a member state, and there is a reasonable nexus (as noted by the jurisdictional norms set forth in the Protocol) between that court and the contract.[41]

---

35. *Id.* at Art. 21.
36. *Id.* at Art. 13.
37. *Id.* at Arts. 24–25.
38. *Id.* at Arts. 14–25.
39. Buenos Aires Protocol, *supra* note 18, at Arts. 1–2.
40. *Id.* The Protocol excludes contracts involving bankrupts, social security, administrative, labor, transport, consumer, insurance and contracts involving family matters, as well as matters involving real estate rights, from coverage under the Protocol. *Id.*
41. *Id.*

a. Choice of Forum Agreements

In international contracts, a written choice of forum agreement freely entered into by the parties gives jurisdiction to the courts or arbitral forums of the member states set forth therein. This written agreement can be set forth in the original contractual document or in a subsequent document, which can be executed even after the commencement of litigation on the contract.[42] Regardless of the existence of such an agreement, the courts of a member state where litigation has been commenced and where the defendant has freely entered an appearance will also have jurisdiction over litigation involving an international contract.

b. Jurisdiction in the Absence of Agreement

In the absence of an agreement by the parties, at the election of the party commencing litigation, the courts of the member state in whose territory lies the place where the contract was to be performed, or the courts of the member state where defendant has its legal domicile will also have jurisdiction in cases involving international contracts.[43]

c. Miscellaneous Jurisdictional Rules

In addition to the jurisdictional rules set forth above, the Buenos Aires Protocol also includes several other jurisdictional rules. First, jurisdiction in an action among partners involving an international contract lies in the courts of partnership's principal administrative office.[44] Second, in cases involving international contracts where there is more than one defendant, the courts of the member state of the domicile of any one of the defendants will have jurisdiction.[45] Third, in cases involving personal guarantees or third party defendants, the courts of the place where the litigation involving the guaranteed obligation or principal litigation will have jurisdiction.[46] Lastly, the courts hearing a mat-

---

42. *Id.* at Arts. 4–5.

43. *Id.* at Art. 7. This shall be understood to be the place where the obligation that serves as the basis for the action was or should have been performed. *Id.* at Art. 8. In contracts involving specific things, this is the place where they existed at the time of the execution of the contract. *Id.* at Art. 8 (a). In contracts involving generic or fungible things, this is the domicile of the debtor at the time the contract was executed. *Id.* at Art. 8(b)-(c). In service contracts, if the services involve things, this is the place where the things existed at the time the contract was executed. *Id.* at Art. 8(d)(1). If the service contract is related to a special place, then this is the place where the contract's performance was to be rendered. *Id.* at Art. 8(d)(2). In all other service contracts, this is the domicile of the debtor at the time of contract execution. *Id.* at Art. 8(d)(3).

44. *Id.* at Art. 10.

45. *Id.* at Art. 12.

46. *Id.*

ter will have jurisdiction to consider any counterclaims based on the facts involved in the original litigation.[47]

As was the case with the Cooperation and Extraordinary Measures Protocol, the member states also agreed in the Buenos Aires Protocol to continue to consult with each other regarding implementation of its provisions and any disputes arising thereunder would be resolved in accordance with the dispute resolution procedures of the Brasilia Protocol.[48] This Protocol became effective on June 15, 1995 after its ratification by the member states.[49]

4. *The Santa María Protocol*

The Santa María Protocol determines international jurisdiction in certain types of consumer matters arising out of contracts where one of the parties is a consumer[50] and the contracts are entered into by a supplier and consumer domiciled in different MERCOSUR member states.[51] The Protocol also applies to contacts where both parties are domiciled in the same member state and performance of the contract will take place in another member state ("international consumer matters").[52]

a. Jurisdictional and Procedural Rules

The courts in whose territory the consumer is domiciled will have jurisdiction in litigation involving international consumer matters and filed either by the consumer or the supplier.[53] Jurisdiction in international consumer mat-

---

47. *Id.* at Art. 13.

48. *Id.* at Arts. 15–16.

49. *Id.* at Arts. 16–18. The Protocol was implemented in Argentina and Brasil on May 10, 1995 and by Paraguay and Uruguay on June 15, 1995. *See* Mercosur Normativa *available at* http:www.mercosur.org.uy/espanol/snor/normativa/incorporacion.

50. Santa María Protocol, *supra* note 20, at Art. 1. These matters include installment sales of movable goods; term loans or other credit operations linked to the financing of a sale of goods; or any other contract whose purpose is the rendering of a service or the supply of movable goods. The latter contracts will be covered by the Protocol only where the execution of the contract was preceded, in the member state where the consumer is domiciled, by a specific offer or sufficiently detailed advertisement; and that the consumer has completed the contract execution formalities required in the member state in which he is domiciled. *Id.*

51. *Id.*

52. In the case of physical persons, the domicile is his habitual residence or the place where he has his principal place of business. In the case of legal persons, domicile is the place where its principal administrative and managerial office is located or the place where its agencies, branches, establishments or other representatives are located. *Id.* at Art. 3.

53. *Id.* at Art. 4.

ters will also lie, at the consumer's exclusive election, in either: the member state where the contract was made, the member state where the performance of the service or delivery of the goods contracted for took place, or the member state of the defendant's domicile.[54] If the defendant is domiciled in a member state and has an agency, establishment, branch or other representative in another member state with which it rendered the operations which created the dispute, litigation may be commenced in the courts of either member state.[55] Similarly, if there are a number of defendants in an action involving the same subject matter, the courts of the member state in which any of the defendants is domiciled will also have jurisdiction.[56] The courts which have jurisdiction over an international consumer matter will also have jurisdiction over any counterclaims or cross claims arising out of the same subject matter.[57]

The Santa María Protocol also has a novel procedural provision which, to the degree allowed by local law, allows the supplier-defendant in litigation involving an international consumer matter to respond to the complaint, introduce evidence, file motions and otherwise litigate the case *before the courts of its own domicile.* In such a situation, the courts of the supplier's domicile will transmit all this documentation, in accordance with the procedures set forth in the Cooperation Protocol,[58] to its Central Authority for transmission to the courts of the member state in which the complaint was filed. This procedure is not available if the defendant has an agency, establishment, branch or other representative in the member state in which the litigation has been commenced.[59]

Judgments entered in all litigation involving international consumer matters which require enforcement in another member state will be transmitted by request or letter rogatory to the appropriate authorities in that member state, again in accordance with the procedures set forth in the Cooperation Protocol.[60]

As was the case with the Cooperation, Extraordinary Measures and Buenos Aires Protocols, the final provisions of the Santa María Protocol also provide that the member states agreed to continue to consult with each other regarding implementation of its provisions and that any disputes arising thereunder would be resolved in accordance with the dispute resolution procedures of the

---

54. *Id.* at Art. 5.
55. *Id.* at Art. 6.
56. *Id.* at Art. 7.
57. *Id.* at Art. 8.
58. *See supra* note 24 and accompanying text.
59. Santa María Protocol, *supra* note 20, at Art. 9.
60. *Id.* at Arts. 11–12.

Brasilia Protocol.[61] As was the case with the other procedural protocols, the Santa María Protocol provided for ratification by at least two member states in order to become effective.[62] The Protocol does indicate, however, that it will not become effective until after the approval by the Council of the "Common MERCOSUR Regulation for the Protection of the Consumer." That Regulation has not yet been passed by the Council.[63]

5. The Penal Matters Protocol

The Penal Matters Protocol creates a mechanism for mutual judicial assistance among the appropriate authorities in the member states in penal matters.[64] This assistance can be quite extensive[65] and is to be rendered both in matters involving ongoing criminal investigations and pending criminal proceedings.[66]

a. Procedures for Rendering Assistance

As was the case with the Cooperation and Extraordinary Measures Protocol, assistance is rendered by the transmission of a Request for Assistance from a court of other governmental authority by the designated Central Authority of a member state to the Central Authority of another member state.[67] The Request for Assistance will be in writing and will contain information identifying the requester, the nature of the matter being investigated or subject to criminal proceedings, the text of any applicable penal legislation, the identity of the accused or parties under investigation, and a detailed description of the nature of

---

61. *Id.* at 13.

62. *Id.* at Arts. 14–15.

63. *Id.* at Arts. 17–18. To date, the MERCOSUR Normativa does not indicate ratification by the member states. *See* MERCOSUR Normativa *available at* http://www.mercosur.org.uy/espanol/snor/normativa/incorporacion.

64. Penal Matters Protocol, *supra* note 19, at Art. 2.

65. *Id.* The assistance can involve notification of judicial actions; reception and production of evidence, such as the taking of testimony and examination of persons or places; citing of witnesses for voluntary appearances to present testimony in the requesting state; transfer of prisoners to the requesting state for the purpose of rendering testimony; production of documents; seizure of goods, transfer or seized goods or similar measures; protection of goods to ensure the enforcement of judicial orders imposing fines or indemnification; or any other measures that are not incompatible with the laws of the member state whose assistance was requested. *Id.* This assistance can also involve the furnishing of copies of official documents in the possession of the authorities of the member state whose assistance is requested, including official documents, files and information not available to the public, under the same conditions they would be furnished to local authorities. *Id.* at Art. 15.

66. *Id.* at Art. 1.

67. *Id.* at Arts. 3–4.

the assistance requested.[68] The Central Authority of the receiving state is to transmit the Request to the appropriate judicial or other governmental authority which will render the requested assistance.[69] Furnishing the requested assistance by the appropriate authorities of the receiving member state is mandatory, with five exceptions. If assistance is denied, the appropriate authority of the receiving state must notify, thorough its Central Authority, the appropriate authorities of the requesting state of their denial and the reasons therefor.[70] The Central Authority of the member state whose assistance has been requested will then notify the Central Authority of the requesting member state, within a reasonable time, of the results of the request and will promptly transmit any information or evidence obtained as a result thereof. The Central Authority of the requesting member state will be immediately notified if the request has not been able to be met wholly or in part, of this fact, and of the reasons therefor.[71]

b. Procedures for Taking Testimony

The request may involve the taking of testimony of witnesses within the territory of the member state whose assistance has been requested. In such a case, the appropriate authority of the member state rendering the assistance will, in accordance with its domestic law, summon the witnesses before it for that purpose. The individual thus summoned must then appear, or be subject to appropriate sanctions under domestic law. This authority may, if authorized by

---

68. *Id.* at Art. 6. The Request may be transmitted by telex, fax or e-mail. In those cases, however, a hard copy of the Request signed by the requesting authority must be transmitted through the Central Authority within ten days of the date of transmission of the original Request. *Id.* at Art. 6(2). The authorities in the requesting state may request that the information or evidence obtained with the assistance of the authorities in the other members be kept confidential, which request will be honored. *Id.* at Art. 10. Forms have apparently been developed for this purpose. *See* "Acuerdo Complementario al Acuerdo de Asistencia Jurídica Mutua en Asuntos Penales entre los Estados Partes del MERCOSUR," (December 5, 2002), *available at* http://www.mercosur.org.uy/espanol/sdyd/acuerdos/2002; and "Acuerdo Complementario al Acuerdo de Asistencia Jurídica Mutua en Asuntos Penales entre los Estados Partes del MERCOSUR y la República de Bolivia y la República de Chile" (December 5, 2002), *available at* http://www.mercosur.org.uy/espanol/sdyd/acuerdos/2002.

69. *Id.* at Art. 4.

70. Assistance may be denied in matters involving: a crime designated as such in military penal legislation; crimes considered by the state whose assistance is requested as political crimes, or as ordinary crimes being prosecuted for political means; tax crimes; matters where the accused has been found not guilty or has already served a sentence in the receiving state for the crime set forth in the Request; and matters where the rendering of the requested assistance will be contrary to the security, public order or other essential interests of the state whose assistance is requested. *Id.* at Art. 5.

71. *Id.* at Art. 11.

local law, permit any individuals named in the request for assistance to appear and participate at this taking of testimony subject to any claims of privilege, immunity or incapacity.[72]

The request may also involve the taking of testimony of witnesses within the territory of the member state requesting the assistance. In such a case, the attendance of the person summoned to testify is purely voluntary, since the authorities of the member state in which the witness is located do not have the power to compel the witness' appearance abroad. If the individual whose testimony has been requested voluntarily agrees to appear, his written consent to appear will be promptly submitted to the Central Authority of the member state requesting assistance. This member state is responsible for the payment of all travel and living expenses incident to such testimony.[73]

The request may also involve the taking of testimony within the territory of the member state requesting assistance of a witness who is subject to criminal proceedings in the other member state. In this situation, no formal extradition proceedings are required. If the witness and the member state whose assistance is requested agree, the witness will be transferred to the requesting state. If the continued presence of the witness in the member state whose assistance is requested is thought to be necessary for the appropriate continuation of the pending criminal proceeding, the witness will be transferred only if the witness and both the requesting and requested member states agree.[74] The witness so transferred to another member state will generally be kept in custody and will be returned as soon as possible to the member state from whence he came. He or she may not be arrested or tried for any crimes allegedly occurring prior to his departure and may be summoned to testify or appear in any proceedings involving a matter not set forth in the Request for Assistance. Any time which the witness spent in custody while testifying will be deducted from any criminal sentence imposed in the pending criminal proceedings.[75]

As was the case with the Cooperation, Extraordinary Measures and Buenos Aires Protocols, the final provisions of the Penal Matters Protocol also provides that the member states agreed to continue to consult with each other regarding implementation of its provisions and that any disputes arising thereunder

---

72. Any claims of privilege, immunity or incapacity under the laws of the member state where the testimony is to be taken will be resolved under local law by the appropriate authorities thereof. Any claims of privilege, immunity or incapacity under the laws of the member state requesting assistance will be referred, through the Central Authority, for resolution to the appropriate authorities in the state requesting assistance. *Id.* at Art. 17.

73. *Id.* at Art. 18.

74. *Id.* at Art. 19. The transfer will not take place if the constitution of the member state whose assistance is requested forbids the extradition of one of its nationals and the witness is such a national. *Id.* at Art. 19(3).

75. *Id.*

would be resolved in accordance with the dispute resolution procedures of the Brasilia Protocol.[76] The Penal Matters Protocol became effective on August 7, 2000 after ratification by the member states.[77]

6. *The International Arbitration Agreement Protocol*

The International Arbitration Agreement is meant to regulate and promote arbitration as a means of alternative dispute resolution in matters arising out of international commercial contracts involving the member states.[78]

The International Arbitration Agreement applies in situations where any of the following circumstances occur: a) the arbitration agreement was entered into among natural or legal persons having their residence, customary place or business, administrative center or branches or agencies in more than one MERCO-SUR member state; b) the contract has a nexus with more than one MERCOSUR member state; c) the parties did not express their will to the contrary and the agreement has a nexus with one of the MERCOSUR member states, as long as the arbitration is held in a MERCOSUR member state; d) the contract has a nexus with a member state and the arbitration is not held in a MERCOSUR member state, as long as all parties agree to be subject to the Arbitration Agreement; and e) the contract has no nexus with a MERCOSUR member state, and the parties have chosen to hold the arbitration in a MERCOSUR member state, as long as the parties expressly agree to be subject to the Arbitration Agreement.[79]

a. The Arbitration Agreement

The Arbitration Agreement[80] must give equitable and non abusive treatment to the contracting parties and must be agreed to in good faith. If the Arbitration Agreement is set forth in a contract clause, this clause must be clearly legible and be placed in a prominent position within the contract document.[81] It must be in writing, and the writing can consist of a telegram, fax, or e-mail.[82] The Arbitration Agreement is separate from the underlying con-

---

76. *Id.* at 25–26.

77. The Penal Matters Protocol became effective on Jan. 8, 2000 for Argentina and Paraguay; on April 28, 2000 for Brasil and on Aug. 7, 2000 for Uruguay.

78. International Arbitration Agreement, *supra* note 21, at Art. 3.

79. International Arbitration Agreement, *supra* note 21 at Art. 1.

80. This term is defined in the International Arbitration Agreement as "the agreement by means of which the parties agree to submit to arbitration all or some controversies that have arisen or may arise among them with respect to contractual relations. It can take the form of a clause included in a contract or that of an independent agreement."(author's translation). *Id.* at Art. 2(e).

81. *Id.* at Art. 4.

82. *Id.* at Art. 6(3). If the Arbitration Agreement is entered into by means of a telegram, fax or e-mail, it must be confirmed by an original hard copy document. *Id.* If

tract and, accordingly, its validity is not affected by the latter's invalidity or lack of existence.[83]

b. The Arbitration Process

The parties to an arbitration have a substantial amount of control over the process. They can designate the arbitration as one at law or in equity,[84] and can chose the law which will be applied to resolve the controversy.[85]

The parties can choose to make the arbitration either institutional or *ad hoc*. If the chosen mechanism is that of an institutional arbitration, its proceedings (including designation of arbitrators, commencement of the arbitration, organizational and procedural formalities, and any other matters) will be regulated by the rules of the arbitral institution chosen by the parties.[86] If the parties choose to make the arbitration *ad hoc*, then the parties can name their own arbitrators, design their own procedural rules and designate the place where the arbitration will be held and the language of the proceedings.[87] In the absence of such a designation, the rules prescribed by the Inter-American Convention on International Commercial Arbitration,[88] as well as the rules promulgated thereunder by the Inter-American Arbitration Commission, will apply.[89]

c. The Panel of Arbitrators

The panel of arbitrators is chosen, if the arbitration is institutional, under the rules of the institution where the arbitration is being held; or, if the arbitration is ad-hoc, under any mechanism set up by the parties. If there is no such mechanism, the arbitrators are chosen, under the procedures set forth under the arbitration rules of the Inter-American Arbitration Commission.[90]

---

the Arbitration Agreement is entered into by an exchange of documents as noted above, it becomes effective at the time and place where the acceptance by the chosen medium (confirmed by a hard copy document) is received. *Id.* at Art. 6(4).

83. *Id.* at Art. 5.

84. *Id.* at Art. 9.

85. *Id.* at Art. 10. This choice must be based on the principles of international private law or of international commercial law. If parties do not make a choice of law in the arbitration agreement, then the arbitrators will resolve the dispute in accordance with the principles of international private law and international commercial law. *Id.*

86. *Id.* at Arts. 11, 12(1), 15.

87. *Id.* at Arts. 12(2), 13–15.

88. Inter-American Convention on International Commercial Arbitration, Jan. 30, 1975 141 I.L.M. 336 (1975) (hereinafter, "Panamá Convention").

89. *Id.* at Art. 12(2)(b).

90. *Id.* at Arts. 16–17. With regard to the appointment of arbitrators, the convention suggests the advisability of appointing arbitrators of different nationality to the parties in the controversy. In ad-hoc arbitration with more than one arbitrator, unless the parties

The arbitration panel is to decide any questions involving its own jurisdiction, authority, the existence, scope and validity of the arbitration agreement, or the arbitrability of any portion of the controversy.[91] The arbitration panel may, at any point in the proceedings, *sua sponte* or at the request of one of the parties, impose extraordinary remedies[92] to preserve the *status quo* among the parties and request their enforcement by any court if competent jurisdiction.[93] Similarly, any party may also request from any court of competent jurisdiction the imposition of extraordinary remedies, and this request will not be deemed contrary to the arbitration agreement or an abandonment of the arbitration process. The arbitration terminates when the arbitration panel renders a final award, when the parties mutually agree to end the arbitration, or where the arbitration panel decides that the arbitration process has become, for some reason, unnecessary or impossible to continue.[94]

d. The Arbitral Award

The arbitral award must be in writing, reasoned and completely resolve all of the matters in controversy. If the award is rendered by more than one arbitrator, it must have been agreed to by a majority of the arbitrators and may contain a dissenting opinion. It must also be signed and served on all the parties.[95] With certain exceptions, the arbitral award is firm, final and unappealable.[96] If the parties settle the case prior to the rendering of an award by the arbitration panel, they may request the arbitration panel to formalize their settlement

---

agree otherwise and designate the reasons therefore, the panel must not be composed solely of arbitrators of the nationality of one of the parties. *Id.* at Art. 16.

91. *Id.* at Art. 18.

92. *See supra* notes 11–15 and accompanying text.

93. Any such extraordinary measures entered in an arbitration would be enforced internationally in accordance with the provision of the Extraordinary Measures Protocol. *Id.* at Art. 19. *See* Extraordinary Measures Protocol, *supra* notes 17, and accompanying text.

94. International Arbitration Agreement, *supra* note 21 at Art. 24.

95. *Id.* at Art. 20.

96. *Id.* The award may be invalidated by a court of competent jurisdiction in the member state in which the arbitration was held if: a) the arbitral agreement is void; b) the arbitral panel has not been appointed properly; c) the procedure followed by the arbitrators did not conform to the regulations of the institution under whose auspices the arbitration was held or to the rules agreed upon by the parties; d) there was a lack of due process in the arbitration; e) one of the arbitrators did not have the legal capacity to serve as an arbitrator; f) the award refers to a controversy that is not arbitrable under the terms of the arbitration agreement; or g) it exceeds the scope of the arbitration agreement. *Id.* at Art. 22.

One of the parties may, within 30 days of service of the award, request from the arbitration panel: a) the correction of any material mistake in the award; the explanation of one or more matters covered in the award; or c) resolve an issue within the controversy that has not been resolved by the award. The panel will respond to such a request within 20 day of its filing. *Id.* at Art. 21.

agreement in the form of an agreed arbitration award.[97] International implementation and enforcement of the arbitral award will take place in accordance with the procedures set forth in the Inter-American Convention on International Commercial Arbitration,[98] the Inter-American Convention on Extraterritorial Enforcement of Foreign Judgments and Arbitral Awards,[99] and the Cooperation Protocol.[100] The International Arbitration Agreement Protocol has not yet become effective.[101]

7. Harmonization of Procedural Matters: An Assessment

The goal behind the Harmonization of Procedural Matters Protocols appears to be quite simple: to encourage the development and expansion of a regional economic market by ensuring that all judicial disputes, especially those "international" ones involving activities or parties in more than one member state, have access to a consistent and expeditious mechanism for their enforcement. Three major themes seem to underlie this goal. The first theme is the simplification and expediting of judicial and administrative processes within the member states. These include the awarding of national treatment to foreign parties to judicial proceedings, the mutual recognition and enforcement of public documents and judicial actions, and the harmonization and simplification of judicial proceedings across national boundaries. The second theme is the harmonization of the rules relating to judicial jurisdiction over certain types of disputes in matters clearly having an "international dimension." A third major theme underlying this goal is the recommendation by the community of alternative dispute resolution, specifically arbitration, as a preferred mechanism for the solution of commercial disputes among nationals of more than one member state. The harmonization of rules regarding the commercial arbitration process, and the creation of procedures for the international enforcement of arbitral awards in the Arbitration Agreement and the Cooperation and Extraordinary Measures Protocol make this preference quite clear.

The mechanisms created by the Harmonization of Procedural Matters Protocols are extremely important because they reverse a long term culture in the

---

97. *Id.* at Art. 20(7).

98. Panamá Convention, *supra* note 88.

99. Inter-American Convention on Extraterritorial Enforement of Foreign Judgement and Aritral Awards, May 8, 1979, Montevideo, Uruguay, 18 I.L.M. 1224 (1979).

100. *See supra* notes 22–28.

101. *See* MERCOSUR Normativa *available at* http:www.mercosur.org.uy/espanol/snor/normativa/incorporacion.

member states (often underscored by legislation and procedural rules) of unequal treatment of foreign litigants and refusal to recognize or assist in foreign judicial or administrative proceedings.[102] An entity in a member state can now more rationally assess its risks (and perhaps be more encouraged) in making an investment elsewhere in the community because of the availability of clearer rules and more expeditious (and therefore less costly proceedings) for the judicial settlement of any disputes that may arise out of that investment. Accordingly, these measures represent an outstanding first step in the process of integration of MERCOSUR's dispute resolution systems.

Another extremely important achievement of these procedural harmonization measures is that they recognize that the rules and processes created therein are only the beginning of a long process of member state cooperation in administrative and judicial proceedings and create a series of mechanisms for the member states to continue to discuss these matters, with a view to the continuation and expansion of the process of cooperation and harmonization.

A note of caution must be inserted, however. The success or failure of the system established in these procedural harmonization measures is highly dependent on the effectiveness of the domestic judicial systems of the member states. Unfortunately, these domestic judicial systems are plagued by too many cases, too few judges and court personnel, insufficient resources, and other similar problems.[103] These have resulted in a substantial judicial backlog of cases, concern by the litigants that the system is inept, unfair or both, and reluctance to rely on the judicial system as a dispute resolution mechanism.[104] These problems must be addressed because, if the domestic judicial system is presently incapable of serving domestic litigants adequately, it will also not be able to do so for international litigants. Accordingly, attention to these problems at the member state judicial system level is crucial for the MERCOSUR system to work. Perhaps these measures at the MERCOSUR level will act as a catalyst for action on judicial reform at the member state level.

---

102. Jorge M. Guira, *MERCOSUR: The Emergence of a Working System of Dispute Resolution*, 6 NAFTA: L & Bus. Rev. Am. 255 (Spring 2000).

103. John Linaelli, *Anglo-American Juisprudence and Latin America*, 20 Fodham Int'l L.J. 50 (November, 1996).

104. T. Leigh Anderson, *For Whom the Bell Tolls...Judicial Selection by Election in Latin America*, 4 Sw.J.L. & Trade Am. 261 (Fall 1997).

D. Harmonization of Substantive Rules: The Stock Exchange Regulation

In 1993, the Council approved a document providing a minimal regulation of the securities markets within MERCOSUR.[105] This regulation has its limitations, since it applies only to international operations executed within MERCOSUR with securities issued by entities registered within MERCOSUR. It also does not cover public debt securities.[106] The Stock Exchanges Regulation does recommend to the member states, however, that its norms be also adopted for domestic securities operations.

1. The Issuer

A company or other entity registered in a MERCOSUR member state ("the issuer") may sell its securities in any other member state. In order to do that, however, they must first register or obtain authorization from the appropriate instrumentality in the member state in which it seeks to issue its securities as a precondition for the issuing of its securities for sale in either stock exchanges or other securities markets.[107] The issuer, once its registration is effected, acquires an obligation to periodically update the information provided to the appropriate regulatory body in its registration.[108] The issuer's registration to sell securities in another MERCOSUR member state may be cancelled, either by the appropriate regulatory body or by the issuer itself. An issuer request for cancellation of its registration must be approved by its shareholders.[109]

---

105. MERCOSUR/CMC/DEC NO. 8/93: Regulación Mínima del Mercado de Capitales (hereinafter, "Stock Exchanges Regulation") *available at* http://www.mercosur.org.uy.http://www.mercosur.org.uy.espanol/snor/normativa/decisions/Dec893.htm.

106. *Id.* at Art. 1.

107. *Id.* at Art. 1.1.2. The registration of such a company must contain information regarding its nature and management, types of securities, number of shareholders, identification of managers and directors (including any links of said individuals to other enterprises), identification of the person with responsibility to disclose information to investors, regulators and exchanges, audited financial statements (including an explanation of the home country accounting standards, if they differ from those of the place of registration), minutes of shareholder meetings, and, if the company is in the pre-operational stage, a financial-economic viability study of the project in which it is involved. *Id.*

108. *Id.* at Art. 1.1.3. The updated information must include: audited annual financial statements, quarterly financial statements, notices and resolutions of shareholder meetings, known shareholder agreements, and a management description of the conduct of the business during the last reporting period. This information must be presented within 45 days after the end of every quarter and within 90 days of the end of the fiscal year. *Id.*

109. *Id.* at Art. 1.1.4.

2. Sales of Securities

The sale of securities to the public in another MERCOSUR member state may be effected by either an intermediary or by the issuer itself, to the extent allowed by local law.[110] An issuer's sale of securities to the public must be approved by a meeting of its shareholders. The notice of this meeting must provide information regarding the type of securities to be proposed to be issued, their characteristics, and the amount thereof to be issued. At this meeting, the shareholders must decide the amount and characteristics of the securities to be issued, the conditions of the issue and the offering price thereof. The shareholders may delegate the decisions the terms of the issue and the offering price to the management.[111]

After shareholder approval is obtained, the issuer must request, from the agency designated for this purpose by local law, authorization for the proposed sale of securities to the public. The request for authorization of the sale must be accompanied by a proposed prospectus, which must contain a substantial amount of information regarding the issuer and its business.[112]

The prospectus must contain information regarding:

- the issuer's capital structure, before and after the sale;
- information regarding the corporate structure in which the issuer operates, including linked and controlled firms and their respective shareholdings therein;
- information regarding the issuer, including type of organization, domicile, principal activity, business registrations, board of directors, linked enterprises, controlled and controlling enterprises, as well as a copy of its articles of incorporations and by laws;
- information regarding its corporate structure, including classes and types of securities, their attributes and number of shares issued and outstanding;
- information regarding the principal managers and administrators of the firm, including names and positions and links with other enterprises;
- the name of the individual responsible for furnishing information to investors, state regulators or stock exchanges. This individual will be responsible for updating all information previously on file regarding the issuer;
- information regarding the issuer's financial condition, including audited financial statements for the last three fiscal years If the issuer has

---

110. *Id.* at Art. 1.2.1.
111. *Id.* at Art. 1.2.2.
112. *Id.* at Art. 1.2.3.

securities traded in other MERCOSUR countries, the financial statements must contain information regarding accounting standards in the
issuer's home country;
- copies of minutes of all shareholder meetings that took place within the
last twelve months;
- if the firm not yet engaged in business operations, a financial-economic
viability study of its business.[113]

The issuer may not publicize pending sale of securities to the public until it
has received approval for the sale from the relevant regulator. If local law authorizes the use of a preliminary prospectus or publicity prior to approval by
the relevant regulator, the material used must indicate that it is preliminary.[114]

In short, a MERCOSUR issuer wishing to sell its securities to the public in
another member state must register twice. It must first register as an issuer
with the relevant regulator in the other member state. Afterwards, the issuer
must register the particular *issue* it wished to market with the appropriate regulator prior to sale.

3. Shareholder Rights

The Stock Exchanges Regulation also states that all member states should
provide in their legislation for certain minimum norms for the protection of
shareholders;[115] including the right of access to certain minimum levels of information (including financial statements and minutes of meetings),[116] pre-
emptive rights,[117] and dissenters' rights.[118]

4. Mutual Funds

The regulation of mutual funds is to be harmonized in all the member
states. A mutual fund wishing to conduct operations in another member state
must meet the following conditions: registration with the appropriate regulator in the MERCOSUR member state in which they are organized; separation
of the manager's assets from those of the fund; certain limitations (unstated)
on the powers of the fund manager, with the purpose of avoiding conflicts of
interest; and certain norms (again unstated) regarding the composition and di-

---

113. *Id.* at Art. 1.1.2.
114. *Id.* at Art. 1.2.4.
115. *Id.* at Art. 1.4.
116. *Id.* at Art. 1.4.1.
117. *Id.* at. Art. 1.4.2.
118. *Id.* at. Art. 1.4.3.

versification of the fund assets. A further prerequisite for operations is the existence of specific rules dealing with custody and deposit of all fund assets.[119]

Mutual funds must also provide their investors, at the time of their investment, with information regarding all rules related to their investment, the value of their shares, and all investment and redemption conditions. Furthermore, mutual funds must periodically provide the appropriate regulatory bodies, in accordance with applicable local law, information relating to the price history of their shares, the composition of their portfolio and a statement showing the result of its investments.[120]

5. Stock Exchanges and Brokers

A MERCOSUR member state stock exchange (or similar entity) wishing to list securities in another MERCOSUR member state must act under the regulation of the appropriate governmental entity in the member state in which it wishes to sell. This regulation must authorize the creation, operations and dissolution of stock exchanges and trading systems; approve the general operational rules and regulations applicable to its members; approve all rules dealing with securities transactions effected by its members, including custody of traded securities; determine the minimum information regarding its economic-financial condition and operations, required to be furnished by the exchange of trading system to the appropriate regulator; and determine the minimum operational information (relating to issuers as well as securities being traded required to be furnished to the public.[121]

Brokers wishing to operate internationally within MERCOSUR must act under the direct or indirect supervision of the appropriate governmental regulator in each state which must: determine the norms that regulate their activities; establish minimum capital and liquidity requirements for operations within the MERCOSUR context; and determine appropriate record keeping requirements for all operations.[122]

6. Payment, Execution and Custody Systems

Payment, execution and custody systems (which must be independent entities chartered exclusively for that purpose) wishing to operate in MERCOSUR shall act under the regulation of the appropriate governmental entity in each

---

119. *Id.* at. Art. 2.1.
120. *Id.* at Art. 2.2.
121. *Id.* at Art. 3.1.
122. *Id.* at Art. 3.2.

member state, which must: authorize their creation, operations and dissolution; approve the limits and utilization of guaranty funds; and have the power to request all registers dealing with securities and depositor funds held in their custody.[123] The Stock Exchanges Regulation also recommends that all payment, execution and custody systems adopt mechanisms for the custody of securities constituted in public documents and integrated mechanisms for the recording of the custody or securities and financial and other transactions.[124] The Regulation has been ratified by the member states.[125]

7. *The Stock Exchanges Regulation: An Assessment*

As was the case with the Harmonization of Procedural Matters Protocols, the purpose of the Stock Exchanges Regulation is to encourage the development and expansion of the MERCOSUR economy by stimulating the investment of capital within the region. The concept is that, with minimum uniform and consistent regulation of securities markets, investors, both within and without MERCOSUR, will feel confident in investing their capital within MERCOSUR. The major regulatory concept found in the Regulation is that of collection and disclosure of information. Issuers of securities wishing to market their securities to the public within the region (including mutual funds) must supply, in a uniform format and on a regular basis, a substantial amount of information regarding their business, operations, management and financial condition. Accounting standards within the issuer's home country which differ from those of the other MERCOSUR member state in which the issuer seeks to operate must be explained to investors. This information is to be available both to their shareholders and to investors within MERCOSUR. Furthermore, the Regulation also creates a system of minimum regulation of the operations of mutual funds, stock exchanges, brokers and payment, execution and custody systems.

These are major improvements. The availability of consistently collected and uniformly disclosed information regarding issuers and their securities gives investors within the MERCOSUR market great ability to choose and evaluate potential investments. Minimum and consistent regulation of mutual funds, stock exchanges and brokers will also increase investor confidence in the capital markets in the region. The Regulation and the regulatory system it creates represent a major step forward.

Two problems arise, however. First, the Regulation and its regulation applies only to MERCOSUR-based "international players" seeking to do business or sell

---

123. *Id.* at Art. 4.1.
124. *Id.*
125. *See* MERCOSUR Normativa *available at* http://www.mercosur.org.uy.http://www.mercosur.org.uy.espanol/snor/incorporacion/consolidado__dec___1993.pdf.

their securities in another MERCOSUR member state. It does not apply to domestic transactions or issuers, who constitute the bulk of the capital market. Although the Protocol does "encourage" the member states to apply these norms to their domestic transaction as a "goal" sometime in the future (subject to "possibilities and economic realities" in each country), it contains no obligation for the member states to do so within the foreseeable future. This norm is clearly aspirational. Thus, this regulation, and the ensuing "comfort" and encouragement to invest its regulatory system may give to investors, will apply only to a small number of "international type" transactions, and will not encourage investor confidence and investment in the capital market itself. Until these norms are extended to cover *all* of the capital markets in the MERCOSUR countries, the Protocol's desired effect will not take place. Unlike the case of similar regulation in the European Union, the Regulation is wholesale harmonization of the basic norms of the securities industry in the member states.[126]

Secondly, the Protocol heavily relies on governmental regulatory bodies within the member states to implement and enforce its norms. While Argentina, Brazil and Chile have fairly extensive and sophisticated governmental regulators of their securities industries who may be able quite easily to fulfill the regulatory functions contemplated in the Protocol, other member states do not.[127] The regulatory bodies of the former may not be able to absorb the new workload and expense contemplated by the Protocol and the latter may not have the facilities of financial wherewithal to create or operate them. Without the Protocol's regulatory system in place (and operating) in all the member states, it may not live up to its full potential.

E. Harmonization of Substantive Norms: The MERCOSUR Competition Policy

1. Introduction

The harmonization of competition norms has long been a concern of MERCOSUR. The Council took the first step in this process by approving, in 1994, Decision 21/94, which was entitled "Basic Elements of the Defense of Competition in MERCOSUR.[128] The purpose of Decision 21/94 was the approval of

---

126. EU Stock Exchange Directives *available at* http://europa.int.eu.htm.

127. Information on securities laws of member states *available at* http://www.natlaw.com.

128. MERCOSUR/CMC/Dec NO. 21/94, "Defensa de Competencia," (hereinafter, "Decision 21/94" or "Basic Elements") *available at* http://www.mercosur.org.uy/espanol/snor/normativa/decisiones/Dec2194.htm.

basic norms that could facilitate the harmonization of national competition law and the creation of a basis for joint action by the member states in the area of competition.[129] It also requested that the member states submit, by March 31, 1995, detailed information concerning the compatibility of their current or proposed competition law with these Basic Elements.[130] This information was to be used by the MCC to prepare a draft protocol on the defense of competition in MERCOSUR.[131]

The Council approved a Protocol for the Defense of Competition in MERCOSUR ("Competition Protocol") in 1996.[132] Regulations for the Competition Protocol ("Competition Regulations") were agreed upon by the member states in 2002[133] and issued as a directive by the MCC in 2003.[134] Both documents are described and evaluated below.

2. The Competition Protocol

a. Applicability

The purpose of the Competition Protocol is the defense of competition within the scope of MERCOSUR.[135] Accordingly, the rules set forth therein apply to those acts undertaken by physical or juridical persons that have as their object producing or which produce effects over competition within the scope of MERCOSUR *and* that affect commerce among the member states.[136] The member states have exclusive jurisdiction over regulation of actions undertaken by any physical or juridical persons domiciled in their territory whose effect on competition is limited to their territory.[137]

---

129. *Id.* at Arts. 1–2. RL+P, *supra* Chptr. 2 note 58 at p. 93.

130. Decision 21/94, *supra* note 128, at Art. 2.

131. *Id.* at Art. 3.

132. MERCOSUR/CMC/Dec. No. 18/96, "Protocolo de Defensa de la Competencia del MERCOSUR" (hereinafter, "Decision 18/96") *available at* http://www.mercosur.org.uy/espanol/snor/normativa/decisiones/1996/9618.htm.

133. "Acuerdo sobre el Reglamento del Protocolo de Defensa de la Competencia del MERCOSUR" (December 5, 2002), *available at* http://www.mercosur.org.uy/espanol/sdyd/acuerdos/2002/Acdo_Rglto_Prot-Defen_Compet.htm.

134. MERCOSUR/CCM/DIR No. 01/03, "Reglamento del Protocolo de Defensa de la Competencia del MERCOSUR," (hereinafter, "Directive 01/03"or "Competition Regulation"), *available at* http://www.mercosur.org.uy/espanol/snor/normativa/directivas/2003/Dir_001_003.htm.

135. Decision 18/96, *supra* note 132, at Art. 1.

136. *Id.* at Art. 2. These include any enterprises that exercise state monopolies, to the degree that the Protocol's rules do not impede the regular exercise of their legal attributes. *Id.*

137. *Id.* at Art. 3.

b. Forbidden Acts

All actions, individual or concerted, that have for their object or effect the limitation, restriction or distortion of competition or of the free access to markets; or that constitute an abuse of a dominant position in the relevant market of goods and service within MERCOSUR and that affect the trade among the member states are forbidden by the Competition Protocol.[138] These practices may include, *inter alia*: direct or indirect price fixing; the imposition of limitations or controls in production, distribution, investment or technological innovation; the division of markets or limitation of access to raw materials; concerted actions in public bidding; adoption, with regard to third parties, of unfair contractual conditions which place them at a competitive disadvantage; conditioning the execution of contracts to other agreements to other matters that do not relate to their subject matter; imposition of unfair prices or contractual conditions; unjustified restrictions in production, distributions or access to technology which results in prejudice to other firms or to consumers; refusals to deal; conditioning of transactions to unfair or unjust commercial uses or practices or to refusals to utilizing goods or services produced by third parties; or selling goods at an artificially low price.[139] The simple control of a market resulting from a natural process based on the greater efficiency of a firm in relation to its competitor does not represent a violation of the Protocol.[140]

c. Control of Acts and Contracts

The member states were to adopt, by 1999, common norms for the control of actions and contracts that could limit or in any form prejudice free competition or result in the domination of the relevant regional market of goods and services, including those which result in economic concentrations, with the purpose of preventing their anti competitive effects within the scope of MERCOSUR.[141]

d. Application of the Protocol

The MCC and the Committee for the Defense of Competition ("CDC") are charged with the enforcement of the policies set forth in the Protocol.[142]

---

138. *Id.* at Art. 4.
139. *Id.* at Art. 6(I-XVII).
140. *Id.* at Art. 5.
141. *Id.* at Art. 7.
142. *Id.* at Art. 8. The CDC is an inter-governmental institution and is composed of the governmental institutions charged with the enforcement of competition policy in the member states ("member state enforcement institutions"). *Id.*

Enforcement proceedings will commence with the member state enforcement institution submitting a complaint from an interested party to the CDC which, after a preliminary technical analysis, will commence an investigation.[143] The CDC will, *inter alia*, establish norms to define the structure of the relevant market, the standards of proof, and the analytical criteria for determining the economic effects of the practice under investigation.[144] The member state enforcement institution in the state where the practice occurred, using the norms established by the CDC, will conduct the investigation in its territory.[145] The other member state enforcement institutions will provide assistance in the form of information, documents and any other means considered necessary for the correct execution of the investigation.[146] The member state enforcement institution performing the investigation will report its conclusions and recommendations to the CDC, which will describe the practices violating the protocol and will recommend the sanctions or other appropriate measures to be imposed.[147] The MCC will then consider the CDC's recommended conclusion and will issue a Directive which will impose the sanctions to be imposed in the case.[148] These sanctions will be enforced by the member state enforcement institution in the member states where the violator resides[149] may include fines, injunctions, or prohibitions on bidding on public contracts or contracting with public financing institutions.[150] The matter under investigation may be resolved at any time through a consent decree.[151] Violations of a consent decree will be subject to sanctions.[152]

e. Cooperation, Dispute Resolution and Other Matters

The member states, through their enforcement institutions, agreed to create mechanisms for the purpose of improving the cooperation and consultation

---

143. *Id.* at Arts. 10–11.

144. *Id.* at Art. 14.

145. *Id.* at Art. 15.

146. *Id.* at Art. 16.

147. *Id.* at Arts. 18–19. If the CDC cannot reach a consensus on the matter, then the disagreement will be resolved by the MCC. *Id.* at Art. 19.

148. *Id.* at Art. 20. If the MCC cannot reach a consensus, it will submit the matter for consideration by the Group. *Id.* The Group's decision will be rendered in the form of a resolution. If the Group cannot reach a consensus, the interested member state may then commence the proceedings set forth in Chapter IV of the Brasilia Protocol for the Resolution of Disputes. *Id.* at Art. 21.

149. *Id.* at Art. 20.

150. *Id.* at Arts. 27–29. *See also* MERCOSUR/CMC/Dec. No. 2/97, "Anexo al Protocolo de Defensa de la Competencia del MERCOSUR,"*available at* http://www.mercosur. org.uy/espanol/snor/normativa/1997/9702. htm.

151. *Id.* at Arts. 22–26.

152. *Id.* at Art. 27.

among them, to ensure a more efficient enforcement of competition policy in MERCOSUR.[153]

Any disputes arising out of the implementation, application or interpretation of the Competition Protocol will be subject to the dispute resolution procedures of the Brasilia and Ouro Preto Protocols.[154]

The Protocol was to become effective thirty days after the deposit of the second instrument of ratification (for the first two ratifying states) and thirty days after the deposit of their respective instrument of ratification by the other member states.[155] As of February 20, 2004, the MERCOSUR website did not reflect any action taken by the member states to ratify the Competition Protocol.[156]

3. The Competition Regulation

a. The CDC

The Competition Regulation first describes the composition of the CDC: the member states enforcement institutions, represented by a member and an alternate.[157] Its coordination functions will be exercised by the member state enforcement institution of the member state currently serving as the President Pro Tem of the Council.[158] The CDC is also authorized to maintain relationships with competition enforcement authorities in other countries, economic integration systems and international organizations.[159] It must meet at least once a quarter and the attendance of at least three representatives is required for a quorum.[160] All decisions are to be taken by consensus of the member states that have ratified the Competition Protocol.[161]

---

153. *Id.* at Art. 30.

154. *Id.* at Art. 31.

155. *Id.* at Art. 33.

156. *See* http://www.mercosur.org.uy/espanol/snor/incorporacion/consolidado_dec_1996.pdf.

157. Competition Regulation, *supra* note 134 at Art. 2. Until all member states have ratified the Competition Protocol, the membership of the CDC shall consist of the representatives of the member states who have deposited instruments of ratification with the MERCOSUR Secretariat. *Id.* at Art. 36. Member states who have not ratified the Protocol may attend meetings of the CDC, but may not participate in the taking of any decisions. *Id.* at Art. 37.

158. *Id.* at Art. 3.

159. *Id.* at Art. 4.

160. *Id.* at Arts. 5–6. Until the Competition Protocol has been ratified by all member states, the presence of the representatives of two member state enforcement institutions shall be sufficient to constitute a quorum. *Id.* at Art. 37.

161. *Id.* at Art. 7. If a decision is taken in the absence of a member, that decision will be final unless the absent member objects thereto within thirty days after the date of the meeting in which the decision was adopted. *Id.* at Art. 8.

b. The Member State Enforcement Institutions

The member state enforcement institutions are charged with the enforcement of the Competition Protocol. They are to: implement or have implemented, within the scope of their jurisdiction, the decisions taken to enforce the Competition Protocol; inform the CDC regarding the norms for the defense of competition that are adopted in their respective states; inform the CDC regarding the process of any investigations they are undertaking under the Protocol; supply any information requested by any other member state enforcement institution in the context of any investigation under the protocol; and inform the CDC regarding the degree of compliance with any registered consent decrees.[162]

c. Substantive Norms

In determining the applicability of the Competition Protocol, the effect on the commerce among the member states and the effect of the relevant market of goods or services in the scope of MERCOSUR, must be considered. The terms "goods or services within the scope of MERCOSUR" shall mean the goods and services that are produced or traded in the territory of one or more of the MERCOSUR member states.[163]

In order to establish an abuse of dominant position in a relevant markets in goods or services within the scope of MERCOSUR, four circumstances, *inter alia,* must be considered: a) the participation in the relevant market of the participating firms; b) the degree to which the good or service involved may be substituted for others of either or national, regional or foreign origin, the conditions of such substitution and the time required therefor; c) the degree to which any normative restrictions limit the access of products, offerors or customers in the market involved; and d) the degree to which the responsible party can unilaterally influence the setting of prices or restrict the supply or demand in the market and the degree to which its competitors may counteract such power.[164]

d. Enforcement Proceedings

The Competition Regulation sets forth a number of specific norms relating to the enforcement proceedings described in the Competition Protocol. These involve the initiation of the process, the content of requests for enforcement, the evaluation and investigation process and the content of recommendations.[165]

---

162. *Id.* at Art. 12.
163. *Id.* at Art. 10.
164. *Id.* at Art. 11.
165. *See Id.* at Arts. 13–30.

Parties contemplating commencing or involved in an enforcement proceeding need to carefully study these norms.

e. Other Topics

The Regulations also contain norms on consent decrees[166] and sanctions. In the event of a failure to comply with a consent decree, the member state enforcement institution may impose a fine on the non compliant party.[167] All fines collected under the Competition Protocol will be remitted to the member state enforcement institution in the member state in whose territory the party against whom the fines were assessed resides.[168] In order to determine the severity of the sanction to be assessed for a violation of the Protocol, the gravity of the violation, the cooperation of the violator with the investigation, and the recidivism of the violator shall be taken into account. In order to determine the gravity of the violation, the following circumstances may, *inter alia*, be considered: the degree of injury or danger of injury to free competition; the negative economic effects produced in the market; the economic position and situation of the violator; and the advantage obtained or sought to be obtained by the violator.[169]

The Regulation also notes that the CDC may, if it wishes, adopt internal rules of procedure.[170]

4. An Evaluation

The Protocol and Regulation represent a welcome effort by MERCOSUR to create common competition norms and enforcement processes. Articles 4 through 6 of the Protocol seem to track the language of Articles 85 and 86 of the European Union's Treaty of Rome.[171] These articles prohibit agreements and concerted practices which have as their object or effect the prevention, restriction or distortion of the common market and abuses of dominant position.[172] The adoption of these norms is highly desirable.

One difference between the system envisioned by the Competition Protocol and Regulations and EU competition norms, however, is the absence of a process similar to that set forth in European Council Regulation 4064/89.[173]

---

166. *Id.* at Art. 31.
167. *Id.* at Art. 33.
168. *Id.* at Art. 34.
169. *Id.* at Art. 35.
170. *Id.* at Art. 39.
171. Treaty of Rome, *supra* Chptr. 2 note 58, at Arts. 85–86.
172. RL+P, *supra* Chptr. 2 note 58, at p. 94.
173. Council Regulation (EEC) No. 4064/89 (21 December 1989) on the Control of Concentrations between Undertakings, OJ L 257/90 P 13, (hereinafter, "Regulation

This Regulation, basing itself on the authority of Article 86 of the Treaty, requires that certain takeovers or mergers ('or concentrations") must be reported to the European Commission before they are effected and allows the Commission to forbid those concentrations if they result in an abuse of dominant position which would significantly impede competition in the common market or in a significant part of it.[174] This lack of a mechanism by means of which an anti-competitive merger or other combination can be stopped before it is effected is regrettable, because it is much harder to undo a completed merger than to stop it before it is implemented.

European competition law is also clear in one critical issue: it applies only in cases where the agreements, concerted practices or abuse of dominant position may affect trade among the member states. Similarly, only concentrations having a "community dimension" (defined in Regulation 4064/89 as a concentration among firms each whose worldwide turnover exceeds 250 million ECU unless each of the firms involves achieves more than two thirds of its aggregate turnover in the Community within one and the same member state)[175] unless exempted, are subject to regulation by the Commission. In short, European competition law applies only to practices which affect competition within the larger community, and not to those practices which affect competition in one member state. This means that practices which affect competition in one member state are still subject to the national competition regimes of the member states of the Union. The boundary between the European and national competition law systems within the European Union appear to be relatively clearly set.[176]

This also appears to be the case in MERCOSUR. As noted above, Articles 2 of the Competition Protocol state that the norms created therein apply to physical or juridical persons that have as their object producing or which produce *effects over competition within the scope of MERCOSUR* and that *affect commerce among the member states*.[177] Similarly, Article 3 appears to make clear that the member states have *exclusive* jurisdiction over the regulation of actions undertaken by any persons (physical or juridical) domiciled whose effect on competition is limited to their territory.[178] That again is a welcome development.

A much more critical concern, however, is the stress that the Protocol and the Regulation place on the need for consensus among the member state en-

---

4064/89") *available at* http://europa.eu.int/smartapi/cgi/sga_doc?smartapi!celexapi!prod! CELEXnumdoc&lg=EN&numd oc=31989R4064&model=guichett.

174. *Id.* RL+P, *supra* Chptr. 2 note 58, at 95.

175. Regulation 4064/89, *supra* note 170 at Art. 1(2).

176. RL+P, *supra* Chptr. 2 note 58, at 95.

177. *See supra* note 140 and accompanying text.

178. *Id.*

forcement institutions before any enforcement action may be commenced and throughout the process of investigation and enforcement. Consensus may be extremely difficult to reach, especially in cases where, because of the differences in the economies of the member states, the competitive effects of an practice or business concentration may differ substantially from one member state or another. Furthermore, the Protocol places the enforcement of any of its norms squarely on the shoulders of the member state enforcement authorities. This is problematic. The competition regimes and institutions of the member states have different histories, financing and norms to apply and their enforcement institutions may not necessarily be equally effective.[179] In addition, because of the interstate nature of some of these practices and concentrations, they may not be able to be policed adequately by one or another member state competition authority. Although the Protocol calls for cooperation, by means of agreements and otherwise, among the member state enforcement institutions, this cooperation may at this point be more theoretical than real.[180]

Lastly, the apparent lack of ratifications of the Protocol by the member states is extremely troubling. Until all the instruments of ratification are deposited, the MERCOSUR competition norms and their enforcement will be purely theoretical.

F. Harmonization of Substantive Norms: Regulation of Commerce in Services

The Regulation of Commerce in Services Protocol[181] means to harmonize regulation by the member states of transnational trade in services.[182]

"Trade in services" includes the rendering of services from one member state to another, from one member state to consumers in other member states, and by

---

179. For background on the competition regimes of the member states, *see* RL+P, *supra* Chptr. 2 note 58, at 25–30, 50–61, 75–77, and 85. *See also* "Breve Análisis Económico de la Ley Argentina de Defensa de la Competencia," *available at* http://www.mecon.gov.arg/cndc/docu1a.htm; Hargain, "Análisis de la Legislación de Defensa de la Competencia," 124 La Justicia Uruguaya (Sept.–Oct. 2001); *available at* http://www.ccee.edu.uy/ensenian/catderco/PubCompHarg02.htm, Hargain, "Defensa de la Competencia y Política de Competencia," 127 Tribuna del Abogado (Mar.–Apr. 2002), *available at* http://www.ccee.edu.uy/ensenian/catderco/PubCompHarg01.htm.

180. *See* Competition Protocol, *supra* note 132, at Art. 30.

181. Montevideo Protocol regarding the Trade in Services in MERCOSUR, MERCOSUR/CMC/DEC No. 13/97 (1997) (hereinafter, "Montevideo Protocol"), *available at* http://www.mercosur.org.uy/http://www.mercosur.org.uy.espanol/snor/normativa/decisions/1997/9713.htm.

182. *Id.* at Art. II.2.

the legal or physical presence of a MERCOSUR service provider in another state.[183]

The regulation of trade in services by member states includes regulations dealing with the access to, rendering, purchase, sale or utilization of services and with the legal or physical presence of MERCOSUR service providers in another member state for the rendering of services.[184]

"Services" includes services on any type other than "governmental services," which are defined services rendered by a governmental entity that are not furnished under commercial conditions or in competition with one or more service providers.[185]

1. National Treatment and Market Access

Each MERCOSUR member state is to grant "immediately and unconditionally" to all service providers from other member states treatment no less favorable than those given to similar services and service providers from any other member state or from any other countries.[186] Furthermore, in all regulations affecting the rendering of services, member states will grant services and service providers from any other member state treatment no less favorable than those given to similar national services or service providers.[187]

Market access to service providers from other member states is another matter, however. The member states are expected to create a "Specific Compromises List" setting forth what access, and under what conditions and limitations, they will grant to services and service providers from other member states and to implement this agreement.[188] These "access agreements," will also permit the movement and repatriation of all capital essential to all services given market access.[189] The member states may also agree on other matter related to trade in services, but which do not involve market access.[190]

Member states may also not, as part of their national legislation, pass or maintain measures limiting the number, type or size of service providers or the number or amount of service transactions within their territory.[191]

---

183. *Id.*
184. *Id.* at Art. II.1.
185. *Id.* at Art. II.3.c. The Protocol also does not apply to services rendered as part of government contracts. *Id.* at Art. XV.
186. *Id.* at. Art. III.
187. *Id.* at Art. V.1.
188. *Id.* at Arts. IV.1, VII.1.
189. *Id.*
190. *Id.* at Art. VI.
191. Specifically, the Protocol describes measures dealing with: the number of service providers, the total value of their assets or service transactions, the total number and

2. Member State Regulation

The protocol first requires that all member state regulation (legislative, judicial or administrative) that affects trade in services shall be administrated in a reasonable, objective and impartial manner.[192] Furthermore, each member state is to maintain or establish courts or judicial, arbitral or administrative proceedings that permit, at the request of a service provider, the prompt review, of administrative decisions affecting trade in services.[193]

Applications for licenses or registration required to become a service provider must be acted upon promptly, and the appropriate authority is to communicate with the applicant during this process.[194] The member states should ensure that all technical norms, requirements and proceedings required for registration or licensing of a service provider do not constitute a barrier to trade in services. Accordingly, these norms, requirements and proceedings are to be based on objective and transparent criteria (such as aptitude and capacity to render the service), are to be the least restrictive necessary to ensure the quality of the service, and, in the case of licensing proceedings, are not per se a restriction on the furnishing of the service.[195]

Each member state also undertakes to urge the appropriate entities in their territory (including governmental entities, as well as professional and other associations) to, in cooperation with their equivalent bodies in all the member states, develop mutually acceptable norms for the exercise of all activities relating to services, including registration and licensing. The member states are then to recommend these norms to the Common Market Group. The Group is then to determine if these norms are consistent with the Protocol. Each member state then undertakes to implement these norms within a mutually agreed upon period of time.[196]

Lastly, all member states will promptly publish, before their effective date, all measures that relate or may affect the operation the Protocol and all international agreements that it has entered into with any country which refer to, or affect, trade in services. Each member state will also promptly notify, at least

---

amount of service transactions, the number of persons that may be employed in a particular service sector or by a particular service provider, the types of business organization by means of which a service provider can operate, or the participation of foreign capital permissible in a service provider. *Id.* at Art. IV.2(a-f).

192. *Id.* at Art. X.1.

193. *Id.* at Art. X. 2. This provision is also not meant to create on a member state the obligation of creating a tribunal or proceeding incompatible with its constitutional structure or the nature of its judicial system. *Id.*

194. *Id.* at Art. X. 3.

195. *Id.* at Art. X.4.

196. *Id.* at Art. XI.

annually, the MERCOSUR Commerce Commission the promulgation of new (or modification to existing) laws, administrative regulations or directives which it considers significantly affect trade in services. Furthermore, each member state will promptly respond to any request from any member state for information regarding any of these measures.[197]

3. Exceptions

None of the provisions of the Protocol is to be interpreted to the effect of prohibiting a member state from enacting or enforcing measures that are necessary for: the protection of morals or the maintenance of public order; the protection of the life and health of persons and animals or the preservation of vegetables; or the obtaining of compliance with laws and regulations not incompatible with the Protocol, and for security.[198] Measures incompatible with Article III of the Protocol (most favored nation treatment) may be undertaken if the different treatment results from an agreement intending to avoid double taxation or from sections dealing with the avoidance of double taxation contained in another international agreement or treaty to which the member state applying the measure is as party.[199] Measures incompatible with Article V of the Protocol (national treatment) may be undertaken if the different treatment is intended to guarantee taxation or the equitable and effective collection of direct taxes relating to services or service providers of the remaining member states.[200] None of these measures, however, may be applied in a way in which results in arbitrary or unjustifiable discrimination when similar conditions prevail among the member states or as a hidden restriction on trade in services.[201]

None of the provisions of the Protocol is to be interpreted as imposing on a member state the obligation to furnish information whose disclosure it deems contrary to its essential security interests; preventing a member state from adopting measures it deems essential to the protection of its essential security interests;[202] or preventing a member state from adopting measures in compliance with its obligations undertaken in connection with the United Nations Charter for the maintenance of international peace and security.[203]

---

197. *Id.* at Art. VIII.
198. *Id.* at Art. XIII.(a-c).
199. *Id.* at Art. XIII.(d).
200. *Id.* at Art. XIII.(e).
201. *Id.*
202. These are measures regarding: the furnishing of services directly or indirectly destined to ensure the supply of the armed forces; fissionable or fusionable materials of those necessary for their fabrication; or norms applied in times of war or grave international tension. *Id.* at Art. XIV.b.
203. *Id.* at Art. XIV (C).

4. *Liberalization Program*

Lastly, the Protocol establishes a liberalization program for trade in services, which the member states will negotiate within a period of ten years.[204] These negotiations will be undertaken on a yearly basis under the supervision of the Common Market Group and will have as their goal the granting of market access within MERCOSUR to all commercial sectors involved in trade in services and the elimination of all barriers to such trade.[205] Member states are expected, during these negotiations, to negotiate and agree to "specific agreements" relating to market access or the elimination of barriers for service providers in particular sectors of the economy. The member states are then expected to implement and enforce these agreements.[206]

5. *Annexes*

Thus far, four Annexes to the Montevideo Protocol have been approved.[207] The most recent Specific Agreements under the Protocol was approved in December 2003.[208] Although the Protocol was signed on December 15, 1997, it

---

204. *Id.* at Art. XIX (1).

205. *Id.* at Arts. XIX (1) and XXII.

206. *Id.* at Art. XIX (2). There are two major exceptions to what otherwise appears to be a very broad commitment to liberalize trade in services, however. First, member states, in order to achieve their policy regarding trade in services, have the right to introduce new regulations which may cover (and presumably limit, or introduce barriers relating to) the subject matters of the liberalization program. These new regulations may not, however, contradict the member state's "specific agreements" made as part of the liberalization program and may not nullify or limit any obligations emerging from the Protocol or any specific agreements. *Id.* at Art. XIX (4). Secondly, any member state may, during the implementation of the trade in services liberalization program, prospectively modify or suspend any specific agreements included in its Specific Agreements list. This is a power that is only meant to be used a member state only in exceptional cases, and the exercise of this power, together with the reasons therefor, must be reported to the Common Market Group. The Group will then consult with the member states which consider themselves affected by this modification or suspension and will attempt to reach a consensus relating to how long this modification or suspension will be in effect and how it will be applied. *Id.* at Art. XX.

207. They cover: the Movement of Physical Persons who Provide Services, Financial Services, Water and Ground Transportation Services and Air Transportation Services. MERCOSUR/CMC/DEC No. 9/98 (1998), Appendix I *available at* http://www.mercosur.org.uy/espanol/snor/normativa/decisiones/1998/9809.htm. The Fourth Round of negotiations on Specific Compromises has recently been launched. MERCOSUR/GMC/Acta No. 01/02, XLV, Reunion Ordinaria del Grupo Mercado Comun (hereinafter, "GMC Acta 01/02") at par. 6.2.1.

208. *Id.* at Appendix II., MERCOSUR/CMC/D. No.1/00(2000), *available at* http://www.merocosur.org.uy. The latter round of negotiations was completed and the specific

has not yet become effective,[209] and none of the member states have completed their incorporation of the Protocol into their domestic legal systems.[210]

6. An Assessment

As was the case with the other protocols we have reviewed, the purpose of the Trade in Services Protocol is to encourage the development and expansion of the MERCOSUR economy by stimulating the movement and growth of trade in services within the region. This Protocol, unlike the Stock Exchanges Protocol, seeks to achieve this by rather than specifying minimally applicable rules, by creating a process which, over the long term, is meant to create free access and eliminate barriers to the trade in services. The Protocol does require member states to give immediate and unconditional national treatment to all service providers from other MERCOSUR countries. However, the major thrust of the Protocol is mostly aspirational: It creates a ten year negotiation process to arrive at mutually agreed upon norms regarding market access, objective and impartial mutual member state regulation and regulatory processes, and the elimination of barriers affecting service providers. These are lofty and laudable goals.

They are, however, not likely to be realized. First, there are very few, and extremely broad and general, norms set forth in the Protocol for the member states to base these negotiations on. The "service sector" in any modern economy is enormous, highly complex, extremely diverse, and constantly expanding. Given this characteristic of the service sector, it is going to be extremely hard for the member states (and the Common Market Group) to know where to start. Furthermore, if one or more of the member states refuses to negotiate, or if the member states cannot reach an agreement, then there is no progress. There is no mechanism in the Protocol or elsewhere that the Common Market Group can use to bring recalcitrant member states to the negotiating table or to pressure them to agree to anything. Given the extremely small number of "specific agreements" reached by the member states so far,[211] and the experience garnished during the negotiations among the members of LAFTA,[212] this is a serious problem.

To make matters worse, a substantial portion of regulation of service providers (such as accountants and attorneys) is carried out by professional as-

---

agreement reached therein is set forth at MERCOSUR/CMC/D n. 22-03, *available at* http://www.mercosur.org.uy.espanol/snor/normativa/decisiones/2003/Dec022_003.htm.

209. *See* Trade Agreements *available at* http://sice.oas.org. *See* MERCOSUR Normativa *available at* http://mercosur.org.uy/espanol/snor/incorporacion/consolidated_dec_1997.pdf.

210. GMC Acta 01/02, *supra* note 207 at par. 6.2.2.

211. *See* MERCOSUR/CMC/DEC No. 9/98, Appendix II, and MERCOSUR/CMC/Dec. No. 1/00 (2000) *supra* note 208.

212. *See supra* Chptr. 1 notes 22–35, and accompanying text.

sociations and other non-governmental organizations. All the member state governments can do is to ask these organizations to cooperate in the negotiations and to agree to changes in their regulation but, as the Protocol itself makes clear, the member states can only "urge" these organizations to cooperate in the process, but cannot compel them to change their rules. Since it may make short term economic sense for some of these organizations to oppose the admission of foreigners" into their ranks, impossible to reach agreement in certain sectors.

The Trade in Services Protocol is therefore trying to do too much with too little. It would have made better sense, as has been done in the European Union, to come to an agreement on specific sectors and norms first, and then to extrapolate general rules from that experience. Such an approach would have worked much better than the present one.

G. Harmonization of Economic Policy: Regulation of Foreign Investment

The Council has began an attempt to harmonize economic policy by issuing two Protocols dealing with the regulation of foreign investment ("Foreign Investment Protocols"). These are the Colonia Protocol, dealing with foreign investment among MERCOSUR countries[213] and a Protocol dealing with investments coming from nationals of non-MERCOSUR member states.[214] As was the case with the Harmonization of Procedural Matters and Stock Exchanges Protocols, the purpose of the Foreign Investment Protocols is to encourage the development and expansion of the MERCOSUR economy by stimulating the investment of capital within the region. Both Protocols are discussed below.

1. The Colonia Protocol

a. "Investments" and "Investors"

The term "investment"is very broadly defined in the Protocol as "the investment of any kind of asset, directly or indirectly, by investors of a member state

---

213. "Colonia Protocol for the Reciprocal Promotion and Protection of Investments in MERCOSUR," MERCOSUR/CMC/DEC No. 11/93 (hereinafter, "Colonia Protocol"), *available at* http://www.mercosur.org.uy. http://www.mercosur.org.uy.espanol/snor/normativa/decisiones/Dec 1193.htm.

214. "Protocol for the Promotion and Protection of Investments Coming from Non MERCOSUR Member States"MERCOSUR/CMC/DEC No. 11/94 and 11/94 Annex (hereinafter, "Non-Member States Protocol"), *available at* http://www.mercosur.org.uy.http://www.mercosur.org.uy.espanol/snor/normativa/decisiones/Dec1946.htm.

in the territory of another member state.[215] Similarly, an "investor" is either a natural person who is a national of a member state who is domiciled or permanently resides therein (a "foreign person"), a legal person organized in accordance with the laws and regulations of a member state and which has its headquarters in the territory thereof (a "foreign legal person"); or a legal person organized in accordance with the laws of the state in which the investment is made, but which is controlled by either foreign persons or foreign legal persons.[216]

b. Promotion and Protection of Investments

Each member state agree to promote the investments from investors from other member states and will admit them into their territory under conditions no less favorable than those given to investments made by their own investors or by investors from non-MERCOSUR member states. The member states, may, however, exempt certain areas of their economy from this requirement, on a temporary and transitory basis.[217] Once a member state admits an investment into its territory, it will expeditiously grant the approvals and authorizations necessary for its development, including the execution of licensing agreements, commercial or administrative assistance, and permission for the entry of all necessary personnel into the country.[218]

The Colonia Protocol essentially requires that a member state give national treatment to investments by MERCOSUR member state nationals. Specifically, each member state must ensure at all times a just and equitable treatment to the investments of investors from another member state and will not prejudice their management, use maintenance, enjoyment or disposition through unjustified or discriminatory measures.[219] Furthermore, each member state must

---

215. Colonia Protocol, *supra* note 213, at Art. 1(1).These may include: a) personal or real property, including rights thereon such as mortgages; b) shares, partnership interests and any other type of participation in an enterprise; c) negotiable instruments; d) intellectual property rights and e) public economic concessions granted in accordance with law, including concessions for the search, cultivation, extraction or exploitation of natural resources. *Id.*

216. *Id.* at Art. 1 (2). The definition does not include a foreign person who, at the time of making the investment, is domiciled or a permanent resident of the country in which the investment is made, unless it can be established that the assets being invested come from outside the country of investment. *Id.*

217. These exceptions are articulated in Annex 1 to the Protocol. For example, Argentina's reservations included real property in border areas, air transport, naval industry, nuclear plants, uranium mining, insurance and fisheries. *Id.* at Annex 1, Article 1.

218. *Id.* at Art. 2.

219. *Id.* at Art. 3(1). This provision does not obligate the member state to extend to investors from other member states the benefits of any international agreement relating, either totally or partially, to tax matters. *Id.* at Art. 3(3).

grant full legal protection to these investments and will grant them treatment no less favorable than that given to investments by its own nationals or by investors from non-MERCOSUR states.[220] Lastly, no member state may impose export agreements, buy local requirements, or similar conditions on any such investment.[221]

c. Expropriations and Compensation

No member state may undertake nationalization or expropriation measures (or measures having the same effect) against investments in their territory that belong to investors from another member state, unless the measure is undertaken for reasons of public utility, on a nondiscriminatory basis, and in accordance with due process of law.[222]

Investors from a MERCOSUR member state who suffer losses from an investment in another member state due to armed conflict, national emergency, revolt or insurrection shall be entitled to compensation or restitution no less favorable than that given to local investors or to investors from non-MERCOSUR states.[223]

d. Transfers

Each member state will allow investors from other member states to freely transfer their investments and profits broadly defined.[224] This transfer will be undertaken without delay, in freely convertible currency, and at the exchange

---

220. *Id.* at Art. 3(2).

221. *Id.* at Art. 3(4).

222. *Id.* at Art. 4(1). Such a measure will include a provision for the payment of prompt, adequate and effective compensation. The amount of this compensation will correspond to the real value of the expropriated investment before the nationalization of expropriation decision was legally announced or publicized by the appropriate authority. This calculation is subject to updating and to the payment of interest to the date of payment. *Id.*

223. *Id.* at Art. 4(2). If a member state or one of its agencies makes a payment to an investor in accordance with a guarantee or insurance policy to cover non commercial risks relating to the investment, the member state in whose territory the investment was made will recognize the subrogation rights, for the purpose of obtaining economic indemnification. of such a member state or agency to any rights or property of the investor. They shall have the same rights that the investor would have been authorized to enforce. An investor shall not file any claim without the authorization of the member state or its agency that made the payment. *Id.* at Art. 6.

224. *Id.* at 5(1). These include: a) capital and the additional sums necessary for the maintenance and development of the investment; b) any gains, return, rent, interest, dividend and other current income; c) loan repayment funds; d) royalties, fees and any other payment relative to intellectual property; e) the yield from the total or partial sale or liquidation of the investment; and f) compensation, indemnities or other payments relating to a nationalization or expropriation. *Id.*

rate in effect on the date of the transfer, in accordance with the proceedings established by the member state in whose territory the investment was made.[225]

e. Applicability of Other Norms

When the law of a member state, the obligations of international law (present or future) or an agreement between an investor and the member state in whose territory the investment was made, contain provisions that grant investments a more favorable treatment than that accorded in the Protocol, those norms will prevail, to the degree that they are more favorable, over the norms set forth in the Protocol.[226]

f. Dispute Resolution

The dispute resolution provisions of the Colonia Protocol cover two types of disputes arising thereunder: those between member states and those between an investor and the member state where the investment took place. The former disputes shall be resolved in accordance with the Brasilia Protocol,[227] or the dispute resolution system that will eventually replace it.[228]

The latter type of disputes are first to be settled by friendly consultations.[229] If these friendly consultations do not resolve the dispute within six months, then the investor has a choice. He could either submit the dispute to the appropriate tribunals of the member state in whose territory the investment was made, to international arbitration.[230]

g. Applicability and Effective Date

The Protocol applies to all investments made before or after its effective date,[231] but its provisions will not be applied to any controversy, claim or dis-

---

225. *Id.* at Art. 5(2). These procedures cannot affect the substance of the rights described above. *Id.*

226. *Id.* at Art. 7.

227. Brasilia Protocol, *supra* Chptr. 2 note 29 and accompanying text.

228. Colonia Protocol, *supra* note 213 at Art. 8. *See* Olivos Protocol, *supra* Chptr. 2 note 29 and accompanying text.

229. *Id.* at Art. 9(1).

230. This arbitration can be either before ACCEDE or before an ad hoc arbitration tribunal established under the UNCITRAL arbitration rules. *Id.* at Art. 9(4). The arbitral tribunal shall decide the controversy in accordance with the Protocol, the law of the member state which is a party to the controversy (including its conflicts of law rules), the terms of the specific agreements made by the parties, and the applicable norms of international law. *Id.* at Art. 9(5). The arbitral award shall be conclusive and obligatory for the parties to the dispute. Each member state will enforce them in accordance with its legislation. *Id.* at Art. 9(6).

231. This effective date was 30 days after the date of deposit of the fourth instrument of ratification of the Protocol. *Id.* at Art. 11.

pute that arose prior to its effective date.[232] The Colonia Protocol was signed on January 17, 1994, but has not yet become effective.[233]

2. The Non-Member States Protocol

The Non-Member States Protocol basically extends the benefits of the Colonia Protocol to investors and investments coming from non-MERCOSUR member states. It first states that the member states agree to grant to investments made by investors from non-MERCOSUR member states treatment no less favorable than that which is established therein.[234] This treatment will then be effected by agreements entered into between each member state and individual non-MERCOSUR member states.[235] The benefits granted by these agreements will not exceed those set forth in the Protocol. The description of the benefits that follows is a mostly *verbatim,* repetition of the language of the Colonia Protocol with some differences. A description of these differences follows.

3. Promotion and Protection of Investments

As was the case in the Colonia Protocol, each member state agrees to promote the investments from investors from non-MERCOSUR member states and will admit them into their territory in accordance with their statutes and regulations. Once a member state admits such an investment into its territory, it will grant the approvals and authorizations necessary for its development, including the execution of licensing agreements, commercial or administrative assistance, and permission for the entry of all necessary personnel into the country.[236]

The Non-Member States Protocol follows the Colonia Protocol by essentially requiring that a member state give national treatment to investments by non-MERCOSUR member state nationals. Specifically, each member state

---

232. *Id.* at Art. 10.

233. *See* Trade Agreement *available at* http://www.sice.oas.org. Argentina and Brasil have ratified the Protocol. The Protocol is in legislative proceedings in Paraguay and while the majority of norms have been incorporated in Uruguay, others are still in legislative proceedings. *See also* MERCOSUR Normativa *available at* http://www.mercosur.org.uy/espanol/snor/normativa.incorporacion.

234. Non-Member States Protocol, *supra* note 214, at Art. 1. The definitions of the terms "investment" and "investors" are identical to those of the Colonia Protocol. *Id.* at Art. 2(a).

235. *Id.* at Art. 2. The minimum term of these agreements will be 10 years. The member state who is a party to such an agreement may stipulate, that, with regard to investments made before the termination of the agreement's term, its provisions will continue in effect for a maximum period of fifteen years from the date of the investment. *Id.* at Art. 2(J).

236. *Id.* at Art. 2.(B).

must ensure at all times a just and equitable treatment to the investments of investors from another member state and will not prejudice their management, use maintenance, enjoyment or disposition through unjustified or discriminatory measures.[237] Furthermore, each member state will grant full legal protection to these investments and will grant them treatment no less favorable than that given to investments by its own nationals or by investors from other states.[238] Lastly, no member state may extend to an investor from a non-Member state the benefits or any treatment, preference or privilege arising from its participation in any free trade zone, customs union, common market, similar regional agreement or international agreement relating to taxation matters.[239]

4. Expropriations and Compensation

The provisions regarding expropriation and compensation are identical to those set forth in the Colonia Protocol with one exception: the provision that required the amount of compensation to equal the value of the investment at the moment the expropriation or nationalization decision was announced or made by the appropriate authority and that this calculation of the real value of the investment would be subject to updating and to the payment of interest to the date of payment is missing. In its place is a provision that simply says that the amount of compensation shall correspond to the value of the expropriated investment.[240]

5. Transfers

The provisions regarding transfers are identical to those of the Colonia Protocol with two exceptions. First, the definition of "investment and profits" includes the remuneration of non-MERCOSUR member state nationals who have obtained authorization to work in the investment are also to be freely transferable and second, the non-Member States Protocol does not include the language that the transfer will be available without delay, in freely convertible currency, and at the exchange rate in effect on the date of the transfer. Instead, it simply states that the transfers are to be made without delay, in freely convertible currency.[241]

---

237. *Id.* at Art. 2(C)(1).
238. *Id.* at Art. 2(C)(2).
239. *Id.* at Art. 2(C)(3).
240. *Id.* at Art. 2(D). *See supra* notes 222–23 and accompanying text.
241. *Id.* at Art. 2 (E) *See supra* note 224 and accompanying text. The Protocol's provision on subrogation is identical to that in the Colonia with one exception: the language that states that a member state or its agency that made a payment shall have the same rights that the investor would have been authorized to enforce and that an investor shall not file any claim without the authorization of the member state or its agency hat made the payment is missing. *Id.* at 2(f).

6. Dispute Resolution

The dispute resolution provisions of the Non-Member States Protocol cover two types of disputes arising thereunder: those between a member state and a non-member state and those between an investor and the member state where the investment took place. The former disputes shall be resolved by diplomatic means. If such a dispute cannot be resolved by diplomatic means, it shall be submitted to international arbitration.[242]

The latter type of disputes are first to be settled by friendly consultations.[243] If these friendly consultations do not resolve the dispute within a reasonable time, then the investor has a choice. He could either submit the dispute to the appropriate tribunals of the member state in whose territory the investment was made, or to international arbitration.[244]

The norms of the agreements to be entered into among the member states and non-member states may be applied to all investments made before or after its effective date,[245] but its provisions would not be applied to any controversy, claim or dispute that arose prior thereto.[246] The Protocol has not yet become effective because it has still to be ratified by the member states.[247]

7. Assessment

As is the case with many of the other Protocols that have been reviewed, the Foreign Investment Protocols are expected to encourage the development and

---

242. *Id.* at Art. 2(G)(2).

243. *Id.* at Art. 2(H)(1)-(2).

244. This arbitration can be submitted to an institutional arbitration tribunal or before an ad hoc arbitration tribunal *Id.* at Art. 2(H)(3). The arbitral tribunal shall decide the controversy in accordance with the Protocol, the law of the member state which is a party to the controversy (including its conflicts of law rules), the terms of the specific agreements made by the parties, and the applicable norms of international law. *Id.* at Art. 2(H)(4).The arbitral award shall be conclusive and obligatory for the parties to the dispute. Each member state will enforce them in accordance with its own legislation. *Id.* at Art. 2 (H)(5).

245. This effective date was 30 days after the date of deposit of the fourth instrument of ratification of the Protocol. *Id.* at Art. 4. The member states also agreed to exchange information regarding any present or future negotiations for promotion and reciprocal protection of investment agreements and agreed to engage in prior consultation regarding any substantial modification to the general norms set forth in the Protocol. The MERCOSUR Administrative Secretariat was to be the clearinghouse and supervisor of all such information exchanges or consultations. *Id.* at Art. 3.

246. *Id.* at Art. 2(I).

247. *See* MERCOSUR Normativa *available at* http://www.mercosur.org.uy/espanol/snor/normativa/incorporacion/consolidado_1994_.pdf.

expansion of the MERCOSUR economy through a community wide harmonization and liberalization of the regulation of foreign investment. The Colonia and the Non-Member States Protocols, in spite of their language similarities, vary widely in their effectiveness.

The Colonia Protocol starts by requiring each Member State to grant national treatment to all investments (broadly defined) made by nationals of another Member State. The basis of this "national treatment" is very comprehensive: it includes equality in the granting of necessary approvals and commercial or administrative assistance, non discriminatory treatment and full legal protection. The Protocol also provides for substantial rights against unfair expropriation or nationalization of these investments and for free transferability of investments and profits (again, very broadly defined).

A cursory reading of the Colonia Protocol may lead to the belief that absolute freedom of investments is now the norm among the MERCOSUR member states. That is not necessarily the case, however. As was seen above, the Protocol allows Member States to exempt certain sectors of their economies from the application of the Protocol.[248] A review of the exceptions that have already been articulated by the Member States are very extensive, and include some of the industrial sectors most attractive to foreign investors.[249]

An extremely crucial question remains, however: how are these rights to be enforced? If, on the one hand, the situation that arises is that a member state, as a matter of general policy, refuses to afford the Colonia Protocol rights to all (or a class) of investors from another member state, then the aggrieved member state can only resort to the dispute resolution proceedings of the Brasilia and Olivos Protocols which, as described above,[250] are extremely ineffectual. A dispute between a foreign investor and a member state is not easily resolved either. The investor must first engage in "friendly consultations" for six months and, if that process doesn't work, then may either seek redress in the courts of the member state in which the investment was made or engage in an international arbitration proceeding. Depending on the nature of the dispute, the investor may not be confident that the courts of the member state that he is litigating against may give him a fair or objective hearing. Furthermore, if the investor chooses this route, and the process in the courts of the member state is not fair or objective, he has no further recourse. The process of international arbitration can be long and expensive. Again, what recourse does the appellant have if the member state refuses to abide by a arbitral award rendered against him?

---

248. *See supra* note 217 and accompanying text.
249. Colonial Protocol, *supra* note 210, at Annex 1.
250. *See supra* Chptr. 3 notes 4–39 and accompanying text.

There is also a substantial logistical process that needs to be undertaken by the Member States in order to implement the Colonia Protocol. Each of them must survey its legislation and administrative regulations to identify all norms that serve as barriers to the absolute freedom of investments by MERCOSUR nationals in their territory and repeal or amend these norms. This is a lengthy, complicated and difficult process. What entity within each member state will undertake this process? How is this process to be undertaken and in what time period is it to be completed? Will this process be centrally supervised by MERCOSUR in any fashion? Will there be a centralized depository of information or data regarding these norms or the process of their amendment or repeal? How much will the process cost? Who will pay for it? Until this process is undertaken and completed, the rights granted by the Colonia Protocol may be more illusory than real.

The Non-Member States Protocol, in spite of tracking the language of the Colonia Protocol almost *verbatim,* is a very different entity. It seeks to extend the rights of the Colonia Protocol to foreign investors from states which are not members of MERCOSUR. There is a catch, however. In order for these rights to apply to investments by non-Member state investors, the Member State in which the investment is to be made has to have entered into an agreement with the state of which the investor is a national to specifically extend these rights. The Non-Member States Protocol makes it clear that Member States *may* enter into these agreements, but does not make it obligatory for them to do so. No such agreements appear to have been entered into so far.[251] Thus, the Non-Member States Protocol is purely aspirational. Even if some of these agreements were negotiated, they would suffer from the shortcomings of the Colonia Protocol described above. Clearly, the harmonization of economic policies is harder to undertake than that of legal norms.

---

251. Currently, there are no such agreements. *See* http://www.mercosur.org.uy or http://www.sice.oas.org.

Chapter 6

The Incorporation of Bolivia and Chile into MERCOSUR

A. Introduction

This Chapter considers an event in MERCOSUR history that has the potential for creating substantial change in MERCOSUR and its operations: the incorporation of Chile and Bolivia into the organization and implementation and development of that relationship.

B. Chile and Bolivia Join MERCOSUR

In 1996, after extensive (and often difficult) negotiations,[1] MERCOSUR entered into Economic Complementation Agreements, first with Chile[2] and then

---

1. Negotiations with Chile took two years and were described in the press as "tough". *See, e.g.,* Raúl Ronzoni, *Trade: Accord with Chile Expands Horizons of MERCOSUR,* March, 26 1996, Inter Press Serv.) (*available at* LEXIS/Nexis, ALLNEWSPLUS Database) (hereinafter, "Ronzoni"). Negotiations with Bolivia were similarly described. *See, e.g.,* Juan Carlos Rocha, *Integration: Mixed Feelings Mark Bolivian Entry into MERCOSUR,* Dec. 12 1996, Inter Press Serv.) (*available at* LEXIS/Nexis, ALLNEWSPLUS Database); Mario Osava, *Integration: MERCOSUR Takes on New Dimensions,* Dec.12 1996, Inter Press Serv.) (*available at* LEXIS/Nexis, ALLNEWSPLUS database); Geoff Dyer, *Bolivia Link to MERCOSUR hit by last-minute Hitch,* Dec.17 1996, Financial Times) (*available at* LEXIS/Nexis, ALLNEWSPLUS Database) (hereinafter, "Dyer"); Fabiana Frayssinet and Mario Osava, *Integration: MERCOSUR takes Two Steps Forward, One Step Back,* Dec.18 1996, Inter Press Serv.) (*available at* LEXIS/Nexis, ALLNEWSPLUS Database). For a detailed analysis of the negotiations between Chile and MERCOSUR, *see* Manuel Valencia, "Negociación de Chile con el MERCOSUR: Realidades y Oportunidades," in CHILE-MERCOSUR, *supra* Chptr. 1 note 56.

2. The agreement with Chile was executed on June 26, 1996 at San Luis, Argentina. Chile Agreement, Intro. note 14.

with Bolivia.[3] Both agreements are highly similar in format and content, and establish a similar relationship.

MERCOSUR chose to incorporate Chile and Bolivia, not by making them full members and party to its existing agreements, but by creating a *separate* relationship with them altogether. This relationship established by the Chile and Bolivia agreements has been described as one of "associate membership" in MERCOSUR.[4] This description is somewhat inaccurate. The agreements, entered into with MERCOSUR, as Economic Complementation Agreements under the framework of ALADI,[5] are not intended to give either Chile or Bolivia any kind of membership status therein. Instead, the agreements establish relationships which have as primary goals the establishment of a free trade area with Chile and Bolivia within a period of 10 years, the creation of judicial in institutional frameworks for economic integration and cooperation, the promotion of economic, scientific, technological and energy cooperation and complementation, the promotion of reciprocal investment and the promotion of the development of physical infrastructure facilities.[6] These relationships are very carefully enumerated and described in the agreements, and are administered and implemented by a separate Administrative Committee for each, and not by any of the MERCOSUR institutions.[7] Chile and Bolivia, do not have, under the agreements, the right to attend or participate in the meetings or the work of any of the MERCOSUR institutions. They also are not bound by MERCOSUR's common external tariff.[8]

1. *The Agreements*

a. Trade Liberalization Program in Brief

The Chile and Bolivia agreements follow the same format and are extremely similar. After describing very similar objectives,[9] they then assert that a free

---

3. The agreement with Bolivia was executed on December 17, 1996 at Fortaleza, Brazil. Bolivia Agreement, *supra* Intro. note 14.

4. *See, e.g.,* Thomas O'Keefe, Esq., "The Chile-MERCOSUR Free Trade Agreement—Effects on Foreign Direct Investment in the Southern Cone," LATIN AMERICAN LAW & BUSINESS REPORT, August 31, 1996 at p.4; Dyer, *supra* note 1.

5. *See* ALADI Treaty Chptr. 1 note 34 and accompanying text.

6. Chile Agreement, Intro. note 14, at Art. 1. Bolivia Agreement, Intro. note 14, at Art. 1.

7. Chile Agreement, *Id.* at Art. 46; Bolivia Agreement, *Id.* at Art. 39. It should be noted, however, that the MERCOSUR component of the Administrative Commission is the Common Market Group.

8. A number of Council Decisions have, however, given Chile and Bolivia the right to participate in the meetings and work of the MERCOSUR institutions, to the degree that Chile and Bolivia are entitled to participate in many if not most or all such meetings or work. *See, e.g.,* MERCOSUR/CMC/DEC No. 12/97; *available at* http://www.mercosur.org.uy/espanol/snor/normativa/decisiones/199797R/htm.

9. *Compare* Chile Agreement, Intro. note 14, Art. 1 with Bolivia Agreement, *supra* Intro. note 14, at Art. 1.

trade area will be established, by means of a trade liberation program, between MERCOSUR and the other contracting party within ten years. This trade liberation program will consist of a program of gradual and automatic tariff reductions over all tariffs[10] on products originating in and proceeding from the territory of the contracting parties.[11] This program of tariff reductions is different for each agreement. The Chile Agreement, for example, sets a general timetable of ten years, starting for the automatic reduction of all tariffs on products not otherwise noted in the agreement.[12] Twelve annexes list categories of products to whom different rules will apply. Some of these products will have their tariffs reduced within ten years, but at a different rate,[13] some within eight years,[14] and others within fifteen to sixteen years[15] Similarly, the Bolivian Agreement contains a general tariff reduction timetable of ten years[16] and special rules with timetables ranging from immediate elimination to fifteen years for seven different categories of products[17]. In both agreements, the parties also agree to impose no new tariffs, increase existing ones in a discriminatory manner or to maintain or apply new non tariff restrictions on imports.[18] Three other characteristics of the Agreements' trade liberalization program include the adoption of rules of origin,[19] national treatment on internal taxation,[20] and the adoption of safeguard measures.[21] The trade liberalization programs set forth in both agreements are described in greater detail below.

---

10. The term "tariff"is broadly defined. It includes customs tariffs and any other charge with equivalent effect, whether of a fiscal, monetary, exchange rate or other nature, that is set on imports. Chile Agreement, *Id.* at Art. 5; Bolivia Agreement, *Id.* at Art. 5.

11. Chile Agreement, *Id.* at Art. 2; Bolivia Agreement, *Id.* at Art. 2.

12. Chile Agreement, *Id.* at Art. 2(a).

13. *Id.* at Arts. 2(c)–(e).

14. *Id.* at Art. 2(b).

15. *Id.* at Arts. 2(f)–(i).

16. Bolivia Agreement, *supra* Intro. note 14, at Art. 2(a).

17. *Id.* at Arts. 2(b)–(h).

18. *Id.* at Arts. 6–8; Chile Agreement, *supra* Intro. note 14 at Arts. 6–8. Certain exceptions to these rules, specifically noted in each agreement's Complementary Notes, are permitted. *Id.*

19. Chile Agreement, *Id.* at Art. 14 and Annex 13; Bolivia Agreement, *Id.* at Art.12 and Annex 9.

20. Chile Agreement, *Id.* at Art. 14, Bolivia Agreement, *Id.* at Art. 13.

21. The concept of safeguard clauses was created and applied in the Treaty of Asunción. *See supra* note 1, and accompanying text. Here both Agreements differ. The Chile agreement provides that the parties will put a system of safeguard measures (not described) in effect by January 1, 1997. Chile Agreement, at Art. 21. The Bolivia Agreement contains a system of safeguard clauses. Bolivia Agreement, at Art. 20 and Annex 10.

b. The Chile Trade Liberation Program in Detail

The Chile Agreement provides for a trade liberation program to be applied to products originating or coming from the territory of Chile and the MER-COSUR member states. This trade liberation program will be completed within a ten year period and will consist of progressive and automatic preferences from the tariffs applicable to imports from third parties. This agreement also incorporates the prior tariff preferences negotiated between the MERCOSUR member states and Chile within the framework of ALADI and replaces any such agreements.[22] The terms "duties" and "charges" mean all customs duties and other charges having an equivalent effect, whether they were related to fiscal, monetary, exchange or other sectors, which are levied on foreign trade.

The parties to the Chile Agreement agree not to establish any different duties or charges having equivalent effect from customs duties, other than those in effect on its effective date.[23] Similarly, no party may impose new duties or charges on exports to their reciprocal trade or increase the terms of existing charges in a discriminatory fashion.[24] Furthermore, no party to the agreement is to impose any new non tariff restrictions on the import or export of its goods to the territory of another party thereto, except as provided for in the World Trade Organization Agreements.[25]

The tariff reduction program for all products not included in a particular Annex to the agreement started on January 1, 1996 with a 40% tariff preference and was to continue yearly until January 1, 2004, where there will be a 100% preference. Future reductions will be 48% in 1997, 55% in 1998, 63% in 1999, 70% in 2000, 78% in 2001, 85% in 2002, and 93% in 2003.[26]

Products set forth in Annex 1 of the Agreement would start on January 1, 1997 and will have different initial preferences, as noted therein. and would continue until January 1, 2004, where there will be a 100% preference. For items starting with a 40% preference, reductions will be 48% in 1997, 55% in 1998, 64% in 1999, 70% in 2000, 78% in 2001, 85% in 2002, and 93% in 2003. For items starting with a 50% preference, reductions will be 56% in 1997, 63% in 1998, 69% in 1999, 75% in 2000, 81% in 2001, 85% in 2002, and 94% in 2003. For items starting with a 60% preference, reductions will be 65% in 1997, 70% in 1998, 75% in 1999, 80% in 2000, 85% in 2001, 90% in 2002, and 95% in 2003. For items starting with a 70% preference, reductions will be 74% in 1997, 78% in 1998, 81% in 1999, 85% in 2000, 89% in 2001, 93% in

---

22. Chile Agreement, *supra* Intro. note 14 at Art. 2.
23. *Id.*
24. *Id.* at Art. 6.
25. *Id.* at Art. 7.
26. *Id.* at Art. 2(a).

2002, and 96% in 2003. For items starting with an 80% preference, reductions will be 83% in 1997, 85% in 1998, 88% in 1999, 90% in 2000, 93% in 2001, 95% in 2002, and 98% in 2003.For items starting with an 90% preference, reductions will be 91% in 1997, 93% in 1998, 94% in 1999, 95% in 2000, 96% in 2001, 98% in 2002, and 99% in 2003.[27]

The tariff reduction program for all products listed in Annex 2 to the agreement started on January 1, 1997 with a 30% tariff preference and will continue yearly until January 1, 2006, where there will be a 100% preference. Future reductions will be 30% through 1999, 50% in 2000 and 2001, 60% in 2002, 70% in 2003, 80% in 2004, and 90% in 2005.[28]

The tariff reduction program for all products listed in Annex 3 to the agreement started on January 1, 1997 with a 0% tariff preference and will continue yearly until January 1, 2006, where there will be a 100% preference. Future reductions will be 0% through 1999, 14% in 2000, 28% in 2001, 43% in 2002, 57% in 2003, 72% in 2004, and 86% in 2005.[29]

Annex 4 to the agreement includes 124 items of auto parts in commerce between Paraguay and Chile. Until December 31, 1999, they were subject to the tariff preference schedule for products listed in Annex 3. Thereafter, they

---

27. *Id.* at Art. 2(b). Annex 1 consists of four lists of previously agreed tariff preferences given by Chile to MERCOSUR (two lists) and MERCOSUR to Chile (two lists). The first list consists of 390 items from ALADI nomenclature numbers 1011.100 ("pure bred breeders") to 9602.0010 ("empty gelatine capsules for products"). It is *available at* http://www.sice.oas.org/trade/msch/A1_1.asp. The second list consists of 164 items ranging from ALADI nomenclature number 0101.1990 ("others") to 9032.1030 "for refrigerators"). It is *available at* http://www.sice.oas.org/trade/msch/A1_2.asp. The third list consists of 597 items ranging from ALADI nomenclature number 1011.100 ("pure bred breeders") to 9701.9000 ("others"). It is *available at* http://www.sice.oas.org/trade/msch/A1_3.asp. The fourth list consists of 340 items ranging from ALADI nomenclature number 0101.1990 ("others") through 9613.8000 ("other lighters") and is *available at* http://www.sice.oas.org/trade/msch/A1_4.asp.

28. *Id.* at Art. 2(c). Annex 2 consists two lists of products. The first list consists of 311 items of preferences from Chile, ranging from ALADI nomenclature numbers 0203.1100 ("pork meat") to 9506.9900 ("others") and is *available at* http://www.sice.oas.org/trade/msch/A-2CH.asp. The second list consists of 311 items of preferences from MERCOSUR, ranging from ALADI nomenclature number 0207.2200 ("turkeys") to 9608.5000 ("games or assorted article appertaining thereto") and is *available at* http://www.sice.oas.org/trade/msch/A_2MS.asp.

29. *Id.* at Art. 2(d). Annex 3 consists two lists of products. The first list consists of 193 items of preferences from Chile, ranging from ALADI nomenclature numbers 2807.0010 ("sulfuric accid") to 8418.2100 ("of compression-refrigerators and freezers") and is *available at* http://www.sice.oas.org/trade/msch/A-3CH.asp. The second list consists of 208 items of preferences from MERCOSUR, ranging from ALADI nomenclature number 0702.0000 ("fresh tomatoes") to 9401.7900 ("others") and is *available at* http://www.sice.oas.org/trade/msch/A_3MS.asp.

would be subject to the tariff preference schedule set forth by the Administrative Commission created to administer the agreement.[30]

Products identified in Annex 5 to the agreement are subject to special treatment, and are subject to the tariff preference schedule set forth therein.[31]

The tariff reduction program for all products listed in Annex 6 to the agreement will start on January 1, 2006 with a 17% tariff preference and will continue yearly until January 1, 2011, where there will be a 100% preference. Future reductions will be 33% through 2007, 50% in 2008, 67% in 2009, an 83% in 2010. Prior to January 1, 2006, they shall have no preference.[32]

Products identified in Annex 7 to the agreement are subject to special treatment, and are subject to the tariff preference schedule set forth therein.[33]

The tariff reduction program for all products listed in Annex 8 to the agreement will start on January 1, 2007 with a 17% tariff preference and will continue yearly until January 1, 2012, where there will be a 100% preference. Future reductions will be 33% through 2008, 50% in 2009, 67% in 2010, an 83% in 2011. Prior to January 1, 2007, they shall have no preference.[34]

---

30. *Id.* Annex 4 is *available at* http://www.sice.oas.org/trade/msch/A-4.asp.

31. *Id.* at Art. 2(e). Annex 5 consists two lists of products. The first list consists of 51 items of preferences from Chile, ranging from ALADI nomenclature numbers 2917.3500 ("anhydrous ftalic") to 9503.9000 ("others") and is *available at* http://www.sice.oas.org/trade/msch/A-5CH.asp. The second list consists of 79 items of preferences from MERCOSUR ranging from ALADI nomenclature number 0603.1000 ("fresh") to 9503.9000 ("others") and is *available at* http://www.sice.oas.org/trade/msch/A_5MS.asp. Both lists indicate particularized treatment for each category of products.

32. *Id.* at Art. 2(f). Annex 6 consists two lists of products. The first list consists of 151 items of preferences from Chile, ranging from ALADI nomenclature numbers 0102.9090 (other live animals of the bovine species") to 9606.1000 ("parts for pressure buttons) and is *available at* http://www.sice.oas.org/trade/msch/A-6CH.asp. The second list consists of 139 items of preferences from MERCOSUR, ranging from ALADI nomenclature number 0207.1000 ("fresh or refrigerated whole birds") to 9606.3000 ("forms for buttons and other parts for buttons") and is *available at* http://www.sice.oas.org/trade/msch/A_6MS.asp.

33. *Id.* at Art. 2(g). Annex 7 consists three lists of products. The first list consists of 32 items of preferences from Chile, ranging from ALADI nomenclature numbers 1006.1010 ("rice with kernel") to 8706.0000("chassis with motor vehicles") and is *available at* http://www.sice.oas.org/trade/msch/A-7CH1.asp. The second list consists of 6 items of meat product preferences from Chile, ranging from ALADI nomenclature number preferences from MERCOSUR ranging from ALADI nomenclature number 0201.1000 ("bovine meat") to 0201.3000 ("bovine meat, boned and frozen")and is *available at* http://www. sice.oas.org/msch/A_CH2.asp. The third list consists of 32 items of preferences from MERCOSUR, ranging from ALADI nomenclature number 0407.0090 ("others") to 8706.0000 ("automobile chassis with cabins") and is *available at* http://www.sice.oas. org/trade/msch/A_7MS.asp. Each lists indicate particularized treatment for each category of products.

34. *Id.* at Art. 2(h). Annex 8 consists one lists of products, with four items of sugar production, ranging from ALADI nomenclature numbers 1701.1100 ("raw cane sugar")

Annex 9 to the agreement includes 3 items of agricultural products. After January 1, 2014, they will enjoy a 100% tariff preference. The Administrative Commission created to administer the agreement has until December 31, 2003, to create a tariff reduction schedule therefor.[35]

Products identified in Annex 10 to the agreement are subject to special treatment, and are subject to the tariff preference schedule set forth therein.[36]

For the Chilean products exported to Argentina and included in Annex 11, the tariff preference applicable is the lower of that set forth in the Annex, compared to that set forth in any other preference schedule.[37]

The applicable tariff for the Chilean exports set forth in the lists set forth in Annex 12 submitted by the MERCOSUR member states shall be that set forth therein, notwithstanding the fact that a it may be subject to a different and lower preference schedule elsewhere in the agreement. Moreover, Chilean exports which appear in Annex 12 and which also appear in Annexes 5 and 7, the tariff to be applied shall be that set forth in the Annex 12 lists. The Administrative Commission overseeing the implementation of the agreement may change the rates in Annex 12, but these changes must consist only of reduction to the residual tariffs then applicable to these exports.[38]

---

to 1701.9900 ("sugar, other") and is *available at* http://www.sice.oas.org/trade/msch/A-8.asp.

35. *Id.* at Art. 2(I). Annex 9 is *available at* http://www.sice.oas.org/trade/msch/A_9.asp.

36. *Id.* at Art. 2(j). Annex 10 consists two lists of products. The first list consists of 45 items of product preferences from Chile, ranging from ALADI nomenclature number 0102 ("live animals of the bovine species") to 1702.9010("malt and malt syrup")and is *available at* http://www.sice.oas.org/msch/A_CH1.asp. The second list consists of 135 items of preferences from MERCOSUR, ranging from ALADI nomenclature numbers 0207 ("meats and edible scraps") to 3926.9000("others) and is *available at* http://www.sice.oas.org/trade/msch/A_10ms_1.asp. Each list indicates particularized treatment for each category of products.

37. *Id.* at Art. 2(k) Annex 11 consists of a list of 91 products, ranging from ALADI nomenclature number 5111 through 6405 and is *available at* http://www.sice.oas.org/trade/msch/A_11.asp. The annex sets forth a 25% ad valorem tariff for all of these products.

38. *Id.* at Art. 4. Annex 12 consists of four lists each submitted by a MERCOSUR member state and including a tariff reduction schedule for certain Chilean exports. The list from Argentina contains 241 items ranging from ALADI nomenclature numbers 2009.1100 through 9403.5000 and is *available at* http://www.sice.oas.org/msch/A_12AR.asp. The list from Brasil contains 28 items ranging from ALADI nomenclature number 2008.7010 through 5112.9000 and is *available at* http://www.sice.oas.org/msch/A_12BR.asp. The list from Paraguay includes 298 items ranging from ALADI nomenclature numbers 0201.1000 through 9403.8000 and is *available at* http://www.sice.oas.org/msch/A_12PA.asp. The list from Uruguay contains 207 items ranging from ALADI nomenclature numbers 402.1010 through 3926.9090 and is *available at* http://www.sice.oas.org/msch/A_12UR1.asp.

The agreement also includes rules of origin, which are very similar to the MERCOSUR rules of origin.[39]

c. The Bolivia Trade Liberation Program in Detail

The Bolivia Agreement provides for a trade liberation program that will be applied to products originating or coming from the territory of Bolivia and the MERCOSUR member states. This trade liberation program will be completed within a ten year period and will consist of progressive and automatic preferences from the tariffs applicable to imports from third parties. This agreement also incorporates the prior tariff preferences negotiated between the MERCOSUR member states and Bolivia within the framework of ALADI and replaces any previous agreements.[40] The terms "duties" and "charges" mean all customs duties and other charges having an equivalent effect, whether they were related to fiscal, monetary, exchange or other sectors, which are levied on foreign trade.[41]

The parties to the Bolivia Agreement also agreed not to establish any different duties or charges having equivalent effect from customs duties, other than those in effect on its effective date.[42] Similarly, no party may impose new duties or charges on exports to their reciprocal trade or increase the terms of existing charges in a discriminatory fashion.[43] Furthermore, no party to the agreement is to impose any new non-tariff restrictions on the import or export of its goods to the territory of another party thereto, except as provided for in the World Trade Organization Agreements.[44]

The tariff reduction program for all products not included in a particular Annex to the agreement started on January 1, 1997 with a 30% tariff preference and will continue yearly until January 1, 2006, where there will be a 100% preference. Future reductions will be 35% in 1998, 40% in 1999, 45% in 2000, 70% in 2000, 50% in 2001, 60% in 2002, 70% in 2003, 80% in 3004 and 90% in 2005.[45]

---

39. These rules of origin are *available at* Annex 13, http://www.sice.oas.org/trade/msch/A_13.asp. Rules of origin for specific products are set forth at Appendices 1 through 4 of Annex 13. Annexes 1–3 are *available at* http://www.sice.oas.org/trade/msch/A_13P1.asp, http://www.sice.oas.org/trade/msch/A_13P2.asp, and http://www.sice.oas.org/trade/msch/A_13P3.asp. Appendix 4 is *available at* http://www.ALADI.org/textacdos.nsf (Sixth Additional Protocol to ACE No. 35.). The rules of origin form for Chile is *available at* http://www.ALADI.org/textacdos.nsf (Appendix 5 to Annex 13 of ACE No. 35.

40. Bolivia Agreement, *supra* Intro. note 14 at Art. 2.

41. *Id.* at Art. 5.

42. *Id.*

43. *Id.* at Art. 6.

44. *Id.* at Art. 7.

45. *Id.* at Art. 2(a).

The tariff reduction program for all products listed in Annex 1 to the agreement started on January 1, 1997 with a 50% tariff preference and will continue yearly until January 1, 2006, where there will be a 100% preference. Future reductions were to be 50% through 2001, 60% in 2002, 70% in 2003, 80% in 2004, and 90% in 2005.[46]

Reductions for products set forth in Annex 2 of the Agreement started on January 1, 1997 and had different initial preferences, as noted therein. and will continue until January 1, 2006, where there will be a 100% preference. For items starting with a 30% preferences, reductions will be 35% in 1998, 40% in 1999, 45% in 2000, 50% in 2001, 60% in 2002, 70% in 2003, 80% in 2004 and 90% in 2005. For items starting with a 50% preference, reductions will be 55% in 1998, 60% in 1999, 65% in 2000, 70% in 2001, 75% in 2002, 80% in 2003, 85% in 2004 and 90% in 2005. For items starting with a 60% preference, reductions will be 64% in 1998, 68% in 1999, 72% in 2000, 76% in 2001, 80% in 2002, 84% in 2003, 88% in 2004 and 92% in 2005. For items starting with a 70% preference, reductions will be 73% in 1998, 76% in 1999, 79% in 2000, 82% in 2001, 85% in 2002, 88% in 2003, 91% in 2004 and 94% in 2005. For items starting with a 80% preference, reductions will be 82% in 1998, 84% in 1999, 86% in 2000, 88% in 2001, 90% in 2002, 92% in 2003, 94% in 2004 and 96% in 2005.[47]

The tariff reduction program for all products listed in Annex 3 to the agreement started on January 1, 1997 with a 15% tariff preference and will continue yearly until January 1, 2006, where there will be a 100% preference. Future reductions were to be 15% through 1999, 20% in 2000, 25% in 2001, 30% in 2002, 40% in 2003, 60% in 2004, and 80% in 2005.[48]

The tariff reduction program for all products listed in Annex 4 to the agreement started on January 1, 1997 with a 10% tariff preference and will continue yearly until January 1, 2006, where there will be a 100% preference. Future re-

---

46. *Id.* at Art. 2(b). Annex 1 consists of a list of products with 79 items of preferences, ranging from ALADI nomenclature numbers 0511.9960 ("fur scraps and cuttings") to 9603.9000 ("the rest") and is *available at* http://www.ALADI.org/nsfALADI/textacdos. nsf/5e800d33de11b31203256a65006bcdd4/515a0c03a7074f8403256c8a006637e4/$FILE/A nexo%201.xls.

47. *Id.* at Art. 2(c). Annex 2 consists of a list of products with 532 items of preferences, ranging from ALADI nomenclature numbers 0210.2000 ("bovine meat") to 9506.91 ("articles for physical fitness") and is *available at* http://www.ALADI.org/nsfAL-ADI/textacdos.nsf/5e800d33de11b31203256a65006bcdd4/5081af59ca40aaa203256c8a006 6d383/$FILE/Anexo%202.xls.

48. *Id.* at Art. 2(d). Annex 3 consists of a list of products with 204 items of preferences, ranging from ALADI nomenclature numbers 0204.10 ("frozen meat") to 8716.4000 ("the   rest")   and   is   *available   at*   http://www.ALADI.org/nsfALADI/textacdos. nsf/5e800d33de11b31203256a65006bcdd4/32bf71b19e2dcdff03256c8a006700c3/$FILE/A nexo%203.xls.

ductions were to be 10% through 2001, 20% in 2002, 40% in 2003, 60% in 2004, and 80% in 2005.[49]

The tariff reduction program for all products listed in Annex 5 to the agreement will start on January 1, 2005 with a 10% tariff preference and will continue yearly until January 1, 2011, where there will be a 100% preference. Future reductions will be 20% in 2006, 30% in 2007, 40% in 2008, 60% in 2009, and 80% in 2010. Prior to January 1, 2005, they shall have no preference.[50]

For all products listed in Annex 6 to the agreement, the tariff reduction program started on January 1, 2005 with a 10% tariff preference and will continue yearly until January 1, 2014, where there will be a 100% preference. Future reductions will be 10% through 2008, 20% in 2009, 30% in 2010, 40% in 2011, 60% in 2012, and 80% in 2013. Prior to January 1, 2006, they shall have no preference.[51]

All products listed in Annex 7 to the agreement will have an initial preference of 100% on the effective date of the agreement.[52]

The agreement also includes rules of origin, which are very similar to the MERCOSUR rules of origin.[53]

---

49. *Id.* at Art. 2(e). Annex 4 consists of a list of products with 342 items of preferences, ranging from ALADI nomenclature numbers 0105.1910 ("ducks") to 9608.1000 ("ball point pens") and is *available at* http://www.ALADI.org/nsfALADI/textacdos.nsf/5e800d33de11b31203256a65006bcdd4/e3d207520c88faaa03256c8a00670c8c/$FILE/Anexo%204.xls.

50. *Id.* at Art. 2(f). Annex 5 consists of a list of 139 items of preferences, ranging from ALADI nomenclature numbers 1701.9100 to 9404.2100 and is *available at* http://www.ALADI.org/nsfALADI/textacdos.nsf/5e800d33de11b31203256a65006bcdd4/15855e42ebbdd9d303256c8a00671685/$FILE/Anexo%205.xls.

51. *Id.* at Art. 2(g). Annex 6 consists of a list of 30 items of preferences, ranging from ALADI nomenclature numbers 11201.0090 to 2306.3000 and is *available at* http://www.ALADI.org/nsfALADI/textacdos.nsf/5e800d33de11b31203256a65006bcdd4/39d5e53516f5cb3d03256c8a006725fe/$FILE/Anexo%206.xls.

52. *Id.* at Art. 2(h). Annex 7 consists of a list of 770 items of preference granted by Bolivia, ranging from ALADI nomenclature numbers 0101.1100 through 9606.3000 and is *available at* http://www.ALADI.org/nsfALADI/textacdos.nsf/a7543a64e65d56c1032567ec004b7572/daa893826bee5ffd032567f2005b1ec7/$FILE/Anexo%207.xls.

53. These rules of origin are *available at* Annex 9, http://www.ALADI.org/nsfALADI/textacdos.nsf/5e800d33de11b31203256a65006bcdd4/5dffd17f798703ae03256a7600549ba4?OpenDocument. Rules of origin for specific products are set forth at Appendices 1 and two of Annex 9. Annexes 1–2 are *available at* http://www.ALADI.org/nsfALADI/textacdos.nsf/5e800d33de11b31203256a65006bcdd4/5dffd17f798703ae03256a7600549ba4/$FILE/_2851ka81j6og42rj5f1ni0c1p5l0n10jechkm6p9064_.doc, http://www.ALADI.org/nsfALADI/textacdos.nsf/5e800d33de11b31203256a65006bcdd4/5dffd17f798703ae03256a7600549ba4/$FILE/_e851ka81j6og42rj5f1ni0c1p5l0n10jechkm6p9068_.doc. The rules of origin form for Bolivia is available at Appendix 3 to Annex 9, *available at* http://www.ALADI.org/nsfALADI/textacdos.nsf/5e800d33de11b31203256a65006bcdd4/5dffd17f798703ae03256a7600549ba4/$FILE/_a851ka81j6og42rj5f1ni0c1p5l0n10jechkm6p906c_.doc.

d. Economic Harmonization, Integration and Cooperation

The Agreements describe in detail a number of initiatives that are meant to promote economic harmonization, integration and cooperation between MERCOSUR and Chile and Bolivia. First, the signatories agree to base their policies in a number of areas on the agreements and standards set forth by the World Trade Organization.[54] The parties to both agreements also agree to promote scientific, industrial, commercial and technical cooperation;[55] the freeing, expanding and progressive diversification of services within their territories;[56] physical integration, defined as the harmonization of land, sea and air routes;[57] and the promotion of reciprocal investments.[58] The Bolivia agreement also provides for the exchange of commercial information and promotion of commercial relations[59] and for the promotion of industrial, commercial and technological harmonization in both economies.[60]

e. Management of the Relationship

The management and evaluation of the relationship between MERCOSUR and Chile and Argentina is undertaken by an Administrative Commission composed of representatives of both MERCOSUR and the individual country involved.[61] The Agreements details a grant to the Administrative Commission

---

54. These areas include dumping, countervailing duties and competition (Chile Agreement, at Arts. 15–20; Bolivia Agreement, at Arts. 14–17); export incentives (Chile Agreement, at Arts. 30–31; Bolivia Agreement, at Arts. 18–19); customs valuation norms (Chile Agreement, at Arts. 23–24; Bolivia Agreement, at Art. 22) sanitary and phytosanitary measures and technical norms and regulations (Chile Agreement, at Arts. 25–29; Bolivia Agreement, at Arts. 23–25). The Chile Agreement also includes intellectual property. Chile Agreement, at Art. 43.

55. Chile Agreement, *Id.* at Arts. 44–45; Bolivia Agreement, *Id.* at Art. 38.

56. Chile Agreement, *Id.* at Arts. 34–35; Bolivia Agreement, *Id.* at Art. 33.

57. Chile Agreement, *Id.* at Arts. 33, 37–40; Bolivia Agreement, *Id.* at Art. 34.

58. Chile Agreement, *Id.* at Arts. 30–31; Bolivia Agreement, *Id.* at Arts. 35–36. The Bolivia Agreement specifically refers to the consideration of the execution of an agreement regarding the reciprocal promotion and protection of investments. This is the type of agreement described in the Non Member States Protocol. *See* Protocol for the Promotion and Protection of Investments at Art. 2. Non Member States Protocol, *supra* Chptr. 5 note 211.

59. Bolivia Agreement, *supra* note 14 at Arts. 30–32.

60. *Id.* at Arts. 26–29. This process includes the promotion of joint business enterprises, joint ventures and multinational enterprises (*Id.* at Art. 27) and the creation of managerial agreements for the production of goods and the rendering of services among public and private enterprises. The latter agreements are meant to create new businesses and harmonize, integrate and rationalize existing industrial enterprises (*Id.* at Art. 28).

61. For the Chile relationship, the Administrative Commission is composed of MERCOSUR's Common Market Group and representatives of the Ministry of Foreign Relations of Chile. Chile Agreement, *supra* Intro. note 14, at Art. 46. The Administrative Commission for the Bolivia Agreement is composed of the MERCOSUR Common Mar-

of very extensive responsibilities, both substantive and administrative, for the management and development of the relationship.[62] Their decisions must be taken by consensus.[63]

Both Agreements provide that any disputes arising between the contracting parties regarding the interpretation, application or compliance with its agreements shall be resolved through the dispute resolution procedures adopted therein.[64] These procedures shall be applicable for a period of three years after the effective date of the Agreements, at the end of which the signatories are to negotiate a new dispute resolution process, which will include an arbitral process.[65]

2. *The Relationship Continues*

As noted above, the parameters of the relationships between MERCOSUR and Bolivia were reached only after extended and contentious negotiations.

The Bolivian negotiations were apparently especially difficult. The Bolivian government appeared especially enthusiastic about the relationship,[66] apparently because it felt both that a MERCOSUR relationship would be the best way to attract investment and technology and that it would strengthen its relationship with Brazil, especially in the energy sector.[67] The private sector appeared to be much less enthusiastic, since they apparently feared competition from the much stronger economies of Argentina and Brazil and were concerned that the Bolivian government had made too many concessions in nego-

---

ket Group and the National Secretariat of International Economic Relations of the Bolivian Foreign Relations Ministry. *Id.* at Art. 39.

62. Chile Agreement, *Id.* at Art. 47(a)-(l); Bolivia Agreement, *Id.* at Art. 40(1)-(17).

63. Chile Agreement, *Id.* at Art. 46, Bolivia Agreement, *Id.* at Art. 39.

64. Chile Agreement, *Id.* at Art. 22. Bolivia Agreement, *Id.* at Art. 21.These procedures require that any dispute first be resolved by reciprocal consultation and direct negotiations. Chile Agreement, *Id.* at Annex 14, Arts. 2–4, Bolivia Agreement, *Id.* at Annex 14, Arts. 2–4. If the dispute is not resolved within thirty days, it can be submitted to the Administrative Commission for resolution. *Id.* at Arts. 5–6. If the dispute cannot readily resolved by the Administrative Commission, it will appoint a Panel of Experts to consider it. The Panel of Experts, once convened, will then consider the matter and report its conclusions to the Administrative Commission, which will then make recommendations to the parties. *Id.* at Arts. 7–13.

65. *Id.* at Art. 14. If the parties cannot come to an agreement regarding such a replacement process within a year, the arbitration procedure set forth in Chapter IV of the Brasilia Protocol will apply. *Id.*

66. Indeed, the President of Bolivia, referred to the new relationship as a "reencounter,"since "Bolivia was once part of the United Provinces of the Rio de la Plata, the Amazon and the Pacific." Marcela Valente, *MERCOSUR: Historic Accords with Chile and Bolivia,*Global Information Network, (June 26 1996 Inter Press Serv.) (*available at* LEXIS/Nexis, ALLNEWSPLUS Database).

67. Dyer, *supra* note 1; Rocha, *supra* note 1.

tiating the agreement.[68] The negotiations were quite contentious, with disagreements regarding preferences over agricultural products, competition policy, protection for struggling industries.[69] Indeed, negotiations were so delayed that the execution of the Bolivian Agreement, scheduled at the same time as the Chilean agreement in June of 1996, had to be postponed for six months.[70] The agreement was finally signed in December of 1996, even after last minute delays,[71] and came into effect on January 1, 1997.[72]

The success of the Bolivia-MERCOSUR relationship is difficult to evaluate. Clearly, trade between Bolivia and MERCOSUR has substantially increased.[73] Unlike the case of Chile, there seems to be little, if any discussion to date about transforming the Bolivian relationship into full membership in MERCOSUR.[74] The Bolivian Minister of Foreign Trade, asserted quite clearly in 2002, however, that Bolivia wanted to become a full member of MERCOSUR. His explanation for Bolivia not having commenced full membership negotiations was that MERCOSUR rules barred a member state from belonging to another regional trading block and Bolivia did not want to leave the Andean Group, to whose members it exported more goods than to MERCOSUR.[75] Given MERCOSUR's recent agreement and development with the Andean Group, this may no longer be an insurmountable problem. The relationship is still in its early years, and its development should be watched carefully. The Bolivian negotiations were so difficult because Bolivia's economy and industrial infrastructure was much less developed than those of Chile or the MERCOSUR states.[76] The success or failure of the integration of Bolivia into the MERCOSUR economic system is extremely important because it will show whether MERCOSUR can

---

68. *Id.*

69. Dyer, *supra* note 1; Osava, *supra* note 1.

70. Comunicado Conjunto de los Presidentes de Los Estados Partes del MERCOSUR, San Luis, Argentina (6/25/96), at paragraph 7 (hereinafter, "Comunicado") *available at* http://www.mercosur.org.uy/espanol/snor/varios/com 0196. htm; Frayssinet & Osava, *supra* note 249.

71. Rocha, *supra* note 1; Dyer, *supra* note 771.

72. Bolivia Agreement, *supra* Intro. note 14, at Art. 47.

73. Sarath Rajapatiara, "Eavaluting Bolivia's Choices for trade integration" World Bank Group, August 1996 *available at* worldbankgroup.org/research/workingpapers. Preliminary Economy of LA and Caribbean, ECLAC Report Dec. 1997, *available at* http://www.ine/gov.bo.mercosur/principal.htm.

74. *See infra* notes 86–101, and accompanying text.

75. "International Agreements: Bolivian Trade Minister Says Nation Wants to be Full Member of MERCOSUR," 17 *International Trade Reporter* (BNA) 1315 (August 24, 2000).

76. *See, e.g.,* "Bolivia is South America's poorest and least developed country" *available at* http://news.bbc.co.uk/hi/english/business/newsid-1896000/1896407. Francisco Bollini Roca, "Bolivia Logra Salvar el Negocio de la Soya" *available at* http://www.bolivinet.com/artiulos/asoya.htm. Information on Bolivia's economy *available at* http:www.boliviabiz.com/business/stats.htm.

successfully integrate other lesser developed economies into its economic system and expand beyond its initial members.[77]

The Chilean situation was very different. Chile had a very highly developed economy with substantial exports to the MERCOSUR countries. These exports tended to be manufactured products, such as computer software and furniture.[78] Chile saw a MERCOSUR relationship as one which would substantially increase its export markets and establish it as an attractive investment venue.[79] Furthermore, a relationship with MERCOSUR would be an indication of Chile's "reinsertion" into Latin America from isolation during the military regime.[80] Chile was also highly attractive to MERCOSUR as a link to Asian and Pacific markets.[81] The comment has also been made that Chile's interest in MERCOSUR was also stimulated by the failure of the United States to grant Chile accession to NAFTA.[82] The negotiations between Chile and MERCOSUR were extended over two years, with disagreements regarding rules of origin, tariff protection of agricultural products, different tariff rates, and the automobile industry.[83]

In purely trade terms, the MERCOSUR-Chile relationship appears to have been quite successful. Trade (including Chilean foreign investment) between Chile and the MERCOSUR countries increased exponentially between 1990 and 1996[84] and has continued to increase since then.[85] Both Chile and MERCOSUR seemed to be quite satisfied with the MERCOSUR relationship and were discussing Chile's full accession to the community.[86] In 2001, however,

---

77. At the time of the Chilean and Bolivian negotiations, negotiations with other ALADI member states and relationships with the Central American and Caribbean states were being contemplated. Comunicado, *supra* note 70, at paragraphs 8–9.

78. These exports grew from $1.8 billion in 1990 to $4.5 billion in 1995. O'Keefe, *supra* note 4 at 3.

79. Chile-MERCOSUR, *supra* Chptr. 1 note 56 at 40–41.

80. *Id.* at 14, 119, 184.

81. *Id.* at 107. O'Keefe, *supra* note 4 at 18–19.

82. *Id.* at 3.

83. Chile-MERCOSUR, *supra* Chptr. 1 note 56 at 77–80.

84. *Id.* at 79–80.

85. "Since 1990 the total bilateral Chilean trade with MERCOSUR countries had expanded from U.S. $1.8 billion to almost U.S. $4.5 billion by 1995 (in 1997 the figure stood at just under U.S. $5 billion." Thomas, Andrew O'Keefe, Esq. "The Evolution of Chilean Trade Policy in the Americas from Lone Ranger to Team Player." Southwestern Journal of Law and Trade in the Americas, Fall 198. 5 SWJLTA 251 (1998). *See also* Preliminary Economy of LA and Caribbean, ECLAC Report Dec. 1997, *available at* http://www.ine.cl. mercosur/principal.htm.

86. The Presidents of Argentina and Chile, in a 2000 joint statement, stressed the opportunity to begin negotiations aimed at intensifying the process of Chile's full integration into MERCOSUR. "Chile Mucho Más Cerca del MERCOSUR.," LA NACION (Buenos Aires) May 20, 2000, available at La Nación On Line (hereinafter, "Chile Mucho Más Cerca") Similarly, in an interview with the Argentine press in May of 2000, the Chilean Foreign Minister described the Chile-MERCOSUR relationship as one of stages.

Chile suspended talks on full membership in MERCOSUR and announced that it was entering into free trade negotiations with the United States.[87] In spite of this suspension, the Presidential Declaration made after the February 18, 2002 meeting of the Council stressed the desire of all parties to continue negotiations between MERCOSUR, Chile and Bolivia to "strengthen the agreements of the integration process."[88] Speculation for the reasons behind Chile's withdrawal included an unwillingness by Chile to increase its already low tariff base to meet the MERCOSUR Common External Tariff or a calculation that greater gains would be available from membership in a United States-led free trade zone, such as the Free Trade Area of the Americas.[89]

The latter reason seems to be supported by Chile's signature, on June 6, 2003, of a free trade agreement with the United States.[90] The Chile Free Trade Agreement constitutes a massive document, with twenty four chapters, three Annexes and four Side Letters covering a number of topics.[91] The principal

---

The first step, she claimed, was economic, and its goals were achieved. The next stage would be more extensive, and would include many other areas, including labor, education and justice. She seemed to feel that the relationship was broadening, that both parties were extremely interested in having Chile become a full member of MERCOSUR, and that there were no insurmountable problems to achieve this goal. "Debemos Definir como Enfrentar la Globalización."LA NACION (Buenos Aires) May 20, 2000, *available at* www.lanacion.com.ar. *See also* "International Agreements: Accession to MERCOSUR will be Priority for Chile in 1999, Official Says," 16 *International Trade Reporter* (BNA) 98 (January 20, 1999); International Agreements: Chile Wants Broad MERCOSUR Mandate for Services, Transportation, Investment," 16 *International Trade Reporter* (BNA) 171 (January 27, 1999); "International Agreements: Chile Shifts Strategy for Achieving Full Member in MERCOSUR Bloc," 17 *International Trade Reporter* (BNA) 983 (June 22, 2000); "International Agreements: Chile, MERCOSUR Leaders Agree on Talks Toward Full Membership," 17 *International Trade Reporter* (BNA) 1130 (July 20, 2000).

87. *Chopping Block: More Troubles for MERCOSUR*, Economist, Dec. 16, 2000 at 40; Jonathan Karp and Pamela Druckerman, *Big Latin Customs Union MERCOSUR reaches a Crossroads*, Wall St. J., Dec. 15, 2000 at A-15; *U.S., Chile sign Free Trade Agreement in Miami*, Associated Press, Jun. 6, 2003, *(hereinafter "U.S.-Chile") available at* http:// www.ajc.com/news/content/news/0603/07uschile.html. *See* Guy de Jonquieres and Edward Alden, *American Ties: This Weekend's Summit of the Americas is an Opportunity for the Region's Leaders to Take Steps Towards Forming the World's Largest Trade Group*, FINANCIAL TIMES (London), April 20, 2001.

88. Communicado Conjunto de los Presidentes del MERCOSUR, Bolivia y Chile, (Feb. 18, 2002) at par. 11 (hereinafter, "Comunicado Conjunto 2002") *available at* http:// www.mercosur.org.uy/espanol/snor/varios/com01-2002.htm.

89. *See infra* notes 91–98 and accompanying text.

90. *U.S, Chile, supra* note 87.

91. Free Trade Agreement between the Government of the United States of America and the Government of the Republic of Chile, Final Text (hereinafter, "Chile Free Trade Agreement") *available at* http://www.sice.oas.org/Trade/chiusa_e/chiusaind_e.asp. These topics include national treatment and market access for goods, rules or origin, customs administration, customs administration, sanitary and phytosanitary measures, technical

provisions of this agreement eliminate about 85% of all tariffs on consumer and industrial products traded between both countries, with most remaining tariffs being eliminated in four years.[92] Furthermore, tariffs on about three quarters of farm goods traded between both countries will be eliminated within four years, with all tariffs and quotas, phased out within twelve years.[93] Other provisions cover provisions according bilateral free access to government procurement,[94] the telecommunications industry,[95] financial institutions,[96] and cross-border trade in services.[97] Chile now shares preferential access to United States markets with Canada, Mexico, Israel and Jordan, the only other countries with whom the United States has free trade agreements.[98] It now has the best of all possible worlds. As a MERCOSUR associate member, Chile's goods have preferential (and eventually tariff-free) access to the MERCOSUR market, without having to be bound by its common external tariff.[99] On the other hand, it also has preferential access to the United States market, its largest trade partner.[100] Neither relationship appears to be inconsistent with the other.[101]

---

barriers to trade, trade remedies, government procurement, investment, cross-border trade in services, financial services, telecommunications, temporary entry for business persons, electronic commerce, competition policy, intellectual property rights, labor, environment, transparency, administration, dispute settlement and exceptions. *Id.*

92. *U.S. and Chile Conclude Historic Free Trade Agreement*, Press Release, Office of the United States Trade Representative (December 11, 2002), (hereinafter, "Press Release 12/11/02") at p. 2 *available at* http://www.ustr/gov/releases/2002/12/02-114.htm.

93. *Id.*

94. Chile Free Trade Agreement, *supra* note 91, at section 9.2.

95. *Id.* at section 13.2.

96. *Id.* at section 12.2.

97. *Id.* at section 11.2.

98. Press Release 12/11/02, *supra* note 92, at p. 1.

99. *See supra* Chptr. 3 notes 33–39 and accompanying text.

100. CIA Factbook, *supra* Chptr. 1 note 52.

101. Chile does bear one risk in this situation. The Chile Free Trade Agreement requires ratification by the United States Congress in order to become effective. Chile, U.S., *supra* note 22. The risk of non ratification by the U.S. Congress appears highly unlikely, however. The House of Representatives approved the agreement on July 25, 2003 and Senate ratification is expected shortly. *Chile, Singapore Free-Trade Pacts Pass House,* THE WALL STREET JOURNAL, July 25, 2003 at A12.

Chapter 7

To Infinity and Beyond: The European Union and Future Expansion

A. Introduction

This chapter explores and evaluates the relationship and negotiations between MERCOSUR and the European Union and the negotiations and agreements with other entities and countries that have been entered into or are currently in negotiation.

B. MERCOSUR and the European Union

1. Introduction

MERCOSUR has had some relationship with the European Community/Eu-
ropean Union[1] almost since the beginning of its existence. An Interinstitutional
Cooperation Agreement was entered into between MERCOSUR and the EU in
May of 1992 and the EU has provided substantial economic and technical assistance to MERCOSUR since then.[2] This relationship was substantially formalized

---

1. Hereinafter, "EU".
2. Agreement of Interinstitutional Cooperation between the European Community
and MERCOSUR, executed on 22 May 1992. This agreement appears to have basically covered funds for technical assistance, instructional seminars and other similar informal contacts. *See, e.g.,* MERCOSUR/GMC/Res 09/93, *available at* http://www.sice.oas.org/trade/
mrcrs/resolutions/RES993.asp and THE EU AND MERCOSUR: OVERVIEW, at 3 (hereinafter,
"EU Overview 2001") (*available at* www.europa.eu.int/comm/external_relations/merco-
sur/intro).

and expanded by an Interregional Framework Agreement on Cooperation, which was signed in December of 1995.[3]

2. The Framework Agreement

The Framework Agreement is a very extensive and ambitious document. Its objectives are to "strengthen existing relations between the parties" and to "prepare the conditions enabling an Interregional Association to be created.[4] This objective will apparently be achieved through three routes: political dialogue,[5] cooperation in trade matters,[6] and the encouragement of the process of integration.[7] This process clearly constitutes a major undertaking, and a Cooperation Council composed of representatives of MERCOSUR, and the EU, is charged by the Framework Agreement with implementing this process.[8]

The political dialogue described by the Framework Agreement is first based on a number of basic political principles which the parties jointly support.[9] MERCOSUR and the EU are to conduct this political dialogue by means of contacts, information exchanges and consultation, including regular meetings between the MERCOSUR heads of state and the highest authorities in the EU, yearly meetings of the Ministers of Foreign Affairs of MERCOSUR, the EU member states and the European Commission, and other periodic meetings of ministerial and other senior officials.[10]

---

3. European Community-Mercosur: Interregional Framework Agreement on Cooperation. Madrid, Spain, Dec. 15, 1995. IELCV-0020. This document is also available as EU Council Document 11133/95 (hereinafter, "Framework Agreement").

4. Framework Agreement, *supra* note 3, at Art. 2(1). These seem to include "trade and economic matters, cooperation regarding integration, and other fields of mutual interest." *Id.* at Art. 2(2).

5. *Id.* at Art. 3.

6. *Id.* at Arts. 4–17.

7. *Id.* at Arts. 18–19, 24.

8. *Id.* at Arts. 25–30.

9. These include such principles as "political and economic freedoms are fundamental to society," "reaffirming human dignity and the promotion of human rights as cornerstones of a democratic society," "reaffirming the essential role of the principles and democratic institutions based on the rule of law," desiring to strengthen international peace and security in accordance with the principles of the United Nations Charter," and "sharing an interest in regional integration as a means of enabling their citizens to achieve sustainable and harmonious development predicated upon social progress and solidarity between their members." *Id.* at DRAFT JOINT DECLARATION ON POLITICAL DIALOGUE BETWEEN THE EUROPEAN UNION AND THE MERCOSUR COUNTRIES PREAMBLE (hereinafter, "Draft Joint Declaration").

10. *Id.* at Art. 3, Draft Joint Declaration, "Mechanisms of the Dialogue." There have been several EU-MERCOSUR ministerial meetings regarding political dialogue, including: Panama, February 1998; Vilamoura Portugal, February 2000; and Santiago, Chile, March 2001. EU Overview 2001, *supra* note 2 at page 3. In the February 2000 meeting,

Cooperation on trade matters seems, however, to be the principal purpose of the Framework Agreement. The objective is to have the parties engage in a process of crafting closer relations with each other, with the purpose of encouraging the increase and diversification of trade. This process is to lead to the "subsequent gradual and reciprocal liberalization of trade" and will promote "conditions which are conducive to the establishment of the Interregional Association."[11] There is no indication in the Framework Agreement itself of what the characteristics of the "Interregional Association" are going to be, or when it is to be completed.[12] This process is clearly going to cover almost every economic sector, including agri-food and industrial standards and certification,[13] customs matters,[14] statistical matters,[15] intellectual property,[16] economic cooperation,[17] business cooperation,[18] investment promotion,[19] energy cooperation,[20] transport cooperation,[21] science and technology cooperation,[22] telecommunications and information technology,[23] and environmental protection.[24] The examination of each of these topics is clearly going to be quite extensive and exhaustive and is to be the subject of very involved negotiations.[25]

---

for example, the ministers presented a "Declaration and Action Programme for Political Cooperation," which identified the main areas of political dialogue to include, *inter alia*, peace and security, prevention of conflicts, confidence and security building measures, promotion and protection of human rights and democracy and the rule of law. JOINT PRESS RELEASE, MINISTERIAL MEETING BETWEEN THE EUROPEAN UNION, THE MERCO-SUR, CHILE AND BOLIVIA, 23 February 2000, at paragraph 4. This document is *available at* http://europa.eu.int/comm/external_relations/mercosur/ass-neg/text/press-rel_vila.htm. Mostly, the ministers agreed to continue their dialogue and reinforce the coordination among themselves. *Id.* at Arts. 5–8.

11. Framework Agreement, *supra* note 3 at Art. 4.

12. The then President of Argentina, Carlos Menem, declared in 1996 that all trade barriers between MERCOSUR and the European Union should be dismantled by the year 2005. *EU/ARGENTINA/MERCOSUR: Free Trade Agreement by the Year 2005,* European Report (June 12, 1996) (*available at* LEXIS/Nexis, ALLNEWSPLUS Database). As shall be seen below, given the pace of the negotiations to date, this timetable may be premature.

13. Framework Agreement, *supra* note 3 at Art. 6.

14. *Id.* at Art. 7.

15. *Id.* at Art. 8.

16. *Id.* at Art. 9.

17. *Id.* at Art. 10.

18. *Id.* at Art. 11.

19. *Id.* at Art. 12.

20. *Id.* at Art. 13.

21. *Id.* at Art. 14.

22. *Id.* at Art. 15.

23. *Id.* at Art. 16.

24. *Id.* at Art. 17.

25. In the area of "business cooperation," for example, the areas to be focused upon include, *inter alia*, increasing the flow of trade, investment, industrial cooperation projects and technology transfer, encouraging modernization and diversification in industry,

Encouraging the process of integration is to occur through cooperation between all parties in all of the areas of the Framework Agreement.[26] This cooperation is apparently envisioned to occur through four venues: information exchange,[27] training and institutional backing,[28] studies and joint projects,[29] and technical assistance.[30]

The negotiations and consultations envisioned in the Framework Agreement are to be undertaken under the direction of a Cooperation Council, composed of members of the EU Council and Commission and members of the MERCOSUR Council and Common Market Group. It is chaired, in turn, by a representative of the EU and a representative of MERCOSUR and creates its own rules of procedure.[31] The Cooperation Council is to be assisted by a Joint Cooperation Committee composed of representatives of the member states of the EU and MERCOSUR. They are to meet at least on a yearly basis and are to assist the Cooperation Council in the performance of its duties. The Council may delegate all or part of its powers to the Committee, with the thought that the Committee shall provide continuity between meetings of the Cooperation Council.[32] The Framework Agreement also creates a Joint Subcommittee on Trade, composed of representatives of the EU and MERCOSUR, which is meant to conduct the preparatory work for the subsequent liberalization of trade envisioned therein.[33] In short, three major organizations are expected to negotiate this relationship.

---

identifying and eliminating barriers to industrial cooperation, promoting industrial innovation, and stimulating cooperation between economic operators, especially small and medium sized enterprises. *Id.* at Art. 11(2). A tall order indeed!

26. *Id.* at Art. 18.

27. *Id.* at Arts. 18(3)(a), 19 & 21.

28. *Id.* at Arts. 18(3)(b), 20.

29. *Id.* at Arts. 18(3)(c), 20, 21.

30. *Id.* at Art. 18(3)(d), 24. An example of this "technical cooperation" is AGREEMENT No. ASR/B-7-311/96/65 FINANCING AGREEMENT BETWEEN THE EUROPEAN UNION AND THE MERCOSUR COUNTRIES (STATISTICAL COOPERATION WITH THE MERCOSUR COUNTRIES) MERCOSUR/CMC/DEC 23/97. This agreement provides for an EU contribution of 4, 135, 000 ECUs for statistical cooperation with the MERCOSUR countries.

31. *Id.* at Art. 25-26. The Council may decide to set up any other body to assist it in the performance of its duties. *Id.* at Art. 28. Several such bodies have been created, including a Biregional Negotiations Committee, three subgroups on specific cooperation areas and three technical groups dealing with trade matters. *See infra* notes 34–37.

32. *Id.* at Art. 27. In particular, the Committee is to make proposals to the Council "with the aim of stimulating preparations for the liberalization of trade and of intensifying cooperation," and "make proposals which contribute to achieving the ultimate aim of the EU-MERCOSUR Interregional Association. *Id.* at Art. 27(5)(c), (d).

33. *Id.* at Art. 29.

3. The EU-MERCOSUR Negotiations

The negotiations between the EU and MERCOSUR contemplated by the Framework Agreement have been quite extensive. The Cooperation Council first met in Brussels in November of 1999.[34] Its principal action was to create a Biregional Negotiations Committee (whose membership was unspecified), which was to be responsible for the general oversight and management of the negotiations on trade matters and cooperation between the parties. The meeting also created a Subcommittee on Cooperation, which was to conduct negotiations on cooperation and report directly to the Biregional Negotiations Committee. The latter was also given the power to create Technical Groups, also directly responsible to the Biregional Negotiations Committee, to examine particular topics forming part of the trade negotiations.[35] The Biregional Negotiations Committee, which had the authority to decide its calendar and agenda, would meet at least three times a year.[36] It would also report to the Cooperation Council (who apparently still had the ultimate power to make actual recommendations to the parties under the Framework Agreement) on a regular basis.[37]

The Biregional Negotiations Committee first met in Argentina in April of 2000.[38] The parties there created and generally described the charge of three different subgroups on cooperation[39] and three different technical groups[40]. The parties also agreed on an extensive program of information exchange between

---

34. Joint Press Release, First Cooperation Council, Brussels, 24 November 1999, *available at* http://europa.eu.int/comm/external_relations/mercosur/ass_neg_text/press-rel_coop.htm (hereinafter, "JPR-FCC").

35. *Id.* at Annex 2, section 1. The Biregional Negotiations Committee will be hereinafter referred to as the "BNC."

36. *Id.* at Annex 2, section 3.

37. *Id.* at Annex 2, paragraph 2.

38. First Meeting of the EU-MERCOSUR Biregional Negotiations Committee (6–7 April 2000, Buenos Aires, Argentina) *available at* http://europa.eu.int/comm/external_relation/mercosur/ass_neg_text/concl/bncl.htm (hereinafter, "First BNC").

39. These were the Subgroups on Economic Cooperation (charged with, *inter alia,* industrial cooperation, cooperation in the field of services, and investment promotion), the Sub Group on Social and Cultural Cooperation (charged, with, inter alia, social cooperation, cultural cooperation, social dialogue and drugs and related organized crime) and the Subgroup on Financial and Technical Cooperation (charged with, *inter alia,* public administration modernization and inter institutional cooperation. *Id.* at sections 3.2–3.3).

40. Technical Group 1 includes, *inter alia,* trade in goods (both tariff and non tariff measures), antidumping and countervailing duties and safeguards and rules of origin. Technical Group 2 includes, *inter alia,* trade in services and intellectual property rights, and Technical Group 3 includes government procurement, competition and dispute settlement. *Id.* at sections 4.2.1.

MERCOSUR and EU officials and agreed on the agenda for their next meeting.[41] The next meeting of the BNC chiefly resulted in the exchange of information among the parties and in beginning discussions on a number of topics.[42] This process continued through the third meeting of the BNC, with the parties considering that enough progress had been made to enable the exchange of draft negotiating texts on a number of issues to occur in the near future.[43]

The fifth meeting of the BNC was held in July of 2001. In that meeting, MERCOSUR, in response to an EC proposal, presented tariff offers and negotiating texts for goods, services and government procurement.[44] Negotiations on political dialogue and cooperation continued[45] and seven draft texts in a num-

---

41. *Id.* at sections 4.2.2–4.2.3. They also agreed that, at the end of each meeting, they would set the specific agenda of the next meeting. *Id.*

42. SECOND MEETING OF THE EUROPEAN UNION-MERCOSUR BIREGIONAL NEGOTIATIONS COMMITTEE (13–16 JUNE 2000, BRUSSELS, BELGIUM) at sections 2–5, *available at* http://europa.eu.int/comm/external_relations/mercosur/ass_neg_text/concl_bnc2.htm (hereinafter, "Second BNC").

43. This meeting was held at Brasilia, Brasil on 7–10 November 2000. THIRD MEETING OF THE EU-MERCOSUR BIREGIONAL NEGOTIATIONS COMMITTEE (7–10 NOVEMBER 2000, BRASILIA, BRASIL.) (hereinafter, "Third BNC"), *available at* http://europa.int.eu/comm/external_relations/mercosur/ass_neg_text/concl_bnc3.htm. At this meeting, for example, enough consensus was found to have the parties prepare a joint text on the preamble, the legal framework of the political dialogue, and various paragraphs of the institutional structure of the future Association Agreement. *Id.* at section 2. *See also* EU SET TO MAKE PROGRESS WITH MERCOSUR IN FOURTH ROUND OF ASSOCIATION NEGOTIATIONS, MEMO 01/91 (BRUSSELS, 16 MARCH 2001) at 3, *available at* http://europa.int.eu/comm/external_relations/mercosur/intro/mem_01_91.htm.

44. By the next meeting, the parties were discussing a draft text on the institutional framework of the future agreement and presented and discussed text proposals on a number of areas related to economic cooperation and social and cultural cooperation. At the fifth meeting of the BNC (in early July of 2001), the EU presented to MERCOSUR an extensive offer dealing with both tariff and non tariff matters, including negotiating texts dealing with goods, services and government procurement. The purpose of this offer, according to the EU, was to substantially and progressively liberalize substantially, all trade, without excluding any sector, during a period of ten years. The MERCOSUR representatives indicated that they would be presenting their own negotiating proposals covering these areas in the near future. Proposals were also exchanged in the areas of cooperation in the agricultural and rural sector, which will be analyzed in the next BNC meeting. On the other hand, the three different Subgroups agreed on joint draft texts in a number of areas. CONCLUSIONS OF THE SIXTH EU-MERCOSUR BIREGIONAL NEGOTIATIONS COMMITTEE, (Brussels, 29–31 October 2001) at par. 1.

45. *Id.* at par. 2-3. These meetings were held in Buenos Aires, Argentina (April of 2002), Brussels, Belgium (November of 2002) and Buenos Aires, Argentina (March of 2003) *See* FINAL CONCLUSIONS OF THE SEVENTH EU-MERCOSUR BIREGIONAL NEGOTIATIONS COMMITTEE, (Buenos Aires, 8–11 April, 2002), *available at* http://europa.eu.int/comm/external_relations/mercosur/ass_neg_text/bnc7.htm; FINAL CONCLUSIONS OF THE EIGHTH EU-MERCOSUR BIREGIONAL NEGOTIATIONS COMMITTEE, (Brussels, 15 November 2002) *available at* http://europa.eu.int/comm/external_relations/mercosur/ass_neg_

ber of areas were agreed to. This process of discussions, review of drafts and further negotiation has continued in the most recent meetings of the BNC.[46]

A meeting of the heads of state of MERCOSUR and the EU was held in May of 2002 and a ministerial meeting was held in March of 2003.[47] At that meeting, the participants lauded that substantial progress had been made in political, institutional and economic trade matter by the BNC[48] and vowed to continue negotiations towards the ultimate objective of the "achievement of further effective access to their respective markets on the basis of progressive and reciprocal trade liberalization in accordance with GATT/WTO rules."[49] They also welcomed a new plan of action on business facilitation[50] and announced the commencement of negotiations on wine and spirits.[51] This meeting was similarly lauded by the MERCOSUR presidents.[52] A meeting of the MERCOSUR and EU trade ministers was held in Brussels in November of 2003. At this meeting, both parties expressed their renewed support for a comprehensive agreement covering market access on goods, services, government procurement and investments, as well as agreements on wine and spirits, competition and intellectual property rights. They also agreed on a timetable of future negotiations, culminating with a final agreement in October of 2004.[53]

---

text/ip02_1684.htm; Final Conclusions of the Ninth EU-MERCOSUR Biregional Negotiations Committee, (Brussels, 17–21 March 2003) *available at* http://europa. eu.int/comm/external_relations/mercosur/ass_neg_text/bnc9.htm.; Final Conclusions, Tenth Meeting of the MERCOSUR-European Union Bi-Regional Negotiations Committee (Asunción, 23–27 June 2003), *available at* http//: europa.eu.int/comm/external_relations/mercosur/ass_neg_test/bnc10.pdf.

46. *Id.* The areas included scientific and technological cooperation, energy, transport, telecommunication, information technology and information society.

47. Second Meeting of Heads of State and of Government of MERCOSUR and of the EU-Joint Communique, Madrid (17 May 2002) (hereinafter, "Madrid Communique"). EU-MERCOSUR-BOLIVIA CHILE Ministerial Meeting, Joint Communique, Athens (27 March 2003), *available at* http://europa.eu.int/comm/external_relations/mercosur/intro/mm27_03_03.htm.

48. *Id.* at par. 2-7.

49. *Id.* at par. 8.

50. EU-MERCOSUR Action Plan on Business Facilitation,(March 16, 2002). This Plan was to intentionally focus on questions of customs, standards, regulations and conformity assessment, sanitary and phytosanitary measures and had the aim of increasing trade flows and facilitating or eliminating potential barriers to trade. *Id.*

51. Madrid Comunique, *supra* note 47, at par. 2.

52. Comunicado Conjunto de los Presidentes de los Estados Partes del MERCOSUR, July 5, 2002 (hereinafter, "Communicado July 2002") at par. 25-27.

53. "EU-MERCOSUR: Trade Ministerial Agrees Roadmap for Final Phase of Free Trade Negotiations,"(Brussels, 12 November 2003), *available at* http//: www.europa.eu. int/comm/external_relations/mercosur/intro/ip03_1544.htm. *See also* "MERCOSUR y UE Comenzaron Nueva Ronda de Negociaciones," EL PAIS(Montevideo, Uruguay), December 3, 2003 (hereinafter, "Nueva Ronda") *available at* http://www.elpais.com.uy/03/12/03/pecono_69761; "Avances entre el MERCOSUR y la UE," LA NACION (Buenos Aires, Ar-

The eleventh meeting of the BNC also commenced at about this time.[54] At that meeting, the EU made an extensive proposal to liberalize trade in agricultural products.[55]

As noted above, as part of its relationship with the EU, MERCOSUR has thus far received substantial amounts of financial assistance meant to be used for the development of its institutions. This financing, and the substantial "technical assistance" provided by the EU and its instititutions to date, could substantially change the organization and operation of MERCOSUR's institutions in the future. Furthermore, a successful completion of these negotiations could mean a highly advantageous entry for MERCOSUR goods into the European market, a state of affairs that could make MERCOSUR far more attractive to other potential members and which could result in more potential applications for membership. This situation could place MERCOSUR in a similar dilemma to that faced by the Union until recently: how to substantially increase the size and membership of the organization without sacrificing its effectiveness and efficiency.

The negotiations described above appeared thus far headed to a mutually agreeable conclusion. That is not to say that these negotiations have not been contentious or difficult. Indeed, there are no guarantees that an agreement can be reached.[56] Indeed, the EU and MERCOSUR negotiators failed to resolve

---

gentina), November 13, 2003, (hereinafter, "Avances") *available at* http://www.lanacion. com.ar/herramientas/printfriendly.asp?nota_id=544853.

54. Nueva Ronda, *Id.*

55. Avances, *supra* note 53. The proposal was described as permitting access, through quotas, to products such as olive oil, milk products, juices, meats and fruits. These products had been excluded from a previous agricultural proposal, meant to include 91% of all agricultural products. *Id.*

56. *See* "International Agreements: MERCOSUR to Play Hardball on Free Trade with EU after Cancún Failure, Argentina Says," 20 *International Trade Reporter* (BNA) 1597 (September 25, 2003); "International Agreements: EU Commissioner Lamy Dampens Hopes for Early Free Trade Accord with MERCOSUR," 20 *International Trade Reporter* (BNA) 1184 (July 10, 2003); "International Agreements: South America's MERCOSUR Presents EU with Duty-Free List in Free Trade Talks," 20 *International Trade Reporter* (BNA) 482 (March 13, 2003); "International Agreements: Patten Rebuffs EU Parliament's Call for More Trade Preferences for MERCOSUR," 19 *International Trade Reporter* (BNA) 1690 (October 3, 2002); "International Agreements: MERCO-SUR, EU Negotiators Agree to Move up Pace of Trade Negotiations," 19 *International Trade Reporter* (BNA) 1358 (August 1, 2002); "International Agreements: EU, MERCO-SUR Pleased with Progress after Latest Round of Free Trade Talks,"19 *International Trade Reporter* (BNA) 713 (April 18, 2002); "International Agreements: Brazilian Business Groups Object to Parts of EU's Farm Offer to MERCOSUR, "18 *International Trade Reporter* (BNA) 1345 (August 23, 2001); Guy de Jonquieres: *Diplomatic Thaw is a Promising Omen,* FINANCIAL TIMES (London) March 8, 2002; "International Agreements: EU Presents MERCOSUR Free Trade Proposal: Brazil Welcomes Offer to Reduce Farm Duties,"18 *International Trade Reporter* (BNA) 1096 (July 12, 2001); "International Agreements: EU Commissioner Wants to Accelerate Trade N egotiations with

their differences over agriculture and market access and were unable to complete an agreement by October of 2004. The negotiators promised to meet again before the end of 2004 to prepare for new cabinet-level negotiations in early 2005.[57] The possibilities of a prompt and comprehensive agreement are now much more uncertain.[58]

4. The European Union and MERCOSUR: Is It a Good Match?

The initial reaction that strikes an observer of the EU-MERCOSUR relationship is the magnitude of the undertaking that the parties have agreed to and the speed at which it has begun to develop. It aims at nothing less than the elimination of all barriers (tariff and non tariff) and the establishment free trade in all goods and services, as well as strengthened political dialogue, between the EU, MERCOSUR and its associate members,[59] whose territory contains a population of 210 million and includes two of the largest and richest countries in Latin America! Should this goal be achieved, the EU and MERCOSUR would constitute the largest trading block in the world.[60]

The parties clearly seem to be quite serious about completing this undertaking successfully. Dozens of experts have exchanged reams of documents and have met and negotiated extensively. They have even gotten to the point of being able to agree on some joint texts and are clearly now exchanging written

---

MERCOSUR, Chile,"18 *International Trade Reporter* (BNA) 380 (March 8, 2001); Guy de Jonquieres, *Altruism with a Bitter Taste: Brussels is Being Forced to Rethink Plans to End Trade Barriers for the Poorest Countries*, FINANCIAL TIMES (London) December 19, 2000; Guy de Jonquieres: *Brussels Fights to Win Support for Reforms to Trade Talks Rules: The Issue is Likely to be Contentious at Nice IGC Conference*, FINANCIAL TIMES (London) December 1, 2000; "International Agreements: EU-MERCOSUR Trade Talks May Begin by End of 1999, Brazilian Official Says,"17 *International Trade Reporter* (BNA) 820 (May 12, 1999); "International Agreements: Divided EU Moves to Negotiate Pact with MERCOSUR, Cites Weak US Stance,"15 *International Trade Reporter* (BNA) 1315 (July 29, 1998).

57. Benson, *New Setback for Europe-Latin Talks*, NEW YORK TIMES, Oct. 28, 2004 at W1.

58. *Por Falta de Consenso, la UE y el MERCOSUR buscan un Pacto Acotado*, LA NACIÓN (Buenos Aires), Oct. 9, 2004, *available at* http://www.nanacion.com.ar/economia/nota.asp?nota_id=643417.

59. EU Overview 2001, *supra* note 2 at 4.

60. EUROPEAN UNION INTERESTS IN MERCOSUR AND CHILE (hereinafter, "EU Interests") at p. 1 *available at* http://europa.eu.int/comm/external_relations/mercosur/background_doc/report_nov99.htm. *See* Lisa Anderon, *The future of Hemisphere Free Trade: Towards a Unified Hemisphere*, 20 Hous. J. Int'l L.635. *See also* http:www.graphicmaps.com/webimage/countrys/sa.htm.

proposals.[61] The stakes are enormous. Trade between MERCOSUR and the European Union and Chile exceeded 49 billion Euros in 1998. Indeed, the EU is MERCOSUR and Chile's main trading partner after the United States and Japan.[62] The EU also projected that, by the beginning of the twenty-first century, EU investments in the MERCOSUR countries and Chile would total $83 billion (US) and would encompass about 50% of the total foreign investment in the region.[63] Financially, the MERCOSUR trade relationship is clearly very important to the EU.

For MERCOSUR, a free trade area relationship with the European Union would grant its products preferential access to one of the largest markets in the world. This liberalized access would represent a massive benefit to the agricultural and industrial export markets of the member states. Furthermore, the relationship would provide a strong attraction (and benefit) for other Latin American nations who would want to consider entry to (or association with) MERCOSUR.

Time, however, is of the essence because the EU has a competitor, the Free Trade Area of the Americas ("FTAA"). The FTAA, which arose out of the 1994 Summit of the Americas in Miami,[64] is meant to be a multilateral, comprehensive regional economic integration treaty to be entered into among the 34 nations that attended the Miami Summit.[65] Negotiations on a draft agreement started in June of 1998[66] and are meant to be concluded no later than January of 2005, with the Treaty coming into effect no later than December of 2005.[67]

The FTAA negotiations process itself is rather extensive and comprehensive. The negotiations are to be guided by a Trade Negotiations Committee,

---

61. *See supra* notes 34–55 and accompanying text.

62. EU Interests, *supra* note 58, at p. 2. The biggest individual customer appears to be Brazil, which received imports from the EU of 15 billion Euros in 1998 and is the EU's ninth largest customer. *Id.*

63. *Id.* at pp. 6–7.

64. Summit of the Americas, Plan of Action, Section II (9), *available at* http://www.sice.oas.org/FTAA/miami/sapoae.asp (hereinafter, "Plan of Action"). The FTAA is only one of a number of initiatives arising out of this Summit. Other initiatives include, inter alia, strengthening democracy, promoting and protecting human rights, promoting cultural values, combating corruption, eradicating poverty and discrimination, and guaranteeing sustainable development and conserving the natural environment. Plan of Action, *Id.*

65. *Id.*; San José Declaration, *supra* Intro. note 19 at paragraphs 1–2.

66. Second Plan of Action, *supra* Intro. note 20, at par. III.A.1.

67. Buenos Aires Declaration, *supra* Intro. note 21. This deadline was last reiterated in Quito, Ecuador in November of 2002. Free Trade Area of the Americas, Seventh Meeting of Ministers of Trade of the Hemisphere, Quito, Ecuador (1 November 2001), *available at* http://www.alca-ftaa.org.ministerials/quito/minist._e.asp at par. 1. (hereinafter, "Quito Declaration").

which will manage the negotiation groups which will deal with specific subject matters.[68] Nine different negotiating groups on market access, investment, services, government procurement, dispute settlement, agriculture, intellectual property rights, subsidies, antidumping and countervailing duties and competition policy, will engage in actual detailed negotiations.[69] The negotiating groups operate subject to general guidelines and specific instructions from the trade ministers.[70] A second draft agreement was produced by the Trade Negotiations Committee in November of 2002 and negotiations continue.[71]

The process described above seems to have some similarities with the ALADI tariff negotiations process, which required extensive negotiations among a large number of parties with different trade relationships and economic systems.[72] Indeed, many observers seem to doubt that negotiations will be completed by the deadline.[73] The United States seems to be primarily focusing on stronger protections for intellectual property, free trade in services, and access to foreign government contracts[74] while other parties, like Brazil, seem to be chiefly interested in the United States ending agricultural subsidies and stopping antidumping measures. Agreement on these issues may be very difficult.[75] As was the case with ALADI, the easy subjects seem to have been agreed upon quickly, and the remaining subjects may prove exceedingly difficult, time consuming, and perhaps impossible to master.[76] Furthermore, provisions in the draft agreement have been criticized, both in the United States and Latin

---

68. San José Declaration, *supra* Intro. note 19 at paragraph 10.

69. *Id.* at par. 12.

70. *See, e.g.,* FTAA-Trade Negotiations Committee, Methods and Modalities for negotiations (October 18, 2002) (FTAA.TNC/20/Rev. 1) *available at* http: www. sice.oas.org/FTAA/M&M_e.asp, FTAA-Trade Negotiations Committee, Guidelines or Directives for the Treatment of the Differences in the levels of Development and Size of Economies, *available at* http://www.sice.oas.org/FTAA/pautas_e.asp (hereinafter, "Different Level Guidelines"). *See, e.g.,* Quito Declaration, *supra* note 65, at Annex 1, Buenos Aires Declaration, *supra* Intro. note 21 at Annex 1.

71. FTAA-Free Trade Area of the Americas, Second Draft Agreement (November 1, 2002) FTAA.TNC/w/133/Rev.2, *available at* http://www-ftaa.alca.org.

72. *See supra* Chptr. 1 notes 5–34 and accompanying text.

73. Trade Wind: Talking up the FTAA and Mercosur, THE ECONOMIST (June 28, 2003) at 34 (hereinafter, "Trade Wind").

74. *See* Press Release, Office of the United States Trade Representative, "U.S. Advances Bold Proposals in FTAA Negotiations to Create World's Largest Free Market in 2005."(February 11, 2003), *available at* http://www.ustr.gov/releases/2003/02/03-08.htm.

75. Trade Wind, *supra* note 71.

76. This does not mean that they cannot be overcome. One suggestion by Brazil appears to have been to move all sensitive topics off the FTAA negotiations and into more generalized WTO negotiations. This would result in a narrower agreement which can be more easily completed. The United States has apparently not been very receptive to this suggestion. *Id.*

America,[77] and these criticisms may influence the finalization, ratification or implementation of the FTAA. Clearly, then the EU and MERCOSUR will have a strong incentive to complete their negotiations in 2004 and create their own free trade area before the FTAA agreement is in place.

On the other hand, if the FTAA agreement has been negotiated and agreed upon by 2005, and an agreement with the EU has *not* been finalized, the MERCOSUR has to consider its position within the context of an FTAA-United States dominated trade environment. MERCOSUR might wish to consider itself becoming a party to the FTAA agreement, or somehow co-existing with the FTAA organization.[78] The incentive for MERCOSUR to join an EU dominated free trade area in that environment would probably diminish substantially.

Concluding the Framework Agreement negotiations will not be easy. First, the Framework Agreement has created a complicated, bureaucratic and essentially consensus driven process for the negotiations themselves. This process requires the Technical Groups and SubGroups to negotiate on their areas of interest and then report their recommendations to the BNC, which must approve them and apparently refer them to the Coordination Council, which must in term approve them. At the same time, the BNC is itself engaged in negotiations covering other topics. All Coordination Council recommendations must then be submitted to the EU and MERCOSUR Councils for approval.[79] The problem with this process is that, while it ensures that the final product will clearly be the product of a consensus of the parties, it is extremely time consuming and dependent on such a consensus. If a consensus is not forthcoming on all or some of the major issues under discussion, the negotiations may break down or be delayed extensively.

Another obstacle to consider is the fact that, until now, the negotiations have been moving steadily apace without interruptions because the difficult issues (such as tariff barriers, especially tariff barriers for agricultural products)

---

77. *See, e.g.,* Latin Americans against the FTAA-Another Americas is Possible, Alliance for Responsible Trade (August 2001), *available at* http://www.art-us.org, Hansen-Kuhn, Free Trade Area of the Americas, vol. 6 no. 12 (April 2001), *available at* http://www.foreignpolicy-infocus.org/briefs/vol6/v6n12ftaa_body.html.

78. The FTAA negotiators have indicated that the FTAA can co-exist with other existing regional integration agreements. It may, however, need to modify its agreements in order to do so. Summit of the Americas, Third Trade Ministerial Meeting, Belo Horizonte, Brazil (May 16, 1997), *available at* http://www.alca-ftaa.org/ministerials/belo_e.asp at par. 5(a)2.

79. *See supra* notes 35–37 and accompanying text. The EU appears to have obtained something akin to Congressional fast track authority in the United States, which may enable it to speedily obtain approval of the final text. Under the MERCOSUR system, once the Council approves such an agreement, it must be ratified by the member states. *See* RF&P, *supra* Chptr. 2 note 58, at pp. 16–19.

have only now begun to be considered. As the EU itself has noted, MERCO-SUR has not been able to agree by itself (or with Chile) on a liberalization regime for certain industrial sectors.[80] Since a substantial portion of the exports from MERCOSUR to the EU involve agricultural products, a major area of contention is likely to be the easing of restriction on agricultural and food exports from MERCOSUR.[81] MERCOSUR is likely to push for substantial liberalization and the EU (with its highly complicated and contentious Common Agricultural Policy and agricultural sectors[82]) more likely to resist such an initiative.[83] This situation may already be manifesting itself. After the EU presentation of its tariff proposal (which included agricultural products), the MERCOSUR reaction was merely to thank the EU side for their proposal and indicate that a counterproposal would be forthcoming. Furthermore, the Common Agricultural Policy is currently the subject of reform as part of the EU's "Agenda 2000". This process of reform, which is also tied to the EU's enlargement is highly sensitive and could be contentious.[84] Until the EU has reformed the Common Agricultural Policy, it is unlikely that a final agreement on agricultural matters will be reached.[85]

Lastly, two cultural issues may interfere with the negotiations themselves. The first is that of organizational culture. Clearly, there is a view among at least some quarters in the EU that it is a more "modern," "advanced," better organized developed international organization than MERCOSUR, which is more a lesser developed "junior partner" which requires mentoring and assistance.[86]

---

80. Overview (July 2000 Situation) (hereinafter, "2000 Overview") at section 1.5. Copy on file with author.

81. Negotiating Market Access, *supra* Intro. note 12 at 3.

82. Common Agricultural Policy, *available at* http://erupa.eu.int/scadplus/leg/en/lvb/104000.htm. *See also* Derek W. Uruin, THE COMMUNITY OF EUROPE, (Longman Group UK Limited, 1991) at 132–135.

83. *See, e.g.,* Brussels Report: Latin Anger at Slow EU Agenda The Grocer, April 22, 2000, *available at* LEXIS/Nexis, All Souces: News Database. Lain America and Europe: Distant Friends, The Economist, May 18, 2002 at 38 (hereinafter, "Distant Friends").

84. Negotiating Market Access, *supra* Intro. note 12 at 11.

85. *Id.* at 3.

86. 2000 Overview, *supra* note 78. This document, referring to MERCOSUR's lack of "autonomous" (supranational) central institutions, describes it as "inspired by the example of the EU, but which did not copy the EU model." *Id.* at paragraph 1.2 It also goes on to note that "At present, MERCOSUR is still in the transition phase towards its common market, comparable to where the EU was during the 1960's." It is an imperfect common market, but one that is moving forwards as part of a process of regional economic integration.... Common commercial policies are being developed...however, their adoption or application is sometimes delayed." *Id.* at paragraph 1.5. The tone of the description of the MERCOSUR integration process in this document is somewhat negative and patronizing. *See Id.* at paragraphs 1.1–1.7. Interestingly enough, this language has been deleted from the current Overview in the EU website, and substituted with much different lan-

Although there is some truth to this perception,[87] the temptation to over-reach, or to attempt to "dictate terms" to the other party may be very strong and hard to resist. Following that impulse could be disastrous, however. Furthermore, the EU is presently in the throes of a very difficult process dealing with its own expansion.[88] This expansion will in all likelihood include the admission to the Union of a number of countries with vastly different economic and political situations and characteristics from those of the current EU members and has been the subject of a substantial amount of controversy.[89] Some of the issues in (or solutions to) the controversies engendered by the expansion of the EU may have unintended consequences spill over into the MERCOSUR negotiations and make these negotiations more complicated and difficult.

C. To Infinity and Beyond?

Bolivia, Chile and the European Union do not seem to be the only candidates for inclusion in some sort of free trade area with MERCOSUR. Since the beginning of MERCOSUR's existence, a number of other countries have expressed an interest in joining MERCOSUR and have commence negotiations toward that end.[90] In 1997, after announcing its withdrawal from the Andean Group, Perú asserted that it wished to open talks with MERCOSUR with the intention of joining Bolivia and Chile as an associate member. These talks, if they have been held, do not appear to have been very successful.[91] Venezuela also expressed an interest in joining MERCOSUR in 1999, but no negotiations seemed to follow this interest.[92] Venezuela is, however, part of the Andean Group, which, as shall be seen below, has negotiated an Economic Complementation Agreement and a free trade agreement with MERCOSUR.

---

guage. Compare: 2001 Overview, *supra* note 2, at paragraphs 2 and 4. The 2000 Overview has been removed from the EU website.

87. Coffey, *supra* Chptr. 1 note 55 at 12. Marta Haines Ferrari, *supra* Chptr. 1 note 36 at 427–428, 327. *See infra* notes 347–49, and accompanying text.

88. White Paper in the 1996 IGC, Summary of Position of the Member States *available at* http://europa.eu.in/en/agenda/igc-home/ev-doc/parlment/peen2.htm;Agenda 2000: For a stronger and wider Europe, COM (97) 2000 final and The Challenge of Enlargement, COM (97) 2000 final/2 *available at* http://europa.eu/com.agenda2000/overview/eu/agenda. htm (hereinafter, "White Paper").

89. Id.

90. *See infra* notes 91–97 and accompanying text.

91. "Peruvians Seek Mercosur Talks," FINANCIAL TIMES (5/16/97). No further public information has appeared regarding any such talks.

92. "Venezuela Seeks to Join MERCOSUR, Menem Says," 16 International Trade Reporter (BNA) 174 (January 27, 1999).

Since 1998, MERCOSUR has either commenced negotiations or entered into agreements seeking to establish free trade areas (or heightened trade relations) with the Andean Community,[93] Mexico,[94] Canada,[95] the European Free Trade Association,[96] India[97] and South Africa.[98] It has also shown an interest in increased relations with Africa.[99]

These efforts follow a similar pattern in the form of a continuum. In the case of the Andean Group, the objective of the agreement is to establish a free trade area between MERCOSUR and the Andean Group and promote the development of integration among the members of the two organizations.[100] After substantial negotiations between the parties over an extended period of time,[101]

---

93. Acuerdo Marco para la Creación de la Zona de Libre Comercio entre la Comunidad Andina y el MERCOSUR (4/16/98) (hereinafter, "Andean Pact Agreement"), *available at* http://www.sice.oas.org/trade/mrcsr/meanco%5Fs.asp.

94. MERCOSUR/CMC/DEC No. 37/00 (6/29/00) *available at* http://www.ice.oas.org/trade/decsisions/dec3700.asp (hereinafter, "Mexican Negotiations") A framework agreement for trade in automotive products was signed in July of 2002. Communicado July 2002, *supra* note 52 at par. 2.

95. "International Agreements: Canada, MERCOSUR Sign Agreement to Eliminate Trade, Investment Barriers." 15 International Trade Reporter (BNA) 1109 (June 24, 1998) (hereinafter, "Canada, MERCOSUR").

96. MERCOSUR/CMC/DEC No. 63/00 (12/14/00) *available at* http://www.sice.oas.org/trade/mrcsrs/decsisions/dec6300.asp (hereinafter, "EFTA Declaration").

97. "Acuerdo Marco entre el MERCOSUR y la República de la India"(June 17, 2003) *available at* http://www.mercosur.org.uy/espanol/sdyd/acuerdos/2003/mercosur_india_junio _asuncion.pdf (hereinafter, "India Agreement").

98. MERCOSUR/CMC/DEC 62/00 (12/14/00) *available at* http://www.sice.oas.org/ trade/mrcsrs/decisions/dec6200.asp (hereinafter, "South African Accord") These negotiations continue. *See* Communicado July 2002, *supra* note 52.

99. *See* "El MERCOSUR Descubre Africa," CLARIN(Buenos Aires, Argentina) October 26, 2003, *available at* http://oldclarin.com/suplementos/economico/2003/10/26/n-00203.htm.

100. Andean Pact Agreement, *supra* note 93, at Art. 1.

101. *See* "International Agreements: Official Says Brazil Pushing for MERCOSUR, Andean Nations FTA by End of Year,"19 International Trade Reporter (BNA) 1606 (September 16, 2002); "International Agreements: MERCOSUR Seeks to Conclude Free Trade Pact with Andean Countries by End of This Year,"19 International Trade Reporter (BNA) 1509 (September 5, 2002); "Trade Policy: MERCOSUR, Andean Nations Agree at Summit to Negotiate an Economic Zone,"17 International Trade Reporter (BNA) 1359 (September 7, 2000); "International Agreements: Andean Community, MERCOSUR Fail to Reach Trade Accord but Talks Continue," 16 International Trade Reporter (BNA) 498 (March 24, 1999); "International Agreements: Andean Pact, MERCOSUR, Continue Efforts Toward Free Trade Accord," 16 International Trade Reporter (BNA) 452 (March 17, 1999); "International Agreements: MERCOSUR, Andean Pact Countries Sign Free Trade Framework Accord,"15 International Trade Reporter (BNA) 707 (April 22, 1998); "International Agreements: MERCOSUR, Andean Nations to Sign Framework Agreement,"15 International Trade Reporter (BNA) 423 (March 11, 1998).

MERCOSUR and the Andean Group signed an Economic Complementation Agreement in December of 2002.[102] This agreement provides that the parties will complete the negotiations for a free trade area, which will include tariff liberalization and the elimination of restrictions and other barriers to reciprocal trade, by December 31, 2003.[103] These negotiations were concluded and a free trade agreement was signed on October 19, 2004.[104] The implementation achievement of this agreement, then, appears to be a high priority one. The cases of South Africa and India seem to have a lesser priority: the goal is to promote the development of commercial interchanges and *establish the conditions* for the creation of a free trade area between the parties, with no target date set.[105] The process with Mexico is not as advanced: all the MERCOSUR Council has done is authorized the Common Market Group to initiate negotiations with Mexico *leading towards the execution* of a free trade agreement.[106] Mexico has, however, recently begun negotiations on a free trade with Argentina, which it hopes will be an entry point to eventual membership in MERCOSUR.[107] The Canadian Agreement, denominated an Trade and Investment Cooperation Agreement, merely establishes a consultative group of senior officials that is to meet at least once year to identify and discuss removal of barriers and calls for customs cooperation and for the negotiation of foreign investment protection agreements with the MERCOSUR member states.[108]

The EFTA Declaration is even less specific from the point of view of results. Its objective is to result in an increase in economic relations, investment and cooperation between the EFTA countries and MERCOSUR through negotiations.[109] It is

---

102. Acuerdo de Complementación Económica celebrado Entre la Comunidad Andina y el Mercado Común del Sur (MERCOSUR) December 6, 2002, *available at* http://www.sice.oas.org/Trade/MRCSR/acMerAns.asp. Also available at MERCOSUR/CMC/Dec. No. 31/02, "Acuerdo entre el MERCOSUR y la Comunidad Andina de Naciones," *available at* http://www.mercosur.org.uy/espanol/snor/normativa/decisiones/2002/Dec_032_002.htm.

103. *Id.* at Art. 1.

104. *América del Sur será toda una Zona de Libre Comercio*, LA NACION (Buenos Aires) Oct. 19, 2004, available at http://www.lanacion.com.ar/economia/nota.asp?note_id+ 646248. The text of the Agreement is not yet available electronically. The Presidents of Brazil and Argentina have noted that they expect the full incorporation of the Andean Group nations into MERCOSUR by 2006. "International Agreements: MERCOSUR Leaders Pledge to Create by 2006 Full-Blown Common Market, Add 4 Members,"20 International Trade Reporter (BNA) 1095 (June 26, 2003).

105. South African Accord, *supra* note 98, at Art. 2; "International Agreements: South Africa to Pursue Closer Ties with MERCOSUR in Trade, Economy,"18 International Trade Reporter (BNA) 26 (January 4, 2001); India Agreement, *supra* note 97 at Art. 2.

106. Mexican Negotiations, *supra* note 94, at Art. 1.

107. "Bilateral Agreements: Mexico holds Second Round of Talks with Argentina on FTA, Looks to MERCOSUR," 20 *International Trade Reporter* (BNA) 32 (January 2, 2003).

108. Canada, MERCOSUR, *supra* note 93.

109. EFTA Declaration, *supra* note 95, at Art. 1.

accompanied by a vague "Plan of Action" that describes some of the substantive areas that the parties agree to negotiate, again with no target dates.[110]

Each of these agreements designates a "negotiating committee" composed of representatives of both parties, that will conclude the required negotiations to achieve the stated goal.[111]

This flurry of additional expansion activity on the part of MERCOSUR is, in balance, problematic. On the one hand, if all of these plans came to fruition, MERCOSUR would form part of a free trade area covering a vast area of the South American and European continents. Free access to this enormous and highly sophisticated capital for its raw materials and manufactured products would be highly advantageous. A close relationship with the European Union, a large, highly sophisticated common market organization with substantial experience in integration, could also assist MERCOSUR in its own internal development.

There are, however, two major problems. First, the FTAA, which seeks to create a free trade area throughout the Southern Hemisphere and is proceeding on an accelerated negotiating posture, is providing stiff competition for MERCOSUR in the negotiation of further free trade agreements.[112] Second, as noted above, MERCOSUR has not yet been able to complete the integration process among its own members and associate members.[113] To extend the integration process, before a template "integration model" has been developed and proven successful, as was done in the European Union, to a number of other countries with whom MERCOSUR does not have current extensive trade relations is to invite a repeat of the LAFTA disaster.[114] Furthermore, engaging at the same time in a process of economic and commercial integration with the European Union, a highly integrated and extremely complex economic and political system, can be even more challenging. Moreover, there is a substantial logistical process involved in implementing the process anticipated by these agreements. As seen by the example of the European Union, these negotiations cover a very large number of different technical areas, economic sectors and concepts and generally involves the participation of dozens of officials and other experts. Supervising the implementation of the MERCOSUR common

---

110. *Id.* at Annex. For example, the "Plan of Action" covers "the interchange of information and technical cooperation in certain essential sectors." *Id.* at Art. 2(a) and the "identification and analysis of measures, including those related to third countries, that influence commerce and investments." *Id.* at Art. 2(b).

111. Andean Pact Agreement, *supra* note 91, at Art. 5, EFTA Declaration, *Id.* at Art.3, South African Accord, *supra* note 96 at Arts. 4–5.

112. *See* notes 62–76 and accompanying text.

113. *See* MERCOSUR Normativa *available at* http://www.mercosur.org.uy/espanol/snor/normativa/incorporacion.

114. *See supra* Chptr. 1 notes 37–48 and accompanying text.

market and negotiating at least four different free trade (or otherwise economic harmonization) agreements at the same time, presents a nearly impossible task for MERCOSUR's small staff.[115]

There is another possible way to consider these agreements. The experience of the European Union shows us that the process of integration is an extremely long term one. Perhaps these agreements and negotiations can be thought of as creating a more symbolic, informal long term relationship rather than an actual short term formal relationship between MERCOSUR and other potential partners. They are chiefly creating a link and a channel of communication. They can be seen as statements of intent, meant to create, nurture and establish a generalized relationship and a tradition of cooperation among its participants rather than an actual free trade area agreement within the short term. In this case, the formal relationship can follow after MERCOSUR has developed its own integration template for expansion and "EU-type negotiations," involving dozens of actors need not follow in every case.[116]

---

115. The current Secretariat consists of 27 persons. *See supra* Chptr. 2 notes 78–79 and accompanying text.

116. The successful conclusion of a framework free trade area agreement between the European Union and MERCOSUR can provide such a template.

Chapter 8

"Relaunching MERCOSUR" and Recent Developments

A. "Relaunching MERCOSUR"

In December of 1999, the presidents of the MERCOSUR member states reiterated that the prompt incorporation of MERCOSUR norms to the national systems of the member states had extremely high priority and noted that measures were needed to ensure this incorporation.[1] Concern had been expressed in the media that the economic problems and frictions that occurred in 1998–1999 between Argentina and Brazil might substantially hamper the progress of the MERCOSUR agenda.[2] Shortly thereafter, in May of 2000, the Council and the member states agreed to "relaunch" MERCOSUR. This relaunching featured an agreement by the economic ministers and central bank presidents of the member states to harmonize their statistics and to engage in macroeconomic coordination to establish "convergence criteria" on fiscal policies, prices and public debt.[3]

Additional agreements included a market access agreement, which forbids member states from adopting any measures which restrict reciprocal trade.[4] This decision required all member states to supply a list by July 30, 2000, of all

---

1. Comunicado de Montevideo *supra* Intro. note 16, at paragraph 11.
2. *The Americas: MERCOSUR's Trial by Adversity,* THE ECONOMIST, May 27, 2000, at p. 37 (hereinafter, "Trial by Adversity").
3. *Id.* Comunicado de Buenos Aires, *supra* Intro. note 16, at paragraph 5. Some have argued that these should be the first steps to a common currency for MERCOSUR. *See, e.g., Economist looks at Prospects for Further MERCOSUR Integration,* O Globo, Dec. 28 1998, (BBC Summary of World Broadcasts) *available at* LEXIS/Nexis ALLNEWS Database), Mario Osava, *Trade-LA-TAM: Fiscal Discipline, New Key to MERCOSUR, Integration,* (May 9, 2000 Inter Press Serv.) *available at* LEXIS/Nexis All Sources/News Database (hereinafter, "*Fiscal Discipline*").
4. MERCOSUR/CMC/Dec.22/00 at Art. 1 *available at* http://www.sice.oas.org/trade/mrcsrs/decisions/Dec2200s.asp.

measures of any type which limited market access and required the Common Market Group to establish, by November 11, 2000, a plan of action to eliminate these restrictions.[5]

The Council also instructed the Common Market Group to formulate, by November 30, 2000, a proposal to limit antidumping investigations and their application to interzonal commerce.[6] The CMG was also to instruct its committees and technical groups to prepare a proposal to eliminate antidumping measures within MERCOSUR and to establish a common regulation on antidumping by non MERCOSUR member states. These proposals were to be submitted to the Council no later than December 31, 2001.[7] In July of 2002, the Council adopted the World Trade Organization Anti-Dumping Agreement as it antidumping regulation.[8]

The Council also reaffirmed its commitment to joint negotiations for commercial agreements granting tariff preferences which involve non member states and barred member states from executing, after June 30, 2001, any new tariff agreements that have not been negotiated by MERCOSUR.[9]

The Council also instructed the Common Market Group to present a proposal for the "institutional strengthening" of the Administrative Secretariat. The language of the decisions implied an expansion in its number of personnel and budgets and required this proposal to be presented to the Council before December 10, 2000.[10] The latest proposals for the year 2004 include a budget of $996,996[11] and currently a staff of 27, including four newly created "technical consultant" positions.

The Council, at its Florianópolis meeting in December of 2000, recognized that the current MERCOSUR dispute resolution mechanism was inadequate

---

5. *Id.*at Arts. 2–3. *See* MERCOSUR/GMC/Res. No. 38/02. Acuerdo del Plan General de Cooperacion y Coordinacion Reciproca para la Seguridad Regional entre los Estados Partes del MERCOSUR, Bolivia y Chile *available at* http://mercosur.org.uy.

6. MERCOSUR/CMC/DEC No. 28/2000 at Art. 1 *available at* http://www.sice.oas.org/trade/mrcsrs/decisions/Dec2800s.asp.

7. *Id.* at Arts. 2–3.

8. MERCOSUR/CMC/Dec. NO. 13/02, "Acuerdo Antidumping de la Organzacion Mundial de Comercio *available at* http://www.mercosur.org/us/espanol/normativa/decisiones/2003/0213.htm.

9. MERCOSUR/CMC/Dec. No. 32/00 at Arts. 1–3 *available at* http://www.sice.oas.org/trade/mrcsrs/decisions/dec3200s.asp.

10. MERCOSUR/CMC/Dec. No. 24/00 at Arts. 1–2 *available at* http://www.sice.oas.org/trade/mrsrs/decisions/dec2400s.asp.

11. *See* Res 01/02, *supra* Chptr. 2 note 79. Res 15/02 *supra* Chptr. 2 note 78 at Art. 3.01. MERCOSUR/GMC/RES. No. 481/03, Presupuesto de la Secretaria del MERCOSUR PARA el EVERCICO 2004 *available at* http://www.mercosur.org.uy/espanol/snor/normativia/resoluciones/2003RES_04_003720.htm.

and established a group of senior officials that are to propose "improvements "to the system, which would consider the establishment of a MERCOSUR arbitral tribunal.[12] These improvements are set forth in the Olivos Protocol.[13] In the same communiqué, the MERCOSUR presidents hailed the agreement, after nine years, of a common policy on the automotive sector[14] and identified a policy agreement on the sugar industry as a high priority, and reiterated the importance of macroeconomic coordination.[15] The process of macroeconomic coordination has gone very slowly. As of July of 2002, the MERCOSUR presidents were reiterating the importance of macroeconomic coordination and agreeing again, to undertake and continue the process.[16]

B. Recent Institutional Changes

As has been noted above, a number of recent institutional changes clearly show an intent by MERCOSUR to strengthen its institutions. First, plans are in progress to transform the "Administrative Secretariat" into a "Technical Secretariat," which can render substantive and technical assistance to the other MERCOSUR institutions.[17] In spite of this reorganization, however, neither the budget nor the number of staff members of the Secretariat has substantially increased.[18] Given the extensive agenda of the various MERCOSUR institutions,[19] the Secretariat needs much more in the way of staff and funds before it can effectively accomplish its new responsibilities.

The Olivos Protocol, substantially changing the MERCOSUR dispute resolution system, has become effective[20] and its regulations have been recently ap-

---

12. Comunicado de Florianopolis, *supra* Intro. note 16.

13. *See* Olivos, *supra* Chptr. 2 note 29 and accompanying text.

14. Comunicado de Florianopolis, *supra* Intro. note 16 at paragraph 11.

15. Comunicado de Florianopolis, *supra* Intro. note 16 at paragraph 12.

16. Communicado, July 2002, *supra* Chptr. 7 note 52 at par. 4-5. *See also* Communicado Conjunto, Feb. 18, 2002, *supra* Chptr. 6 note 88 at par. 5.

17. *See supra* Chptr. 2 notes 84–88 and accompanying text.

18. The 2002 budget proposal for the Secretariat called for 27 positions and a budget of $980,000. The 2004 budget calls for 26 positions and a budget of $996,996. *See supra* Chptr. 2 note 79 and accompanying text.

19. *See* MERCOSUR/CMC/Dec/ No. 26/03, "Programa de Trabajo 2004–2006" (hereinafter, "Programa de Trabajo"), *available at* http://www.mercosur.org.uy/espanol/snor/normativa/decisiones/2003/Dec_026_003.htm.

20. *See* "Comunicado Conjunto de los Presidentes de los Estados Partes del MERCOSUR, (December 16, 2003) (hereinafter, "Comunicado Conjunto 2003"), *available at* http://www.mercosur.org.uy/espanol/actas/cmc/2003/comunicado%conjunto.htm at paragraph 15.

proved.[21] The Tribunal was therefore expected to be in place and functioning by January 1, 2004.[22]

A Committee of Permanent Representatives has been established, which is meant to provide some continuity for the work of the Council and serve a valuable liaison role.[23]

An agreement was entered into between the Parliament and the Council, which was meant to strengthen the role of the former within the context of MERCOSUR, and serve as the basis for a MERCOSUR Parliament.[24] The prologue to the Agreement notes the creation of a true regional Parliament as a major goal of MERCOSUR.[25] Moreover, the Agreement also sets forth an undertaking by the Council to consult the Joint Parliamentary Commission in those matters that require legislative approval for their incorporation into the legal systems of the member states and an undertaking by the Joint Parliamentary Commission to promote, through its national delegations, the incorporation of the MERCOSUR norms into the legal systems of the member states.[26]

C. The 2004–2006 Work Plan

An ambitious work plan for the next two years was approved by the Council on December 15, 2003. It included eighteen different economic topics.[27] Among these economic topics were included the completion of antidumping regulations by the end of 2004,[28] harmonization of indirect tariffs,[29] substantial work on macroeconomic coordination,[30] the implementation of measures leading to the development of a regional stock exchange by 2006,[31] the continuation of external negotiations,[32] and the continuation of complementary

---

21. *See supra* Chptr. 3 note 2 and accompanying text.
22. Comunicado Conjunto 2003, *supra* note 20, at paragraph 15.
23. *See supra* Chptr. 3 notes 13–27 and accompanying text.
24. *See* Comunicado Conjunto 2003, *supra* note 20, at paragraph 19. Acuerdo Interinstitucional Consejo Mercado Común-Comisión Interparlamentaria Conjunta (October 6, 2003), *available at* http://www.mercosur.org.uy/espanol/sdyd/acuerdos/2003/03_ACUERDO%20INTERINSTITUCIONAL.htm (hereinafter, "Acuerdo Interinstitucional").
25. Acuerdo Interinstitucional, *supra* note 24, at Prologue.
26. Acuerdo Interinstitucional, *supra* note 24, at Arts. 1–2.
27. Programa de Trabajo, *supra note* 19, at paragraphs 1.1–1.18.
28. *Id.* at paragraph 1.4.
29. *Id.* at paragraph 1.11.
30. *Id.* at paragraph 1.12.
31. *Id.* at paragraph 1.13.
32. *Id.* at paragraph 1.17.

work leading towards the effective implementation of the MERCOSUR Public Contracts Protocol.[33]

Seven social topics are also included in the plan, dealing with, *inter alia*, promoting the expansion of participation in civil society,[34] designing and developing investigation centers in the member states to research social betterment programs,[35] improving educational programs,[36] and deepening the exchange of information of, and promoting respect for, human rights in the region.[37]

Thirdly, two institutional development programs also appear in the work plan. These include working towards the creation of a MERCOSUR parliament,[38] ensuring functioning of the Tribunal, establishing Center for the Promotion of Government of Laws, and completing, by the end of 2004, the transformation of the Secretariat into a technical secretariat.[39]

Lastly, the work plan calls for the establishment of a cooperation program in science and technology,[40] and continuing work in physical and energy integration.[41] These are welcome developments. They clearly recognize that substantial areas of the MERCOSUR agreements and agenda need to be incorporated and implemented into the domestic legal and economic systems of the member states. They also show that, even one of the most intractable tariff problems facing MERCOSUR, that of the automotive sector, can eventually be resolved and showed some level of commitment by the organization and its members to a continuation of the integration process. By imposing short deadlines for continued progress, they seek to energize it.

They also have recognized the absolute need for an effective Administrative Secretariat and dispute resolutions systems and have undertaken a commitment to strengthen and expand the former and create the latter.

They illustrate, however, obstacles to the MERCOSUR integration process. There seems to be a substantial lag and gap between the agreement on policy at the MERCOSUR level and the implementation of this policy at the member state level. Neither the Administrative Secretariat nor any other MERCOSUR institution has the resources to effectively supervise, on a current basis, the negotiation of new norms, the implementation of established norms and the ne-

---

33. *Id.* at paragraph 1.18.
34. *Id.* at Art. 2.1.
35. *Id.* at Art. 2.2.
36. *Id.* at Art. 2.6.
37. *Id.* at Art. 2.7.
38. *Id.* at Art. 3.1
39. *Id.* at Art. 3.2.
40. *Id.* at Art. 4.1.
41. *Id.* at Art. 4.2.

gotiations to expand the Union. The member states may be too preoccupied with their domestic concerns, perspectives and priorities to be able to do either.

Relaunching and developing MERCOSUR, in the sense of expediting the integration process and making it more effective and efficient, will require a paradigm change. Given all the progress that has been made, the future agenda, and its implementation, has become far too extensive and complex for MERCOSUR's current framework. The supranational integration process, by now very successful, needs to be managed by a supranational actor with adequate resources and authority. The supranational norms created by this process need a mechanism to ensure that they are implemented by the member states in an expeditious and uniform fashion. Some sort of effective enforcement mechanism needs to be created to ensure that norms are kept and those who fail to do so are sanctioned.

Appendices

MERCOSUR BASIC DOCUMENTS

Appendix I

Treaty of Asunción
30 I.L.M. 1041 (March 26, 1991)

Appendix I: Treaty of Asunción.
SOUTHERN COMMON MARKET (MERCOSUR) AGREEMENT
(Original: Spanish)

Treaty Establishing a Common Market between the Argentine Republic, the Federal Republic of Brazil, the Republic of Paraguay and the Eastern Republic of Uruguay.

The Argentine Republic, the Federative Republic of Brazil, the Republic of Paraguay and the Eastern Republic of Uruguay, hereinafter referred to as the "States Parties",

CONSIDERING that the expansion of their domestic markets, through integration, is a vital prerequisite for accelerating their processes of economic development with social justice,

BELIEVING that this objective must be achieved by making optimum use of available resources, preserving the environment, improving physical links, coordinating macroeconomic policies and ensuring complementarity between the different sectors of the economy, based on the principles of gradualism, flexibility and balance,

BEARING IN MIND international trends, particularly the integration of large economic areas and the importance of securing their countries a proper place in the international economy.

BELIEVING that this integration process is an appropriate response to such trends,

AWARE that this Treaty must be viewed as a further step in efforts gradually to bring about Latin American integration, in keeping with the objectives of the Montevideo Treaty in 1980,

CONVINCED of the need to promote the scientific and technological development of the States Parties and to modernize their economies in order to expand the supply and improve the quality of available goods and services, with a view to enhancing the living conditions of their populations,

REAFFIRMING their political will to lay the bases for increasingly close ties between their peoples, with a view to achieving the above-mentioned objectives,

HEREBY AGREE AS FOLLOWS:

CHAPTER I: PURPOSES, PRINCIPLES AND INSTRUMENTS

Article 1

The States Parties hereby decide to establish a common market, which shall be in place by 31 December 1994 and shall be called the "common market of the southern cone" (MERCOSUR).

This common market shall involve:

The free movement of goods, services and factors of production between countries through, inter alia, the elimination of customs duties and non-tariff restrictions on the movement of goods, and any other equivalent measures;

The establishment of a common external tariff and the adoption of a common trade policy in relation to third States or groups of States, and the co-ordination of positions in regional and international economic and commercial forums;

The co-ordination of macroeconomic and sectoral policies between the States Parties in the areas of foreign trade, agriculture, industry, fiscal and monetary matters, foreign exchange and capital, services, customs, transport and communications and any other areas that may be agreed upon, in order to ensure proper competition between the States Parties;

The commitment by States Parties to harmonize their legislation in the relevant areas in order to strengthen the integration process.

Article 2

The common market shall be based on reciprocity of rights and obligations between the States Parties.

Article 3

During the transition period, which shall last from the entry into force of this Treaty until 31 December 1994, and in order to facilitate the formation of the common market, the States Parties shall adopt general rules of origin, a system for the settlement of disputes and safeguard clauses, as contained in Annexes 11. III and IV respectively to this Treaty.

Article 4

The States Parties shall ensure equitable trade terms in their relations with third countries. To that end, they shall apply their domestic legislation to restrict imports whose prices are influenced by subsidies, dumping or any other unfair practice. At the same time, States Parties shall co-ordinate their respective domestic policies with a view to drafting common rules for trade competition.

Article 5

During the transition period, the main instruments for putting in place the common market shall be:

(a) A trade liberalization programme, which shall consist of progressive, linear and automatic tariff reductions accompanied by the elimination of non-tariff restrictions or equivalent measures, as well as any other restrictions on trade between the States Parties, with a view to arriving at a zero tariff and no non-tariff restrictions for the entire tariff area by 31 December 1994 (Annex I);

(b) The co-ordination of macroeconomic policies, which shall be carried out gradually and in parallel with the programmes for the reduction of tariffs and the elimination of non-tariff restrictions referred to in the preceding paragraph;

(c) A common external tariff which encourages the foreign competitiveness of the States Parties;

(d) The adoption of sectoral agreements in order to optimize the use and mobility of factors of production and to achieve efficient scales of operation.

Article 6

The States parties recognize certain differentials in the rate at which the Republic of Paraguay and the Eastern Republic of Uruguay will make the transition. These differentials are indicated in the trade liberalization programme (Annex 1).

Article 7

In the area of taxes, charges and other internal duties, products originating in the territory of one State Party shall enjoy, in the other States Parties, the same treatment as domestically produced products.

Article 8

The States Parties undertake to abide by commitments made prior to the date of signing of this Treaty, including agreements signed in the framework of the Latin American Integration Association (ALADI), and to co-ordinate their positions in any external trade negotiations they may undertake during the transitional period. To that end:

(a) They shall avoid affecting the interests of the States Parties in any trade negotiations they may conduct among themselves up to 31 December 1994;

(b) They shall avoid affecting the interests of the other States Parties or the aims of the common market in any agreements they may conclude with other countries members of the Latin American Integration Association during the transition period;

(c) They shall consult among themselves whenever negotiating comprehensive tariff reduction schemes for the formation of free trade areas with other countries members of the Latin American Integration Association;

(d) They shall extend automatically to the other States Parties any advantage, favour, exemption, immunity or privilege granted to a product originating in or destined for third countries which are not members of the Latin American Integration Association.

CHAPTER II: Organizational Structure

Article 9

The administration and implementation of this Treaty, and of any specific agreements or decisions adopted during the transition period within the legal framework established thereby, shall be entrusted to the following organs:

(a) The Council of the common market

(b) The Common Market Group

Article 10

The Council shall be the highest organ of the common market, with responsibility for its political leadership and for decision-making to ensure compliance with the objectives and time-limits set for the final establishment of the common market.

Article 11

The council shall consist of the Ministers for Foreign Affairs and the Ministers of the Economy of the States Parties.

It shall meet whenever its members deem appropriate, and at least once a year with the participation of the Presidents of the States Parties.

Article 12

The presidency of the Council shall rotate among the States Parties, in alphabetical order, for periods of six months.

Meetings of the Council shall be co-ordinated by the Minister for Foreign Affairs, and other ministers or ministerial authorities may be invited to participate in them.

Article 13

The Common Market Group shall be the executive organ of the common market and shall be co-ordinated by the Ministries of Foreign Affairs.

The Common Market Group shall have powers of initiative. Its duties shall be the following:

- to monitor compliance with the Treaty;
- to take the necessary steps to enforce decisions adopted by the Council;
- to propose specific measures for applying the trade liberalization programme, co-ordinating macroeconomic policies and negotiating agreements with third parties;
- to draw up programmes of work to ensure progress towards the formation of the common market.

The Common Market Group may set up whatever working groups are needed for it to perform its duties. To start with, it shall have the working groups mentioned in Annex V.

The Common Market Group shall draw up its own rules of procedure within 60 days of its establishment.

Article 14

The Common Market Group shall consist of four members and four alternates for each country, representing the following public bodies:

- Ministry of Foreign Affairs;
- Ministry of Economy or its equivalent (areas of industry, foreign trade and/or economic co-ordination);
- Central Bank.

In drafting and proposing specific measures as part of its work up to 31 December 1994, the Common Market Group may, whenever it deems appropriate, call on representatives of other government agencies or the private sector.

Article 15

The Common Market Group shall have an administrative secretariat whose main functions shall be to keep the Group's documents and report on its activities. It shall be headquartered in the city of Montevideo.

Article 16

During the transition period, decisions of the Council of the common market and the Common Market Group shall be taken by consensus, with all States Parties present.

Article 17

The official languages of the common market shall be Spanish and Portuguese, and the official version of its working documents shall be that drafted in the language of the country in which each meeting takes place.

Article 18

Prior to the establishment of the common market on 31 December 1994, the States Parties shall convene a special meeting to determine the final institutional structure of the administrative organs of the common market, as well as the specific powers of each organ and its decision-making procedures.

CHAPTER III: Period of Application

Article 19

This Treaty shall be of unlimited duration and shall enter into force 30 days after the date of deposit of the third instrument of ratification. The instruments of ratification shall be deposited with the Government of the Republic of Paraguay, which shall notify the Governments of the other States Parties of the date of deposit.

The Government of the Republic of Paraguay shall notify the Governments of each of the other States Parties of the date of entry into force of this Treaty.

CHAPTER IV: Accession

Article 20

This Treaty shall be open to accession, through negotiation, by other countries members of the Latin American Integration Association; their applications may be considered by the States Parties once this Treaty has been in force for five years.

Notwithstanding the above, applications made by countries members of the Latin American Integration Association who do not belong to subregional integration schemes or an extraregional association may be considered before the date specified.

Approval of applications shall require the unanimous decision of the States Parties.

CHAPTER V: DENUNCIATION

Article 21

Any State Party wishing to withdraw from this Treaty shall inform the other States Parties of its intention expressly and formally and shall submit the document of denunciation within 60 days to the Ministry of Foreign Affairs of the Republic of Paraguay, which shall distribute it to the other States Parties.

Article 22

Once the denunciation has been formalized, those rights and obligations of the denouncing State deriving from its status as a State Party shall cease, while those relating to the liberalization programme under this Treaty and any other aspect to which the States Parties, together with the denouncing State, may agree within the 60 days following the formalization of the denunciation shall continue. The latter rights and obligations of the denouncing Party shall remain in force for a period of two years from the date of the above-mentioned formalization.

CHAPTER VI: General Provisions

Article 23

This Treaty shall be called the "Treaty of Asuncion".

Article 24

In order to facilitate progress towards the formation of the common market, a Joint Parliamentary Commission of MERCOSUR shall be established. The executive branches of the States Parties shall keep their respective legislative branches informed of the progress of the common market established by this Treaty.

DONE at the city of Asuncion, on 26 March 1991, in one original in the Spanish and Portuguese languages, both texts being equally authentic. The Government of the Republic of Paraguay shall be the depositary of this Treaty and shall send a duly authenticated copy thereof to the Governments of signatory and acceding States Parties.

For the Government of the Argentine Republic:

Carlos Saul Menem

Guido di Tella

For the Government of the Federative Republic of Brazil:

Fernando Collor

Francisco Rezek

For the Government of the Republic of Paraguay:

Andres Rodriguez

Alexis Frutos Vaesken

For the Government of the Eastern Republic of Uruguay:

Luis Alberto Lacalle Herrera

Hector Gros Espiell

ANNEX I: Trade Liberalization Programme

Article 1

The States Parties hereby agree to eliminate, by: 31 December 1994 at the latest, any duties, charges and other restrictions applied in their reciprocal trade.

With regard to the schedules of exceptions submitted by the Republic of Paraguay and the Eastern Republic of Uruguay, the period for their elimination shall extend to 31 December 1995, on the terms of article 7 of this annex.

Article 2

For the purposes of the preceding article:

(a) "Duties and charges" shall mean customs duties and any other charges of equivalent effect, whether related to fiscal, monetary, foreign exchange or other matters, levied on foreign trade. This concept does not cover fees and similar charges corresponding to the approximate cost of services rendered; and

(b) "Restrictions" shall mean any administrative, financial, foreign exchange or other measures by which a State Party unilaterally prevents or impedes reciprocal trade. This concept does not cover measures taken in the situations envisaged in article 50 of the Montevideo Treaty of 1980.

Article 3

As of the date of entry into force of the Treaty, the States Parties shall begin a programme of gradual, linear and automatic tariff reductions, which shall benefit products classified according to the tariff nomenclature used by the Latin American Integration Association, observing the following timetable:

Date	30 June 1991	31 Dec. 1991	30 June 1992	31 Dec. 1992	30 June 1993	31 Dec. 1993	30 June 1994	31 Dec. 1994
% Tariff Reduction	47	54	61	68	75	82	89	100

Preferences shall apply to the tariff in force at the time of their application and shall consist of a percentage reduction in the most favourable duties and charges applied to imports of products coming from third countries not members of the Latin American Integration Association.

If one of the States Parties increases this tariff for imports from third countries, the established timetable shall continue to apply at the tariff level in force on 1 January 1991.

If tariffs are reduced, the corresponding preference shall apply automatically to the new tariff on the date on which that new tariff enters into force.

For the above purposes, the States Parties shall exchange among themselves and shall transmit to the Latin American Integration Association, within 30 days of the entry into force of the Treaty, updated copies of their customs tariffs and of those in force on I January 1991.

Article 4

Preferences agreed to in partial scope agreements concluded by the States Parties among themselves in the framework of the Latin American Integration Association shall be expanded, under the present tariff reduction programme, according to the following timetable:

DATE/PERCENTAGE TARIFF REDUCTION

31 Dec. 1990	30 June 1991	31 Dec. 1991	30 June 1992	31 Dec. 1992	30 June 1993	31 Dec. 1993	30 June 1994	31 Dec. 1994
00–40	47	54	61	68	75	82	89	100
41–45	52	59	66	73	80	87	94	100
46–50	57	64	71	78	85	92	100	
51–55	61	67	73	79	86	93	100	
56–60	67	74	81	88	95	100		
61–65	71	77	83	89	96	100		
66–70	75	80	85	90	95	100		
71–75	80	85	90	95	100			
76–80	85	90	95	100				
81–85	89	93	97	100				
86–90	95	100						
91–95	100							
96–100								

These reductions shall apply only in the context of the corresponding partial scope agreements and shall not benefit other members of the common market; nor shall they apply to products included in the respective schedules of exceptions.

Article 5

Without prejudice to the mechanism described in articles 3 and 4, States Parties may also expand preferences by means of negotiations conducted in the framework of the agreements envisaged in the Montevideo Treaty of 1980.

Article 6

The tariff reduction timetable referred to in articles 3 and 4 of this annex shall not apply to products included in the schedules of exceptions submitted by each of the States Parties with the following quantifies of ALADI nomenclature items:

Argentine Republic:	394
Federative Republic of Brazil:	324
Republic of Paraguay:	439
Eastern Republic of Uruguay:	960

Article 7

The schedules of exceptions shall be reduced at the end of each calendar year in accordance with the following timetable:

(a) For the Argentine Republic and the Federative Republic of Brazil, by 20 per cent per year of the component items; this reduction applies from 31 December 1990;

(b) For the Republic of Paraguay and the Eastern Republic of Uruguay, the reduction shall be at the following rates:

10 per cent on the date of entry into force of the Treaty

10 per cent on 31 December 1991

20 per cent on 31 December 1992

20 per cent on 31 December 1993

20 per cent on 31 December 1994

20 per cent on 31 December 1995

Article 8

The schedules of exceptions contained in appendices I, II, III and IV include the first reduction envisaged in the preceding article.

Article 9

Products which are removed from schedules of exceptions on the terms set forth in Article 7 shall automatically benefit from the preferences resulting from the tariff reduction programme established in Article 3 of this annex.

They shall benefit, at the least, from the minimum percentage reduction provided on the date on which they are removed from the schedules.

Article 10

States Parties may apply up to 31 December 1994, to products included in the tariff reduction programme, only the non-tariff restrictions expressly mentioned in the notes supplementing the complementarity agreement to be concluded by the States Parties in the framework of the Montevideo Treaty of 1980.

As of 31 December 1994, all non-tariff restrictions shall be eliminated from the common market area.

Article 11

In order to ensure observance of the tariff reduction timetable established in Articles 3 and 4, and also the formation of the common market, the States Parties shall co-ordinate any macroeconomic and sectoral policies which may be agreed upon and to which the Treaty establishing the common market refers, beginning with those connected with trade flows and the composition of the States Parties' productive sectors.

Article 12

The provisions of this Annex shall not apply to the partial scope agreements, economic complementarity agreements Nos. 1, 2, 13 and 14 or trade and agricultural agreements signed in the framework of the Montevideo Treaty of 1980, such agreements being governed exclusively by their own provisions.

(The Spanish and Portuguese read: THIS IS A TRUE COPY OF THE ORIGINAL WHICH IS IN THE POSSESSION OF THE TREATY DEPARTMENT OF THE MINISTRY OF FOREIGN AFFAIRS)

(Signed) Bernardino H. Saguier Caballero

Under-Secretary for Foreign Affairs

ANNEX II: GENERAL RULES OF ORIGIN

Chapter I: General Rules for Classification of Origin

Article 1

The following shall be classified as originating in the States Parties:

(a) Products manufactured wholly in the territory of any of the Parties, when only materials originating in the States Parties are used in their manufacture;

(b) Products included in the chapters or headings of the tariff nomenclature of the Latin American Integration Association referred to in Annex 1 of resolution 78 of the Committee of Representatives of that Association, simply by virtue of the fact that they are produced in their respective territories.

The following shall be classified as produced in the territory of a State Party:

(i) Mineral, plant and animal products, including hunting and fishing products, extracted, harvested or gathered, born and raised in its territory or in its territorial waters or exclusive economic zone;

(ii) Marine products extracted outside its territorial waters and exclusive economic zone by vessels flying its flag or leased by companies established in its territory; and

(iii) Products resulting from operations or processes carried out in its territory by which they acquire the final form in which they will be marketed, except when such processes or operations simply involve assembly, packaging, division into lots or volumes, selection and classification, marking, the putting together of assortments of goods or other equivalent operations or processes;

(c) Products in whose manufacture materials not originating in the States Parties are used, when such products are changed by a process carried out in the territory of one of the States Parties which results in their reclassification in the tariff nomenclature of the Latin American Integration Association under a heading different from that of such materials, except in cases where the States Parties determine that the requirement of Article 2 of this Annex must also be met.

However, products resulting from operations or processes carried out in the territory of a State Party, by which they acquire the final form in which they will be marketed, shall not be classified as originating in the States Parties when such operations or processes use only materials or inputs not originating in their respective countries and simply involve assembly, division into lots or volumes, selection, classification, marking, the putting together of assortments of goods or other similar operations or processes;

(d) Until 31 December 1994, products resulting from assembly operations carried out in the territory of a State Party using materials originating in the States Parties and third countries, when the value of those materials is not less than 40 per cent of the f.o.b. export value of the final product; and

(e) Products which, in addition to being produced in their territory, meet the specific requirements established in Annex 2 of Resolution 78 of the Committee of Representatives of the Latin American Integration Association.

Article 2

In cases where the requirement of Article 1 (c) cannot be met because the process carried out does not involve a change in nomenclature heading, it shall suffice that the c.i.f. value of the third country materials at the port of destination or the maritime port does not exceed 50 per cent of the f.o.b. export value of the goods in question.

In considering materials originating in third countries for States Parties with no outlet to the sea, warehouses and free zones granted by the other States Parties when the materials arrive by sea shall be treated as the port of destination.

Article 3

The States Parties may establish, by mutual consent, specific requirements of origin which shall prevail over general classification criteria.

Article 4

In determining the specific requirements of origin referred to in Article 3 and in reviewing those already established, State Parties shall take the following elements, individually or jointly, as a basis:

I. Materials and other inputs used in production:

　(a) Raw materials:

　　(i) Preponderant raw material or that which essentially characterizes the product; and

　　(ii) Main raw materials.

　(b) Parts or components:

　　(i) Part or component which essentially characterizes the product;

　　(ii) Main parts or components; and

　　(iii) Percentage of parts or components in relation to total weight.

　(c) Other inputs.

II. Type of processing used.

III. Maximum proportion of the value of materials imported from third countries in relation to the total value of the product arrived at using the valuation procedure agreed to in each case.

Article 5

In exceptional cases, where specific requirements cannot be met because of circumstantial supply problems: availability, technical specifications, delivery date and price, taking into account the provisions of Article 4 of the Treaty, materials not originating in the States Parties may be used.

In the situation envisaged in the preceding paragraph, the exporting country shall issue the corresponding certificate informing the importing State Party and the Common Market Group, together with any background information and evidence justifying the issue of that document.

If such cases occur repeatedly, the exporting State Party or the importing State Party shall inform the Common Market Group of the situation so that the specific requirement can be reviewed.

This article does not cover products resulting from assembly operations and shall apply pending the entry into force of the common external tariff for products subject to specific requirements of origin and their materials or inputs.

Article 6

Any State Party may request that requirements of origin established pursuant to Article 1 above be reviewed. Such requests shall propose and justify the requirements applicable to the product or products in question.

Article 7

For the purpose of meeting requirements of origin, materials and other inputs originating in the territory of any State Party and used by a State Party in the manufacture of a given product shall be classified as originating in the territory of this latter State Party.

Article 8

The criterion of maximum use of materials or other inputs originating in States Parties may not be taken into account in establishing requirements which involve the imposition of materials or other inputs of those States Parties when, in their view, such materials or inputs do not meet adequate supply, quality or price standards or are not adapted to the industrial processes or technologies used.

Article 9

In order for originating goods to benefit from preferential treatment, they must have been shipped directly from the exporting country to the importing country. For these purposes, the following shall be deemed direct shipment:

(a) Goods not shipped through the territory of a country that is not a party to the Treaty;

(b) Goods shipped in transit through one or more countries that are not parties to the Treaty, with or without transshipment or temporary storage, under the supervision of the competent customs authority in such countries, provided that:

(i) Transit is justified by geographical reasons or transport considerations;

(ii) The goods are not intended for trade or use in the country of transit; and

(iii) The goods are not subjected, during shipment and storage, to any operation other than loading, unloading or handling to keep them in good condition or ensure their conservation.

Article 10

For the purposes of these general rules, it shall be understood that:

(a) Products coming from free zones located within the geographical boundaries of any of the States Parties shall meet the requirements envisaged in these general rules;

(b) The term "materials" shall include raw materials, intermediate products and parts and components used in the manufacture of goods.

CHAPTER II: Declaration, Certification and Verification

Article 11

In order for imports of products originating in the States Parties to benefit from the reductions in duties, charges and restrictions they have granted each other, the export documentation for such products must include a declaration certifying that they meet the requirements of origin established in accordance with the preceding chapter.

Article 12

The declaration referred to in the preceding article shall be issued by the final producer or the exporter of the goods and certified by an official department or professional association with legal personality, authorized by the Government of the exporting State Party.

In authorizing professional associations, States Parties shall make sure that they are organizations which have national jurisdiction and can delegate authority to regional or local associations while remaining directly responsible for the veracity of the certifications issued.

The States Parties undertake to establish, within a period of 90 days from the entry into force of the Treaty, a harmonized regime of administrative penalties for cases of false certification, without prejudice to the corresponding criminal proceedings.

Article 13

Certificates of origin issued for the purposes of this Treaty shall be valid for 180 days from the date of their issue.

Article 14

In all cases, the standard form annexed to agreement No. 25 of the Committee of Representatives of the Latin American Integration Association shall be used until such time as another form approved by the States Parties comes into effect.

Article 15

States Parties shall transmit to the Latin American Integration Association the list of official departments and professional associations authorized to issue the certification referred to in the preceding article. with a record and exact copy of the authorized signatures.

Article 16

If a State Party considers that the certificates issued by an official department or professional association authorized by another State Party are not in compliance with the provisions of these general rules, it shall inform that State Party accordingly so that the latter can take whatever steps it deems necessary to solve the problems that have arisen.

In no case may the importing country hold up import procedures for products covered by the certificates referred to in the preceding paragraph. It may, however, in addition to requesting the corresponding additional information from the governmental authorities of the exporting country, take whatever measures it deems necessary to safeguard fiscal interests.

Article 17

For the purposes of subsequent verification, copies of certificates and the corresponding documents shall be kept for two years from the date of their issue.

Article 18

The provisions of these general rules and any amendments thereto shall not affect goods already loaded for shipment on the date of their adoption.

Article 19

The provisions of this Annex shall not apply to the partial scope agreements, economic complementarity agreements Nos. 1, 2, 13 and 14 or trade and agricultural agreements signed in the framework of the Montevideo Treaty of 1980, such agreements being governed exclusively by their own provisions.

(The Spanish and Portuguese versions read: THIS IS A TRUE COPY OF THE ORIGINAL WHICH IS IN THE POSSESSION OF THE TREATY DEPARTMENT OF THE MINISTRY OF FOREIGN AFFAIRS.)

(Signed) Bernardino H. Saguier Caballero Under-Secretary for Foreign Affairs

ANNEX III: Settlement of Disputes

1. Any dispute arising between the States Parties as a result of the application of the Treaty shall be settled by means of direct negotiations.

   If no solution can be found, the States Parties shall refer the dispute to the Common Market Group which, after evaluating the situation, shall within a period of 60 days make the relevant recommendations to the Parties for settling the dispute. To that end, the Common Market Group may establish or convene panels of experts or groups of specialists in order to obtain the necessary technical advice.

   If the Common Market Group also fails to find a solution, the dispute shall be referred to the Council of the common market to adopt the relevant recommendations.

2. Within 120 days of the entry into force of the Treaty, the Common Market Group shall propose to the Governments of States Parties a system for the settlement of disputes which shall apply during the transition period.

3. Before 31 December 1994, the States Parties shall adopt a permanent disputes settlement system for the common market.

(The Spanish and Portuguese read: THIS IS A TRUE COPY OF THE ORIGINAL WHICH IS IN THE POSSESSION OF THE TREATY DEPARTMENT OF THE MINISTRY OF FOREIGN AFFAIRS.)

(Signed) Bernardino H. Saguier Caballero Under-Secretary for Foreign Affairs

ANNEX IV: Safeguard Clauses

Article 1

Each State Party may, up to 31 December 1994, apply safeguard clauses to imports of products benefiting from the trade liberalization programme established under the Treaty.

The States Parties hereby agree that they shall use these rules only in exceptional cases.

Article 2

If imports of a given product damage or threaten serious damage to its market as a result of a significant increase in imports of that product from the other States Parties over a short period of time, the importing country shall request the Common Market Group to hold consultations with a view to ending such a situation.

The importing country shall accompany its request with a detailed statement of the supporting facts, reasons and justifications.

The Common Market Group shall begin consultations within a maximum of 10 calendar days from the submission of the request by the importing country and shall conclude them, having taken a decision thereon, within 20 calendar days from the start of consultations.

Article 3

The existence or otherwise of damage or the threat of serious damage within the meaning of these rules shall be determined by each country, taking into account trends, inter alia, in the following aspects related to the product in question.

(a) Production level and capacity used;

(b) Employment level;

(c) Share of the market;

(d) Level of trade between the parties concerned or participating in the consultations;

(e) Performance of imports and exports in relation to third countries.

None of the above-mentioned factors shall, on its own, be decisive for determining the existence of damage or the threat of serious damage.

In determining the existence of damage or the threat of serious damage, factors such as technological changes or shifts in consumer preferences towards similar and/or directly competitive products in the same sector shall not be taken into account.

Application of the safeguard clause shall be subject, in each country, to the final approval of the national section of the Common Market Group.

Article 4

In order not to interrupt any trade flows which may have been generated, the importing country shall negotiate a quota for imports of the product in respect of which the safeguard clause has been invoked. This quota shall be governed by the same preferences and other conditions established in the trade liberalization programme.

The above-mentioned quota shall be negotiated with the State Party in which the imports originate, during the period of consultation referred to in Article 2. If the period of consultation ends without an agreement being reached, the importing country which considers itself affected may fix a quota which shall be maintained for one year.

In no event may a quota fixed unilaterally by the importing country be less than the average physical volume imported in the last three calendar years.

Article 5

Safeguard clauses shall apply for a year and may be extended for a further consecutive year on the terms established in this Annex. Such measures may be adopted only once for each product.

In no event may the application of safeguard clauses extend beyond 31 December 1994.

Article 6

The application of safeguard clauses shall not affect goods already loaded for shipment on the date of their adoption. Such goods shall be computed into the quota provided for in article 4.

Article 7

During the transition period, any State Party which considers itself affected by serious difficulties in its economic activities shall request the Common Market Group to hold consultations so that the necessary corrective measures can be taken.

Within the periods established in Article 2 of this Annex, the Common Market Group shall evaluate the situation and decide on the measures to be taken, according to the circumstances.

(The Spanish and Portuguese versions read: THIS IS A TRUE COPY OF THE ORIGINAL WHICH IS IN THE POSSESSION OF THE TREATY DEPARTMENT OF THE MINISTRY OF FOREIGN AFFAIRS.)

(Signed) Bernardino H. Saguier Caballero Under-Secretary for Foreign Affairs

ANNEX V: Working Groups of the Common Market Group

For the purposes of co-ordinating macroeconomic and sectoral policies, the Common Market Group shall establish. within 30 days of its formation, the following working groups:

Sub-Group 1: Commercial issues

Sub-Group 2: Customs issues

Sub-Group 3: Technical standards

Sub-Group 4: Fiscal and monetary policies relating to trade

Sub-Group 5: Inland transport

Sub-Group 6: Maritime transport

Sub-Group 7: Industrial and technological policy

Sub-Group 8: Agricultural policy

Sub-Group 9: Energy policy

Sub-Group 10: Co-ordination of macroeconomic policies

(The Spanish and Portuguese versions read: THIS IS A TRUE COPY OF THE ORIGINAL WHICH IS IN THE POSSESSION OF THE TREATY DEPARTMENT OF THE MINISTRY OF FOREIGN AFFAIRS.)

(Signed) Bernardino H. Saguier Caballero Under-Secretary for Foreign Affairs

DECLARATION NO. 1 OF THE FOREIGN MINISTERS
OF THE MERCOSUR COUNTRIES

1. The Foreign Ministers of the Argentine Republic, the Federative Republic of Brazil, the Republic of Paraguay and the Eastern Republic of Uruguay, meeting at Asunción on the occasion of the signing of the Treaty establishing the common market or tho southern cone (MERCOSUR), emphasize the importance of the Treaty For achieving the objectives set forth in the Montevideo Treaty of 1980, within whose scope it falls.

2. In this context, the Foreign Ministers of the countries members of MERCOSUR are convinced that the prospects offered by the consolidation Of subregional groupings facilitate the development of economic ties and the integration of the region as a whole.

3. They reiterate their readiness to maintain and expand agreements concluded in the framework of the Latin American Integration Association. They will also consider, with the utmost interest, future applications to accede to the Treaty, in accordance with the rules established therein.

4. The Foreign Ministers of the MERCOSUR countries also reiterate their Governments' political determination that the instrument they are now signing should contribute to increased trade flows and to securing their economies D competitive place on the international market.

Asunción, 26 March 1991

DECLARATION NO. 2 OF THE FOREIGN MINISTERS
OF THE MERCOSUR COUNTRIES

The Foreign Ministers of the Argentine Republic, the Federative Republic of Brazil, the Republic of Paraguay and the Eastern Republic of Uruguay, meeting at Asunción on the occasion of the signing of the Treaty establishing the common market of the southern cone (MERCOSUR).

Considering and sharing the interest shown by the Republic of Bolivia in joining in efforts to establish the common market of the southern cone.

Considering tho close economic ties that exist between the five countries in the context of the Latin American Integration Association, the River Plate Basin and such integration projects as the Paraguay-Paraná (Puerto Cáceres-Nueva Palmira) waterway.

Hereby express their interest in exploring jointly with the Government of Bolivia the various approaches and alternatives that exist for formalizing its ties with MERCOSUR in due course, in accordance with the rules established in the Treaty of Asunción.

Asunción, 26 March 1991

DECLARATION NO. 3 OF THE FOREIGN MINISTERS OF THE MERCOSUR COUNTRIES

The Foreign Ministers of the Argentina Republic, the Federative Republic of Brazil, the Republic of Paraguay and the Eastern Republic of Uruguay, meeting at Asunción on the occasion of the signing of the Treaty establishing tho common market of the southern cone (MERCOSUR), considering the message sent by the President of the Republic of Chile, Mr. Patricio Alwyn, express their profound gratitude for the views set forth therein, which are an important display of support for the integration process being launched today.

The four Foreign Ministers share the views expressed by the President of the Republic of Chile concerning the historic importance of this Treaty for Latin American integration and warmly welcome the determination of the Chilean Government to strengthen its ties with the countries members of the common market of the southern cone.

Asunción, 26 March 1991

Appendix II

Protocol of Ouro Preto Regarding the Institutional Structure of MERCOSUR (December 17, 1994)

SUPPLEMENTARY PROTOCOL TO THE ASUNCIÓN AGREEMENT
ON THE INSTITUTIONAL STRUCTURE OF THE MERCOSUR
—OURO PRETO PROTOCOL—

The Argentine Republic, the Federative Republic of Brazil, the Republic of Paraguay and the Oriental Republic of Uruguay, hereinafter referred to as the "Party States:"

In compliance with Article 18 of the Treaty of Asunción of March 26, 1991;

Considering the importance of the advances already achieved and the implementation of a joint customs union as a stage in the creation of a common market;

Reaffirming the principles and objectives of the Treaty of Asunción and mindful of the need for special considerations towards the lesser developed countries and regions within the Mercosur;

Mindful of the dynamics implicit in the entire integration process and the consequent need to adapt the institutional structure of the Mercosur to changes that have taken place;

Recognizing the outstanding job performed by the existing administrative bodies during the transition period;

Agree:

Chapter I

Mercosur Structure

Article 1

The institutional structure of Mercosur shall comprise the following administrative bodies:

I—The Common Market Council ("CMC");

II—The Common Market Group ("CMG");

III—The Mercosur Commerce Commission ("MCC");

IV—The Joint Parliamentary Commission ("JPC");

V—The Socio-Economic Consultative Forum ("SECF")

VI—The Administrative Secretariat of Mercosur ("ASM")

Sole paragraph—Any auxiliary organs deemed necessary to attain the objectives of the integration process may be created under the terms of this Protocol.

Article 2

The Common Market Council, the Common Market Group and the Mercosur Commerce Commission are intergovernmental organizations with decision-making powers.

Section I

The Common Market Council

Article 3

The Common Market Council is the highest administrative body of the Mercosur. It is charged with political leadership of the integration process, and with making those decisions necessary to ensure that the objectives established by the Asunción Agreement are met and that the common market becomes fully established.

Article 4

The Common Market Council shall consist of the Ministers of Foreign Relations and Economics, or their equivalents, from each Party State.

Article 5

The Common Market Council's Chairmanship shall rotate among the Party States, in alphabetical order, for six-month terms.

Article 6

The Common Market Council shall meet as often as it deems necessary, but no less than once every six months, with participation by the Presidents of each Party State.

Article 7

The Ministers of Foreign Relations shall coordinate the meetings of the Common Market Council, and other Ministers or authorities at the cabinet level may be invited to participate.

Article 8

The following are functions and powers of the Common Market Council:

I—To ensure the implementation of the Treaty of Asunción, its Protocols and the agreements signed within its framework;

II—To formulate policies and promote necessary actions that will constitute the common market;

III—To assume the legal personality of Mercosur;

IV—To negotiate and sign agreements, on behalf of Mercosur, with third countries, groups of countries and international bodies. Said functions may be delegated by express mandate to the Common Market Group under the conditions set by Article XIV, paragraph VII;

V—To rule on proposals submitted to it by the Common Market Group;

VI—To organize the Ministers' meetings and rule on agreements submitted to it from those meetings;

VII—To create, modify or eliminate whatever administrative bodies it deems appropriate;

VIII—To clarify the contents and scope of its Decisions, when deemed appropriate;

IX—To nominate the Director of the Mercosur Administrative Secretariat;

X—To issue financial and budgetary Decisions;

XI—To approve the internal operating procedures of the Common Market Group.

Article 9

The Common Market Council shall issue Decisions that are binding on the Party States;

Section II

The Common Market Group

Article 10

The Common Market Group is the executive body of the Mercosur.

Article 11

The Common Market Group shall comprise four regular members and four alternates per country, appointed by their respective governments, and must include representatives of the Ministries of Foreign Relations and Economics (or their equivalents) and of the Central Banks. The Common Market Group shall be coordinated by the Ministers of Foreign Relations.

Article 12

The Common Market Group, in the course of drafting and proposing concrete measures in fulfillment of its duties, may convene representatives of other governmental bodies, or of the institutional structure of Mercosur, when it deems appropriate.

Article 13

The Common Market Group shall hold regular and special meetings as often as necessary, in accordance with its operating procedures.

Article 14

The Common Market Group has the following functions and powers:

I—To monitor, within its jurisdictional limits, compliance with the Treaty of Asunción, its Protocols, and agreements signed within its framework;

II—To propose draft Decisions to the Common Market Council;

III—To take the necessary measures for implementation of Decisions adopted by the Common Market Council;

IV—To set up work programs that further the establishment of the common market;

V—To create, modify or eliminate entities such as work subgroups and specialized meetings in order to fulfill its objectives;

VI—Within its jurisdiction, to rule on proposals or recommendations submitted to it by other Mercosur bodies;

VII—To negotiate agreements on behalf of Mercosur with third countries, groups of countries and international organizations, with participation by Representatives of all Party States, when the Common Market Council expressly so delegates, and within the limits established by special mandates issued for this purpose. When so mandated, the Common Market Group shall proceed to sign said agreements. The Common Market Group, when so authorized by the Common Market Council, may delegate the above powers to the Mercosur Commerce Commission;

VIII—To approve the budget and annual account statements presented by the Mercosur Administrative Secretariat;

IX—To adopt financial and budgetary Resolutions based on guidelines provided by the Council;

X—To submit its internal operating procedures to the Common Market Council;

XI—To organize the Common Market Council's meetings and prepare any reports and studies requested by it;

XII—To select the Director of the Mercosur Administrative Secretariat;

XIII—To supervise the activities of the Mercosur Administrative Secretariat;

XIV—To approve the internal operating procedures of the Commerce Commission and the Socio-Economic Consultative Forum;

Article 15

The Common Market Group shall issue Resolutions which shall be binding on the Party States.

Section III

The Mercosur Commerce Commission

Article 16

It shall be the duty of the Mercosur Commerce Commission, the body responsible for assisting the Common Market Group, to ensure the application of common trade policy instruments, as agreed by the Party States, for operation of the joint customs union, and to monitor and review any subjects and questions related to common trade policies, to trade within the Mercosur and with third countries.

Article 17

The Mercosur Commerce Commission shall comprise four regular members and four alternates per Party State, and shall be coordinated by the Ministers of Foreign Relations.

Article 18

The Mercosur Commerce Commission shall meet at least once a month, or as often as requested by the Common Market Group or any Party State.

Article 19

The following are functions and powers of the Mercosur Commerce Commission:

I—To monitor the application of common trade policy instruments in intra-Mercosur trade, trade with third countries, international organizations and in trade agreements.

II—To consider and rule on requests submitted by the Party States regarding the application and implementation of the common external tariff and other instruments of common trade policy;

III—To monitor the application of instruments of common trade policy within the Party States;

IV—To analyze the development of common trade policy instruments for operation of the joint customs union, and to submit Proposals in this regard to the Common Market Group;

V—To make decisions relating to the administration and application of the common external tariff and of the common trade policy instruments agreed to by the Party States;

VI—To report to the Common Market Group on the development and application of common trade policy instruments, the processing of requests received and the decisions adopted regarding such requests.

VII—To propose new rules, or modifications to existing Mercosur trade and customs rules, to the Common Market Group;

VIII—To propose tariff rate review for specific items of the common external tariff, including the consideration of cases covering new production activities within the Mercosur sphere;

IX—To set up, direct and supervise technical committees needed for adequate performance of its operations;

X—To carry out any tasks requested by the Common Market Group relating to common trade policy;

XI—To adopt internal operating procedures which shall be submitted to the Common Market Group for approval.

Article 20

The Mercosur Commerce Commission shall issue rulings either by Directives or Proposals. The Directives shall be binding on the Party States.

Article 21

In addition to the functions and powers set forth in Articles 16 and 19 of this Protocol, the Mercosur Commerce Commission shall be responsible for evaluating claims presented by the National Sections of the Mercosur Commerce Commission initiated by Party States or private parties—whether individuals or legal entities—relating to situations covered by Article 1 or 25 of the Brasilia Protocol, when said claims fall within its jurisdiction.

1. Consideration of the above-referenced claims by the Mercosur Commerce Commission shall not bar an action by the complaining Party State under the Brasilia Protocol for the Settlement of Disputes.

2. Claims originating under the situations established by this Article shall be processed in accordance with the procedures set forth in the Annex to this Protocol.

Section IV

The Joint Parliamentary Commission

Article 22

The Joint Parliamentary Commission is the body that represents the Parliaments of the Party States within the context of the Mercosur.

Article 23

The Joint Parliamentary Commission shall comprise an equal number of Parliamentary representatives from each Party State.

Article 24

Members of the Joint Parliamentary Commission shall be appointed by their respective national Parliaments, in accordance with their own internal procedures.

Article 25

The Joint Parliamentary Commission shall endeavor to expedite the applicable internal procedures of each Party State to ensure that the rules promulgated by Mercosur administrative organs created under Article 2 of this Protocol are put into effect promptly. In addition, it shall assist with legislative harmonization, when necessitated by the advancing integration process. The Council shall, when necessary, request that the Joint Parliamentary Commission analyze priority issues.

Article 26

The JPC shall submit Recommendations to the Common Market Council through the Common Market Group.

Article 27

The JPC shall adopt internal operating procedures.

Section V

The Socio-Economic Consultative Forum

Article 28

The Socio-Economic Consultative Forum is the body that represents the economic and social sectors, and shall comprise an equal number of representatives from each Party State.

Article 29

The Socio-Economic Consultative Forum shall serve a consultative function, and shall express its positions through Recommendations to the Common Market Group.

Article 30

The Socio-Economic Consultative Forum shall submit its operating procedures to the Common Market Group for approval.

Section VI

The Mercosur Administrative Secretariat

Article 31

The Mercosur shall have an Administrative Secretariat who provides operational support. The Mercosur Administrative Secretariat shall be responsible for providing services to the other Mercosur organs, and shall be permanently headquartered in the city of Montevideo.

Article 32

The Mercosur Administrative Secretariat shall perform the following functions:

I—Serve as the official archive for Mercosur documentation;

II—Publish and disseminate rules adopted within Mercosur's framework. In this context, it shall be responsible for:

 i) Procuring true Spanish and Portuguese translations, in coordination with the Party States, of all decisions adopted by the institutional bodies within the Mercosur structure, in conformity with the provisions of Article 39;

 ii) Publishing the Mercosur Official Gazette.

III—Arrange meeting logistics for the Common Market Council, the Common Market Group and the Mercosur Commerce Commission, and to the extent possible, for the other Mercosur subdivisions, when said meetings are held at its permanent headquarters. With respect to meetings held outside its permanent headquarters, the Mercosur Administrative Secretariat shall provide support to the State hosting the meeting;

IV—Report regularly to the Party States on the measures implemented by each country to incorporate into its legal system the rules promulgated by the Mercosur administrative organs established by Article 2 of this Protocol;

V—Register the national arbitrator and expert rosters, and perform other tasks, per the Brasilia Protocol of December 17, 1991;

VI—Perform those tasks requested by the Common Market Council, the Common Market Group and the Mercosur Commerce Commission;

VII—Prepare budget estimates and, once these have been approved by the Common Market Group, carry out all actions necessary to ensure their proper implementation;

VIII—File annual balance and activity reports with the Common Market Group;

Article 33

The Mercosur Administrative Secretariat shall be under the supervision of a Director who shall be a national of one of the Party States. The Director shall be elected by the Common Market Group on a rotating basis, after consultation with the Party States, and shall be designated by the Common Market Council. The Director shall serve a two-year term, without reelection.

Chapter II

Legal Status

Article 34

The Mercosur shall have legal status under international law.

Article 35

In the exercise of its functions, Mercosur may perform all necessary actions to achieve its objectives, including the signing contracts, buying and selling personal or real property, making court appearances and making conveyances.

Article 36

The Mercosur shall enter into agreements regarding its headquarters.

Chapter III

Decision-Making Procedures

Article 37

Decisions by the Mercosur administrative organs shall be taken by consensus, with all Party States present.

Chapter IV

Internal Application of Rules Promulgated by the Mercosur Organs

Article 38

The Party States formally agree to take all necessary measures to ensure compliance, within their respective territories, with the rules promulgated by the Mercosur administrative organs established by Article 2 of this Protocol.

Sole Paragraph—The Party States shall report to the Mercosur Administrative Secretariat on the measures taken to this end.

Article 39

The content of the Decisions of the Common Market Council, the Resolutions of the Common Market Group, the Directives of the Mercosur Commerce Commission and the Arbitral Awards in Dispute Resolutions shall be published, in full, in Spanish and Portuguese, in the Mercosur Official Gazette, together with any action which, in the opinion of the Common Market Council or the Common Market Group, requires official publicity.

Article 40

In order to ensure that the rules promulgated by the Mercosur administrative organs established by Article 2 of this Protocol come into effect simultaneously in all Party States, the following procedure shall be followed:

i) Once a rule has been approved, the Party States shall take the necessary measures to incorporate it into their national legal systems, and shall report said measures to the Mercosur Administrative Secretariat.

ii) Once each Party State has reported incorporation of same into its respective national legal system, the Mercosur Administrative Secretariat shall notify all State Parties.

iii) The rules shall become effective simultaneously in all Party States 30 days after the Mercosur Administrative Secretariat has given notice in accordance with the preceding subparagraph. With this objective in mind, the Party States shall, within the time limit set forth above, publish the entry in force of the above mentioned norms in their respective official gazettes.

Chapter V

Legal Sources of the Mercosur

Article 41

The legal sources of Mercosur are:

I—The Treaty of Asunción, its protocols, and additional or supplementary instruments;

II—Agreements signed within the framework of the Treaty of Asunción and the protocols thereto;

III—The Decisions of the Common Market Council, the Resolutions of the Common Market Group and the Directives of the Mercosur Commerce Commission adopted since the effective date of the Treaty of Asunción.

Article 42

The rules promulgated by the Mercosur administrative organs established by Article 2 of this Protocol shall be binding, and, when necessary, shall be incorporated into the national legal systems of each Party State in accordance with the procedures set forth by each country's legislation.

Chapter VI

Dispute Resolution System

Article 43

Disputes arising among the Party States concerning the interpretation, application or non-implementation of the provisions of the Treaty of Asunción, the agreements signed within its framework, the Decisions of the Common Market Council, the Resolutions of the Common Market Group, or the Directives of the Mercosur Commerce Commission shall be subject to the dispute settlement procedures set forth in the Brasilia Protocol of December 17, 1991.

Sole Paragraph—The Directives of the Mercosur Commerce Commission are hereby incorporated into Articles 19 and 25 of the Brasilia Protocol.

Article 44

Before the Common External Tariff convergence process is concluded, the Party States shall review the current Mercosur dispute resolution system with the aim of adopting the permanent system referred to in paragraph 3 of Annex III to the Treaty of Asunción.

Chapter VII

Budget

Article 45

The Mercosur Administrative Secretariat shall have a budget to cover its operating expenses as well as expenses incurred by order of the Common Market Group. Said budget shall be funded by contributions from each Party State, in equal shares.

Chapter VIII

Languages

Article 46

Spanish and Portuguese are the official languages of Mercosur. Official versions of working documents shall be written in the language of the country hosting the meeting.

Chapter IX

Review

Article 47

Party States, as they deem appropriate, shall convene diplomatic conferences for purpose of reviewing the institutional structure of Mercosur established by this Protocol, as well as the specific functions of each of its subdivisions.

Chapter X

Validity

Article 48

This Protocol, which constitutes an integral part of the Treaty of Asunción, shall have indefinite duration, and shall come into force 30 days after the date of deposit of the third ratification instrument. This Protocol and its ratification instruments shall be deposited with the Government of Paraguay.

Article 49

The Government of the Republic of Paraguay shall notify the governments of the other Party States of the date of deposit of the ratification instruments, and of this Protocol's effective date.

Article 50

With regard to accession or denunciation, the rules established by the Treaty of Asunción shall apply in their entirety to this Protocol. Accession to or denunciation of the Treaty of Asunción, or this Protocol, shall constitute, *ipso jure,* accession to or denunciation of the Treaty of Asunción and this Protocol.

Chapter XI

Transitional Provisions

Article 51

The institutional structure provided by the Treaty of Asunción of March 26, 1991, and the administrative organs created thereby, shall remain in place until this Protocol comes into force.

Chapter XII

General Provisions

Article 52

This Protocol shall be referred to as the "Ouro Preto Protocol."

Article 53

All provisions of the Treaty of Asunción of March 26, 1991 that conflict with the terms of this Protocol, and with the Decisions adopted by the Common Market Council during the transition period, are hereby repealed.

Signed in the City of Ouro Preto, Federative Republic of Brazil, on the seventeenth day of the month of December of nineteen hundred ninety four, in one original, in Portuguese and Spanish, both texts being equally official.

The Government of Paraguay shall send authenticated copies of this Protocol to the governments of the other Party States.

FOR THE ARGENTINE REPUBLIC, Carlos Saul Menem Guido Di Tella

FOR THE FEDERATIVE REPUBLIC OF BRAZIL, Itamar Franco Celso L.N. Amorin

FOR THE REPUBLIC OF PARAGUAY, Juan Carlos Wasmosy Luis Maria Ramirez Boettner

FOR THE ORIENTAL REPUBLIC OF URUGUAY, Luis Alberto Lacalle Herrera Sergio Abreu

ANNEX TO THE OURO PRETO PROTOCOL
GENERAL PROCEDURES FOR CLAIMS BROUGHT BEFORE THE MERCOSUR COMMERCE COMMISSION

Article 1

Claims submitted by the National Sections of the Mercosur Commerce Commission that were initiated by a Party State, or private party—be it an individual or legal entity—, in accordance with Article 21 of the Ouro Preto Protocol shall be subject to the procedures set forth in this Annex.

Article 2

The Complaining Party State shall submit its claim to the Pro-Tempore Chair of the Mercosur Commerce Commission, who shall take the necessary steps to include the item on the Agenda of the next Mercosur Commerce Commission meeting, providing at least one-week's advance notice. If no decision is reached at said meeting, the Mercosur Commerce Commission shall, without taking any further action, forward the record to a Technical Committee.

Article 3

The Technical Committee shall prepare and submit to the Mercosur Commerce Commission a joint opinion on the issue within thirty (30) calendar days. Said opinion, or the conclusions of each expert member of the Technical Committee, if no joint opinion is reached, shall be taken into consideration by the Mercosur Commerce Commission in reaching a decision on the claim.

Article 4

The Mercosur Commerce Commission shall rule on the claim at its first regular meeting following receipt of the joint opinion, or should there be none, then the experts' conclusions. A special meeting may also be convened for this purpose.

Article 5

If a consensus cannot be reached at the first meeting referred to in Article 4, the Mercosur Commerce Commission shall submit to the Common Market Group the various alternatives proposed, together with the joint opinion or the conclusions of the experts on the Technical Committee, in order to reach a decision on the referred claim. The Common Market Group shall rule within thirty (30) days of receipt by the Pro-Tempore Chair of the proposals submitted by the Mercosur Commerce Commission.

Article 6

If there is agreement that the claim has merit, the Responding Party State shall adopt the measures approved by the Mercosur Commerce Commission or the

Common Market Group, as the case may be. In either case, the Mercosur Commerce Commission or, subsequently, the Common Market Group, shall fix a reasonable time period for the implementation of said measures. If this period expires without the Responding State's compliance with the decision adopted by either the Mercosur Commerce Commission or the Common Market Group, the Complaining State may resort directly to the procedures set forth in Chapter IV of the Brasilia Protocol.

Article 7

If no consensus is reached by the Mercosur Commerce Commission, and subsequently, by the Common Market Group, or if the Responding State does not comply with the decision within the time period set by Article 6, the Complaining State may resort directly to the procedures established in Chapter IV of the Brasilia Protocol, and shall inform the Mercosur Administrative Secretariat accordingly.

The Arbitral Panel, before ruling, and within fifteen (15) days from being convened, shall announce the interim measures it deems appropriate under Article 18 of the Brasilia Protocol.

Appendix III

Protocol of Brasilia for the Solution of Controversies

DECISIONS OF THE COMMON MARKET COUNCIL

MERCOSUR/CMD/DEC NO. 01/91—ANNEX—Brasilia Protocol for the Settlement of Disputes

BRASILIA PROTOCOL FOR THE SETTLEMENT OF DISPUTES

The Argentine Republic, The Federative Republic of Brazil, the Republic of Paraguay and the Oriental Republic of Uruguay, hereinafter the "Party States";

In compliance with the provisions of Article 3 and Annex III to the Treaty of Asunción subscribed to on March 26, 1991 and according to which the Party States commit to adopting a Dispute Resolution System to be in effect during the transition period;

RECOGNIZING

the importance of having an effective instrument to ensure implementation of said Treaty and the provisions deriving from it;

CONVINCED

that the Dispute Resolution System contained herein shall contribute to the strengthening of relations among the Parties based on principles of justice and equity;

AGREE as follows:

CHAPTER 1

SCOPE OF APPLICATION

Article 1.

Disputes arising among the Party States concerning the interpretation, application or non-implementation of the Treaty of Asunción, the agreements entered into within its framework, the Decisions of the Common Market Council and the Resolutions of the Common Market Group, shall be submitted to the settlement procedures established herein.

CHAPTER II
DIRECT NEGOTIATIONS

Article 2.

The Party States involved in a dispute shall attempt to resolve it, first and foremost, by direct negotiations.

Article 3.

1. Party States involved in a dispute shall inform the Common Market Group, through the Administrative Secretariat, concerning the steps that take place during negotiations and the results thereof.

2. Direct negotiations shall not, absent the parties' agreement otherwise, exceed a term of fifteen (15) days from the date that a Party State raises the dispute.

CHAPTER III
INTERVENTION BY THE COMMON MARKET GROUP

Article 4.

1. If agreement is not reached through direct negotiations, or if the dispute is only partially resolved, any Party State involved in a dispute may submit the matter to the Common Market Group for consideration.

2. The Common Market Group shall evaluate the situation, allowing the disputing parties to present their respective positions and requiring, when deemed necessary, the advice of experts selected from the roster referred to in Article 30 of this Protocol.

3. The expenses incurred in connection with said expert advice shall be shared equally by the Party States involved in the dispute, or in whatever proportion the Common Market Group determines.

Article 5.

At the close of these proceedings, the Common Market Group shall make recommendations to the Party States involved in the dispute aimed at resolving the dispute.

Article 6.

The proceedings described in this Chapter shall not last more than thirty (30) days from the date the dispute was submitted to the Common Market Group for consideration.

CHAPTER IV
ARBITRAL PROCEEDINGS

Article 7.

1. Where a dispute has not been resolved through application of the procedures outlined in Chapters II and III, any Party State involved in the dispute may inform the Administrative Secretariat of its intention to resort to arbitration proceedings under this Protocol.

2. The Administrative Secretariat shall immediately so notify the other State or States involved in the dispute and the Common Market Group, and shall undertake whatever steps are required for elaboration of the proceedings.

Article 8.

The Party States stipulate that the Arbitral Panel has exclusive jurisdiction *ipso facto* and without necessity of special agreement in each case it is constituted to hear and resolve all disputes referred to in this Protocol.

Article 9.

1. The arbitration proceedings shall be conducted before an ad hoc Panel comprising three (3) arbitrators from the roster referred to in Article 10.

2. The arbitrators shall be designated as follows:

Each Party State involved in the dispute shall designate one (1) arbitrator. The third arbitrator, who cannot be a national of the Party States involved in the dispute, shall be designated by mutual agreement of the Party States involved in the dispute and shall preside over the Arbitration Panel. The panelists shall be designated within fifteen (15) days after notice by the Administrative Secretariat to the Party States involved in the dispute that one of them intends to resort to arbitration.

Each Party State involved in the dispute shall also appoint an alternate arbitrator, with the same qualifications, to replace the permanent arbitrator in the event of his inability or disqualification from the Arbitral Panel, either at the time it is composed or during the proceedings.

Article 10.

Each Party State shall designate ten (10) arbitrators who shall comprise a roster to be registered with the Administrative Secretariat. The roster, and its successive modifications, shall be made known to the Party States.

Article 11.

If a Party State involved in the dispute fails to appoint its arbitrator by the deadline set in Article 9, the Administrative Secretariat shall appoint one from that State's panelists, in order of listing on the respective roster.

Article 12.

1. If the Party States involved in the dispute cannot agree regarding selection of the third arbitrator by the deadline set by Article 9, the Administrative Secretariat, at the request of any of them, shall proceed to designate him by lot from a roster of sixteen (16) arbitrators drawn up by the Common Market Group.

2. Said roster, which shall also be registered with the Administrative Secretariat, shall be composed in equal parts by nationals of the Party States and of other countries.

Article 13.

The arbitrators that comprise the rosters referred to in Articles 10 and 12 shall be jurists of recognized expertise in the areas that might be subject of disputes.

Article 14.

If two or more Party States have the same position in the dispute, they shall unify their representation before the Arbitral Panel and shall designate an arbitrator by mutual agreement, within the period established by article 9.2 i).

Article 15.

The Arbitral Panel for each such dispute shall establish its headquarters in one of the Party States and shall adopt its own rules of procedure. Said rules shall guarantee that each party involved in the dispute has ample opportunity to be heard and present its proofs and allegations and shall also ensure that proceedings are conducted in an expeditious manner.

Article 16.

The Party States involved in the dispute shall inform the Arbitral Panel about proceedings that have taken place prior to the arbitration proceedings, and shall file a brief statement of the legal or factual grounds for their respective positions.

Article 17.

The Party States involved in the dispute shall designate their representatives before the Arbitral Panel and may designate consultants for the defense of their rights.

Article 18.

1. The Arbitration Panel may, at the request of the interested party and to the extent that well-founded grounds exist that continuing the current situation would cause severe and irreparable damage to one of the parties, enter interim measures deemed appropriate under the circumstances and in accordance with the terms set by the Panel to prevent said damage.

2. The Party States involved in the dispute shall implement, immediately or by the deadline set by the Arbitral Panel, any provisional measures until the award referred to in Article 20 is rendered.

Article 19.

1. The Arbitration Panel shall decide the dispute on the basis of the provisions of the Treaty of Asunción, the agreements entered into within its framework, the Decisions of the Common Market Council, and the Resolutions of the Common Market Group, as well as applicable principles and provisions of International Law.

2. This provision does not restrict the authority of the Arbitral Panels to decide a dispute *ex aequo et bono*, if the parties so agree.

Article 20.

1. The Arbitral Panel shall render a written decision within a sixty (60) day period, extendible a maximum of thirty (30) days, from the date the Presiding Arbitrator was appointed.

2. Arbitral Panel awards shall be adopted by majority vote, shall state the reasons therefor and shall be signed by the Panel Chair and other panelists. Members of the Arbitral Panel may not write dissenting opinions and shall maintain voting confidentiality.

Article 21.

1. Arbitral Panel awards are final and binding on the disputing Party States upon receipt of the respective notices and, with respect to same, shall have *res judicata* effect.

2. Awards shall be implemented within fifteen (15) days, unless the Arbitral Panel sets a different deadline.

Article 22.

1. Any Party State involved in the dispute may, within fifteen (15) days after notification of the award, request clarification of same, or an interpretation of the manner in which it should be implemented.

2. The Arbitral Panel shall issue the requested clarification within the following fifteen (15) days.

3. The Arbitral Panel may suspend implementation of the award, if the circumstances so merit, until it rules on any such request.

Article 23.

If a Party State fails to implement the Arbitral Panel's award within the thirty (30)-day deadline, the other Party States involved in the dispute are entitled to adopt temporary compensatory measures, such as the suspension of benefits or other equivalent measures, tending to induce the award's implementation.

Article 24.

1. Each Party State involved in the dispute shall cover the expenses incurred for the services of the arbitrator it appointed.

2. The Chair of the Arbitral Panel shall receive pecuniary compensation, which, together with the other expenses of the Arbitral Panel, shall be paid in equal parts by the disputing Party States, unless the Panel decides to allocate them differently.

CHAPTER V

PRIVATE CLAIMS

Article 25.

The proceedings established by this Chapter shall apply to claims brought by private parties (individuals or legal entities) in connection with the sanction or application, by any of the Party States, of legal or administrative measures having a restrictive, discriminatory or unfairly competitive effect, in violation of the Treaty of Asunción, the agreements entered into within its framework, the Decisions of the Common Market Council, or the Resolutions of the Common Market Group.

Article 26.

1. The affected private parties shall file their claims with the National Section of the Common Market Group in the Party State of their usual residence or principal place of business.

2. The private parties shall adduce evidence that permits the aforementioned National Section to determine the likelihood of the violation, and the existence or threat of harm.

Article 27.

1. Unless the claim refers to an issue that has been the subject of dispute resolution proceedings under Chapters II, III or IV of this Protocol, the National Section of the Common Market Group that allowed the claim pursuant to Article 26 of this Chapter may, in consultation with the affected private party:

Initiate direct contact with the National Section of the Common Market Group of the Party State charged with the violation in order to seek, through consultation, an immediate resolution of the issue raised; or

submit the claim summarily to the Common Market Group.

Article 28.

If the matter has not been resolved within fifteen (15) days from notice of the claim under Article 27 a), the National Section giving the notice may, at the affected private party's request, submit it summarily to the Common Market Group.

Article 29.

1. Upon receipt of the claim, the Common Market Group shall evaluate, at its first meeting thereafter, the grounds forming the basis of the National Section's allowance of the claim. If it concludes that the requirements necessary to allow the claim to proceed have not been satisfied, it shall summarily reject the claim.

2. If the Common Market Group does not reject the claim, it shall immediately proceed to convene a group of experts who shall issue an opinion regarding the claim's legitimacy within a non-extendible thirty (30)-day period from the date of their appointment.

3. Within that time period, the group of experts shall provide the claiming private party and the State against whom the claim has been filed the opportunity to be heard and to present their arguments.

Article 30.

1. The group of experts referred to in Article 29 shall comprise three (3) members appointed by the Common Market Group, or, in the absence of agreement regarding one or more experts, they shall be chosen by vote of the Party States from among the members of a roster of twenty-four (24) experts. The Administrative Secretariat shall inform the Common Market Group of the name of the expert or experts that received the most votes. In the latter event, and unless the Common Market Group decides differently, one of the designated experts shall not be a national of the Responding State nor of the State where the private party filed its claim pursuant to Article 26.

2. For purposes of drawing up a roster of experts, each Party State shall designate six (6) persons of recognized expertise in the areas that might be subject of disputes. Said roster shall be registered with the Administrative Secretariat.

Article 31.

The expenses incurred for the services of the expert group shall be paid in shares allotted by the Common Market Group, or, in the absence of agreement, in equal shares by the Parties directly involved.

Article 32.

The group of experts shall submit its report to the Common Market Group. If said report verifies the legitimacy of the claim filed against a Party State, any other Party State may require it to adopt corrective measures or to withdraw the challenged measures. If this requirement does not yield results within fifteen (15) days, the Party State making same may have direct recourse to arbitration proceedings under the conditions established in Chapter IV of this Protocol.

CHAPTER VI

FINAL PROVISIONS

Article 33.

This Protocol, an integral part of the Treaty of Asunción, shall become effective once the four Party States have filed their respective ratification instruments. Said instruments shall be filed with the government of the Republic of Paraguay, who shall notify the governments of the other Party States of the filing date.

Article 34.

This Protocol shall remain in effect until the Permanent Dispute Settlement System for the Common Market referred to in paragraph 3 of Annex III of the Treaty of Asunción enters into effect.

Article 35.

Accession by a State to the Treaty of Asunción shall imply *ipso jure* accession to this Protocol.

Article 36.

The official languages in all proceedings under this Protocol shall be Spanish and Portuguese, as applicable.

Entered into in the City of Brasilia on the seventeenth day of the month of December of the year nineteen hundred ninety one in one original in Spanish and Portuguese, both texts being equally authentic. The government of the Republic of Paraguay shall be the depository for this Protocol and shall send duly authenticated copies of same to the governments of the other Party States.

FOR THE GOVERNMENT OF THE ARGENTINE REPUBLIC:

CARLOS SAUL MENEM

GUIDO DI TELLA

FOR THE GOVERNMENT OF THE FEDERATIVE REPUBLIC OF BRAZIL:

FERNANDO COLLOR

FRANCISCO REZEK

FOR THE GOVERNMENT OF THE REPUBLIC OF PARAGUAY:

ANDRES RODRÍGUEZ

ALEXIS FRUTOS VAESKEN

FOR THE GOVERNMENT OF THE ORIENTAL REPUBLIC OF URUGUAY:

LUIS ALBERTO LACALLE HERRERA

HECTOR GROS ESPIELL

Appendix IV

Olivos Protocol for the Solution of Controversies

OLIVOS PROTOCOL
1. FOR THE SETTLEMENT OF DISPUTES IN THE MERCOSUR

==

The Argentine Republic, the Federative Republic of Brazil, the Republic of Paraguay and the Oriental Republic of Uruguay, hereinafter the "Party States";

BEARING IN MIND the Treaty of Asunción, the Brasilia Protocol and the Ouro Preto Protocol;

RECOGNIZING that as the integration process within the Mercosur evolves, the dispute resolution system requires improvement;

CONSIDERING the need to consistently and systematically ensure the correct interpretation, application and implementation of the fundamental instruments of the integration process and of the body of rules of the Mercosur;

CONVINCED of the importance of making specific modifications to the dispute resolution system so as to consolidate jurisdiction and authority within the Mercosur;

AGREE as follows:

CHAPTER I
DISPUTES AMONG PARTY STATES
Article 1
Scope of Application

1. Disputes arising among Party States regarding the interpretation, application, breach or non-implementation of the provisions of the Treaty of Asunción, the Ouro Preto Protocol, the protocols and agreements entered into within the framework of the Treaty of Asunción, the Decisions of the Common Market Council, the Resolutions of the Common Market Group, and the Directives of the Mercosur Commerce Commission shall be subject to the procedures established herein.

2. Disputes falling within the scope of application of this Protocol that could also be subject to the dispute resolution system of the World Commerce Orga-

nization, or to other preferential trade schemes to which the Mercosur Party States belong individually, shall be amenable to presentation in either forum at the election of the Complaining Party. Notwithstanding the above, the parties involved in a dispute shall be able to set the forum by mutual agreement.

Once a dispute resolution proceeding has commenced in conformity with the preceding paragraph, none of the parties shall have recourse to the procedures established by the other fora with regard to the same dispute, as defined by Article 14 of this Protocol.

Notwithstanding the above, the Common Market Council shall regulate any aspects related to forum selection within the framework of this paragraph's provisions.

CHAPTER II
PROCEDURES REGARDING TECHNICAL ASPECTS
Article 2
Establishing the Procedures

1. When deemed necessary, expedited procedures may be established to resolve disagreements among Party States about technical aspects governed by instruments of common trade policy.

2. The rules of operation, scope of such procedures and the nature of the pronouncements issued in accordance with them shall be defined and approved by Decision of the Common Market Council.

CHAPTER III
ADVISORY OPINIONS
Article 3
Requesting Procedures

The Common Market Council may establish a process regarding requests for advisory opinions to the Permanent Appelate Tribunal setting their scope and procedures.

CHAPTER IV
DIRECT NEGOTIATIONS
Article 4
Negotiations

Party States involved in a dispute shall first endeavor to resolve it by direct negotiations.

Article 5
Procedures and Time Limits

1. Absent agreement otherwise by the disputing parties, direct negotiations shall not exceed fifteen (15) days from the date that the party initiating the dispute gives notice.

2. The disputing Party States shall notify the Common Market Group, through the Mercosur Administrative Secretariat, of the negotiation proceedings and the results obtained.

CHAPTER V
INTERVENTION BY THE COMMON MARKET GROUP
Article 6
Optional Procedures before the Common Market Group

1. If direct negotiations do not result in an agreement, or if the dispute is only partially resolved, any of the disputing Party States may directly proceed to initiate arbitration proceedings pursuant to Chapter VI.

2. Without waiving the provisions of the preceding section, the Party States involved in the dispute may, if they unanimously agree, submit the matter to the Common Market Group for its consideration.

i) In this event, the Common Market Group shall evaluate the situation, giving the disputing parties the opportunity to present their respective positions, and requiring, when it deems necessary, the opinion of experts selected from the roster referred to in Article 43 of this Protocol.

ii) the costs incurred in connection with these opinions shall be paid by the Party States involved in the dispute in equal parts, or in whatever proportion the Common Market Group sets.

3. A third-party State, not involved in the dispute, may also bring the dispute before the Common Market Group for consideration, if requiring such proceeding is justified at the close of direct negotiations. In that event, the arbitration proceeding commenced by the claiming Party State shall not be interrupted, absent agreement by the Party States involved in the dispute.

Article 7
Powers of the Common Market Group

1. If the dispute is submitted to the Common Market Group by the Party States involved in the dispute, it shall, if possible, make detailed and specific recommendations aimed at resolving the dispute.

2. If the dispute is brought before the Common Market Group at the request of a third-party State, the Common Market Group may make comments or recommendations regarding the matter.

Article 8
Time Limits for Intervention and Pronouncements
by the Common Market Group

The proceedings described in this Chapter shall not last more than thirty (30) days from the date of the meeting at which the dispute was submitted to the Common Market Group.

CHAPTER VI
AD HOC ARBITRATION PROCEEDINGS
Article 9
Commencement of the Arbitration Stage

1. When a dispute has not been resolved in accordance with the procedures set out in Chapters IV and V, any State that is party to the dispute may inform the Mercosur Administrative Secretariat of its decision to resort to the arbitration proceedings established by this Chapter.

2. The Mercosur Administrative Secretariat shall in turn immediately notify such decision to the other State or States involved in the dispute and to the Common Market Group.

3. The Mercosur Administrative Secretariat shall undertake whatever administrative steps are required for the proceedings.

Article 10
Composition of the Ad Hoc Arbitration Panel

1. The arbitration proceedings shall be conducted before an Ad Hoc Panel comprised of three (3) arbitrators.

2. The arbitrators shall be appointed as follows:

i) Each disputing State shall designate one (1) permanent arbitrator from the roster established by Article 11.1, within fifteen (15) days of notification by the Mercosur Administrative Secretariat to the Party States involved in the dispute that one of them intends to resort to arbitration.

It shall simultaneously designate, from this same roster, one (1) alternate arbitrator to replace the permanent one in case of inability or disqualification during any stage of the arbitration proceeding.

ii) If a Party State involved in the dispute fails to name its arbitrators within the period indicated in subsection 2 i), the Mercosur Administrative Secretariat shall select them by lot within two (2) days after expiration of the first period, from among that State's arbitrators on the roster established under Article 11.1.

3. The Chair of the Arbitral Panel shall be designated as follows:

i) The Party States involved in the dispute shall appoint the third arbitrator by mutual agreement, from the roster mentioned in Article 11.2 iii) within fifteen (15) days of notice to the Party States involved in the dispute by the Mercosur Administrative Secretariat that one of them intends to resort to arbitration. The third arbitrator shall preside over the Ad Hoc Arbitration Panel.

Simultaneously, the Party States involved in the dispute shall designate an alternate arbitrator from the same roster to replace the permanent arbitrator in case of inability or disqualification during any stage of the arbitration proceedings.

The Panel Chair and alternate cannot be nationals of any of the Party States involved in the dispute.

ii) If the Party States involved in the dispute fail to agree within the specified time regarding selection of the third arbitrator, the Mercosur Administrative Secretariat, at the request of any Party, shall designate such panelist by lot from the roster established pursuant to Article 11.2 iii), excluding nationals from the Party States involved in the dispute.

iii) Individuals designated to act as third arbitrators shall respond within three (3) days of notification of their designation regarding their willingness and ability to act as panelists in the dispute.

4. The Mercosur Administrative Secretariat shall notify the arbitrators of their appointment.

Article 11

Roster of Arbitrators

1. Each Party State shall draw up a roster comprised of twelve (12) arbitrators to be registered with the Mercosur Administrative Secretariat. This roster, accompanied by a detailed *curriculum vitae* of each arbitrator, shall be distributed simultaneously to the other Party States and the Mercosur Administrative Secretariat.

i) Each Party State may request additional information regarding the persons designated by the other Party States to comprise the roster described in the preceding paragraph, within thirty (30) days from the date of notification.

ii) The Mercosur Administrative Secretariat shall provide the consolidated roster of arbitrators for Mercosur, as well as its successive modifications, to the Party States.

2. Each Party State shall likewise propose four (4) candidates for the roster of third arbitrators. At least one arbitrator selected by each Party State for inclusion in the roster shall not be a national of any Party State of Mercosur.

i) The other Party States shall be provided the roster, as well as the *curriculum vitae* of each proposed candidate, through the Pro Tempore Presidency.

ii) Each Party State may request additional information regarding the panelists proposed by the other Party States, or present justifiable objections to the selected candidates pursuant to the criteria set by Article 35, within thirty (30) days of receiving notice.

The objections shall be communicated through the Pro Tempore Presidency to the proposing Party State. If no agreement has been reached within thirty (30) days of notice, the objection shall be upheld.

iii) The consolidated roster of third arbitrators, as well as its successive modifications, together with the curriculum vitae of each arbitrator, shall be conveyed by the Pro Tempore Presidency to the Mercosur Administrative Secretariat, who shall register it and notify the Party States.

Article 12

Representatives and Consultants

The disputing Party States shall designate their representatives before the Ad Hoc Arbitration Panel and may also designate counsel for the defense of their rights.

Article 13

Joint Representation

If two or more Party States allege the same position in a dispute, they may consolidate their representation before the Ad Hoc Arbitration Panel and shall designate an arbitrator by mutual agreement, within the period established by Article 10.2 i).

Article 14

Subject of the Dispute

1. The subject of the dispute shall be determined by the written demand and answer thereto filed with the Ad Hoc Arbitration Panel, and shall not be expanded subsequently.

2. The allegations made by the parties in the documents mentioned in the preceding paragraph shall be based on issues considered in earlier stages conducted under this Protocol and under the Appendix to the Ouro Preto Protocol.

3. Within the documents mentioned in paragraph 1 of this Article, the Party States involved in the dispute shall provide the Ad Hoc Arbitration Panel with a description of any proceedings taking place prior to the arbitration proceedings, and shall file a statement of the legal and factual grounds for their respective positions.

Article 15

Interim Measures

1. The Ad Hoc Arbitration Panel, at the request of the interested party, and to the extent a well-founded presumption exists that continuing the current situation would cause serious and irreparable harm to one of the disputing parties, may take whatever interim measures it deems necessary to prevent said injury.

2. The Panel may, at any time, repeal such measures.

3. Where an petition for review of the Arbitral Award is filed, any interim measures not repealed prior to the Award shall remain in effect until the first

meeting of the Permanent Appellate Tribunal, at which time it shall decide whether the measures shall continue or cease.

Article 16

Arbitral Award

The Ad Hoc Arbitration Panel shall render its decision within a sixty—(60)—day period, which period may, at the Panel's discretion, be extended up to an additional thirty (30) days from the date that the Mercosur Administrative Secretariat notifies the Parties and other arbitrators that the Panel Chairperson has accepted the appointment.

CHAPTER VII

REVIEW PROCEDURES

Article 17

Appeal for Review

1. Within fifteen (15) days from notification of said award, any disputing Party may request that the Permanent Appellate Tribunal review the Ad Hoc Arbitral Panel's award.

2 The appeal shall be limited to those issues of law involved in the dispute and the judicial interpretations developed in the Ad Hoc Arbitral Panel's award.

3. The awards of the Ad Hoc Arbitral Panel based on principles of *ex aequo et bono* shall not be made the subject of review.

4. The Mercosur Administrative Secretariat shall take charge of the administrative functions entrusted to it for management of the proceedings and shall keep the disputing Party States and the Common Market Group informed.

Article 18

Composition of the Permanent Appellate Tribunal

1. The Permanent Appellate Tribunal shall comprise five (5) arbitrators.

2. Each Mercosur Party State shall designate one (1) arbitrator and an alternate for a period of two (2) years, renewable for a maximum of two consecutive periods.

3. The fifth arbitrator shall be a national of one of the Mercosur Party States, and shall be appointed for a three (3)-year period that shall be non-renewable except as the Party States may otherwise agree. Said arbitrator shall be elected unanimously by the Party States from the roster referred to below, at least three (3) months before the expiration of the fifth arbitrator's term. None of the above shall affect the provisions of section 4 of this Article.

If unanimity cannot be reached, the Mercosur Administrative Secretariat shall make the appointment by lot from among the roster panelists within two (2) days from the above deadline.

The roster for designating the fifth arbitrator shall consist of eight (8) members. Each Party State shall propose two (2) members who shall be nationals of Mercosur countries.

4. The Party States may define, by mutual agreement, other criteria for designation of the fifth arbitrator.

5. At least three (3) months before the end of the arbitrators' term, the Party States shall announce whether they will reappoint the current arbitrators or propose new candidates.

6. In the event that an arbitrator's term expires while hearing a dispute, the arbitrator shall remain in office until it concludes.

7. The provisions of Article 11.2 shall apply, when appropriate, to proceedings described in this Article.

Article 19

Permanent Availability

Upon acceptance of their appointments, members of the Permanent Appellate Tribunal shall be permanently available to act whenever convened.

Article 20

Operation of the Tribunal

1. Where the dispute involves two Party States, the Tribunal shall comprise three (3) arbitrators. Two (2) arbitrators shall be nationals, respectively, of each Party State involved in the dispute. The Director of the Mercosur Administrative Secretariat shall appoint the third arbitrator by lot from among the remaining arbitrators who are not nationals of the Party States involved in the dispute. This third arbitrator shall chair the Tribunal. The Chair shall be designated the day after the petition for review is filed, on which date the Tribunal shall be duly constituted for all intents and purposes.

2. Where there are more than two disputing Party States, the Tribunal shall comprise five (5) arbitrators.

3. The Party States may, by mutual consent, define other criteria for the operation of the Tribunal established pursuant to this Article.

Article 21

Response to the Appeal for Review and Award Deadline

1. Once an appeal has been filed, the opposing party shall be entitled to respond within fifteen (15) days of receiving notice of same.

2. The Permanent Appellate Tribunal shall rule on the appeal within thirty (30) days from the filing date of the response referred to above, or from the deadline for filing same, as the case may be. At the Tribunal's discretion, the thirty (30) day deadline may be extended up to an additional fifteen (15) days.

Article 22

Scope of the Ruling

1. The Permanent Appellate Tribunal may affirm, modify or reverse the legal grounds and awards of the Ad Hoc Arbitral Panel.

2. Awards rendered by the Permanent Appellate Tribunal shall be conclusive and shall govern over awards rendered by the Ad Hoc Arbitral Panel.

Article 23

Direct Access to the Permanent Appellate Tribunal

1. The Parties involved in the dispute may, at the conclusion of proceedings pursuant to Articles 4 and 5 of this Protocol, expressly agree to submit the matter directly and without right of appeal to the Permanent Appellate Tribunal, in which case it shall have the same jurisdiction as an Ad Hoc Arbitral Panel, and Articles 9, 12, 13, 14, 15 and 16 of this Protocol shall apply.

2. In this event, the Permanent Appellate Tribunal's award shall be binding on the disputing Party States upon receipt of the corresponding notice, shall not be susceptible to review and, with respect to the parties, shall have *res judicata* effect.

Article 24

Special and Emergency Measures

The Common Market Council may establish special proceedings to attend to special emergency cases that might cause irreparable damage to the Parties.

CHAPTER VIII

ARBITRAL AWARDS

Article 25

Adoption of Awards

The awards of the Ad Hoc Arbitral Panel and the Permanent Appellate Tribunal shall be adopted by majority vote, shall state the reasons therefor and shall be signed by the Chair and other panelists. The arbitrators may not write dissenting opinions and shall maintain voting confidentiality. Deliberations shall also be confidential and shall remain so at all times.

Article 26

Binding Effect of the Awards

1. All Ad Hoc Arbitral Panels' awards are binding on the disputing Party States upon their notification and, with respect to the Parties, shall have *res judicata* effect if no appeal has been filed by the deadline specified in Article 17.1 for filing of same.

2. The Permanent Appellate Tribunal's awards are final and binding on the disputing Party States upon their notification, and shall have *res judicata* effect with respect to them.

Article 27

Compulsory Implementation of Awards

Awards shall be implemented in the form and with the scope they were rendered. The adoption of compensatory measures under this Protocol shall not discharge a Party State from its obligation to implement the award.

Article 28

Motion for Clarification

1. Any of the disputing Party States may request clarification of the award rendered by the Ad Hoc Arbitration Panel or the Permanent Appellate Tribunal, or the manner in which same should be implemented, within fifteen (15) days of its notification.

2. The Panel or Tribunal, as applicable, shall rule on the request within fifteen (15) days from its filing, and may grant an extension of time for implementing the award.

Article 29

Time Periods and Mode of Implementation

1. Awards rendered by the Ad Hoc Arbitral Panels or the Permanent Appellate Tribunal, as the case may be, shall be implemented within the time periods set in the relevant decision. If no time period is set, the awards shall be implemented within thirty (30) days of notification.

2. In the event that a Party State files a petition for review, implementation of the award rendered by the Ad Hoc Arbitral Panel shall be suspended while the appeal is pending.

3. Within fifteen (15) days from notification of the award, the Party State obligated to implement same shall inform the other party involved in the dispute, as well as the Common Market Group, through the Mercosur Administrative Secretariat, regarding the measures it will adopt to implement the award.

Article 30

Disagreements Regarding Implementation of Awards

1. In the event that the State benefiting from the award believes the measures adopted do not implement the award, it shall have a period of thirty (30) days from adoption of such measures to bring the matter to the attention of the Ad Hoc Panel or the Permanent Appellate Tribunal, as applicable.

2. The Panel or Tribunal shall have thirty (30) days from the date it undertakes the matter to settle the issues referred to in the preceding paragraph.

3. If the Ad Hoc Arbitral Panel that heard the matter cannot be convened, another one shall be formed with the necessary alternate(s) provided for in Articles 10.2 and 10.3.

CHAPTER IX
COMPENSATORY MEASURES
Article 31
Compensatory Measures

1. If a Party State involved in the dispute totally or partially fails to comply with the Arbitral Panel's award, the other Party involved in the dispute shall have the right, for a period of one (1) year, commencing the day following the expiration of the deadline set forth in Article 29.1, and independently from having recourse to the proceedings of Article 30, to initiate the application of temporary compensatory measures, such as the suspension of benefits or other equivalent obligations tending to induce implementation of the award.

2. The Party State benefited by the award shall endeavor first to suspend benefits or equivalent obligations in the affected sector or sectors. In the event that it considers suspension in the affected sector to be impracticable or ineffective, it shall have the right to suspend benefits or obligations in another sector, indicating the reasons that support that decision.

3. The Party State to be taking compensatory measures shall give formal notice a minimum of fifteen (15) days in advance to the non-complying Party State.

Article 32
Right to Challenge Compensatory Measures

1. When the Party State benefited by the award applies compensatory measures due to non-compliance with said award, and the non-complying Party State deems that the measures it has taken are satisfactory, the latter shall have fifteen (15) days from the notification provided in Article 31.3 to bring the situation to the consideration of the Ad Hoc Arbitral Panel or the Permanent Appellate Tribunal, as applicable, which in turn shall have thirty (30) days from the date it is convened to adjudicate the matter.

2. In the event that the non-complying Party State considers the compensatory measures applied to be excessive, it may request, up until fifteen (15) days after the application of said measures, that the Ad Hoc Arbitral Panel or the Permanent Appellate Tribunal, as applicable, rule with respect to this matter within a period of thirty (30) days from being convened.

i) The Panel or Tribunal shall rule on the compensatory measures adopted. It shall evaluate, as the case may be, the grounds stated for applying the measures in a different sector than the one affected, as well as their proportionality to the consequences of non-implementation of the award.

ii) In analyzing proportionality, the Panel or Tribunal shall take into consideration, among other elements, the volume and/or value of commerce in the affected sector, as well as all other harm or factors that influenced the determination of the level or amount of compensatory measures.

3. The Party State taking the compensatory measures shall align them with the decision of the Panel or Tribunal within ten (10) days, unless the Panel or Tribunal sets another time period.

CHAPTER X
PROVISIONS COMMON TO CHAPTERS VI AND VII
Article 33
Jurisdiction of the Panels

The Party States stipulate, *ipso facto* and without necessity of special agreement, that the jurisdiction of the Ad Hoc Arbitration Panels constituted in each case to hear and resolve the disputes referred to in this Protocol is exclusive, as is the Permanent Appellate Tribunal's jurisdiction to hear and resolve disputes in accordance with the powers conferred upon it by this Protocol.

Article 34
Choice of Law

1.The Ad Hoc Arbitration Panels and the Permanent Appellate Tribunal shall decide disputes in conformity with the Treaty of Asunción, the Ouro Preto Protocol, the protocols and agreements entered into within the framework of the Treaty of Asunción, the Decisions of the Common Market Council, the Resolutions of the Common Market Group and the Directives of the Mercosur Commerce Commission as well as applicable principles and provisions of International Law.

2. This provision does not restrict the authority of the Ad Hoc Arbitration Panels, or the Permanent Appellate Tribunal when acting directly and as sole recourse in conformity with Article 23, to decide disputes *ex aequo et bono,* if the parties so agree.

Article 35
Qualifications of Arbitrators

1. The members of the Ad Hoc Arbitration Panels and of the Permanent Appellate Tribunal shall be jurists of recognized expertise in fields that might be the subject of disputes and shall possess knowledge of the regulatory scheme of Mercosur.

2. The arbitrators shall observe the necessary impartiality and functional independence from the central government or direct administration of the Party States and should have no direct interest whatsoever in the dispute. They shall be appointed according to their objectivity, reliability and sound judgment.

Article 36
Expenses

1. The expenses and fees incurred for the services of the arbitrators shall be paid by the country who designated them, and the expenses of the Chair of the

Ad Hoc Arbitration Panel shall be paid in equal parts by the disputing Party States, unless the Panel decides to allot them differently.

2. The expenses and fees incurred for the services of the arbitrators of the Permanent Appellate Tribunal shall be paid in equal parts by the disputing Party States, unless the Board decides to allot them differently.

3. The expenses referred to in the paragraphs above may be paid through the Mercosur Administrative Secretariat. Payments may be made by means of a Special Fund that the Party States may create by depositing their respective contributions to the account of the Administrative Secretariat, pursuant to Article 45 of the Ouro Preto Protocol, or upon commencement of the proceedings provided for in Chapters VI or VII of this Protocol. The Fund shall be managed by the Mercosur Administrative Secretariat, who shall render an account annually regarding the use of said funds to the Party States.

Article 37

Fees and Other Expenses

Fees, traveling and lodging expenses, *per diems* and other arbitrators' expenses shall be determined by the Common Market Group.

Article 38

Headquarters

The Permanent Appellate Tribunal shall be headquartered in the city of Asunción. Notwithstanding, for good cause the Tribunal may hold special sessions in other Mercosur cities. The Ad Hoc Arbitration Panels may meet in any city of the Mercosur Party States.

CHAPTER XI

CLAIMS BY PRIVATE PARTIES

Article 39

Scope of Application

The proceedings established by this Chapter shall apply to claims brought by private parties (individuals or legal entities) in connection with the adoption or application, by any of the Party States, of legal or administrative measures having a restrictive, discriminatory or unfairly competitive effect, in violation of the Treaty of Asunción, the Decisions of the Common Market Council, the Resolutions of the Common Market Group and the Directives of the Mercosur Commerce Commission.

Article 40

Commencement of Proceedings

1. The private parties affected shall present their claims before the National Section of the Common Market Group in the Party State of their usual residence or principal place of business.

2. The private parties shall adduce evidence that permits determination of the likelihood of the violation and the existence or threat of harm, in order to have the claim recognized by the National Section and evaluated by the Common Market Group or a group of experts, if convened.

Article 41

Procedure

1. Unless the claim refers to an issue that has been the subject of dispute resolution proceedings in accordance with Chapters IV to VII of this Protocol, the National Section of the Common Market Group that recognized the claim pursuant to Article 40 of this Chapter shall initiate consultations with the National Section of the Common Market Group of the Party State charged with the violation in order to seek, thereby, an immediate resolution of the issue raised. Said consultations shall automatically and summarily be deemed concluded if the issue has not been resolved within fifteen days from the date the claim is notified to the Party State charged with the violation, unless the parties set a different deadline.

2. If the consultation period expires without a resolution having been reached, the National Section of the Common Market Group shall refer the claim directly to the Common Market Group.

Article 42

Intervention by the Common Market Group

1. Upon receipt of the claim, the Common Market Group shall evaluate the requirements established by Article 40.2 that formed the basis of the National Section's allowance of the claim at the first meeting following its receipt. If it concludes that the requirements necessary to allow the claim to proceed have not been satisfied, it shall reject the claim without further procedural steps, ruling by consensus.

2. If the Common Market Group does not reject the claim, it shall be deemed allowed. In this event, the Common Market Group shall immediately proceed to convene a group of experts that shall issue an opinion regarding its validity within a non-extendible thirty (30) day period from their designation.

3. Within this time period, the group of experts shall provide the claiming private party and the States involved the opportunity to be heard and to present their arguments at a joint hearing.

Article 43

Group of Experts

1. The group of experts referred to in Article 42.2 shall be formed by three (3) members designated by the Common Market Group, or, in the absence of agreement regarding one or more experts, these shall be chosen by vote of the Party States from a roster of twenty-four (24) experts. The Mercosur Adminis-

trative Secretariat shall inform the Common Market Group of the name of the expert or experts that received the most votes. In the latter event, and unless the Common Market Group decides differently, one (1) of the designated experts shall not be a national of the Responding State, nor of the State where the private party filed its claim pursuant to Article 40.

2. For purposes of drawing up the roster of experts, each Party State shall designate six (6) persons of recognized competence in areas that might be the subject of claims. Said roster shall be registered with the Mercosur Administrative Secretariat.

3. Any expenses arising from the participation of the group of experts shall be borne as determined by the Common Market Group or, in the absence of such agreement, shall be borne equally by each party to the dispute.

Article 44

Opinion of the Group of Experts

1. The group of experts shall submit its report to the Common Market Group.

i) If the validity of the claim against a Party State is verified by unanimous opinion, any other Party State may require it to adopt corrective measures or to discontinue the challenged measures. If this requirement does not yield results within fifteen (15) days, the Party State making same may have direct recourse to arbitration proceedings, pursuant to the conditions established in Chapter VI of this Protocol.

ii) Upon receipt of a unanimous opinion that a claim is without merit, the Common Market Group shall immediately deem the claim concluded in terms of this Chapter.

iii) In the event that the group of experts is unable to reach a unanimous opinion, it shall submit its separate conclusions to the Common Market Group, who shall immediately consider the claim concluded in terms of this Chapter.

2. The conclusion of the claim, in terms of subsections ii) and iii) of the preceding section, shall not preclude the Claiming Party State from initiating proceedings pursuant to Chapters IV through VI of this Protocol.

CHAPTER XII

GENERAL PROVISIONS

Article 45

Settlement or Voluntary Dismissal of Claim

At any stage of the proceedings, the party bringing forth the dispute or claim may withdraw the same, or the parties involved may reach a settlement. In either event, thereby concluding the dispute or claim. The Common Market Group, the Panel or the Tribunal, as the case may be, shall be informed of voluntary dismissals or settlements through the Mercosur Administrative Secretariat.

Article 46
Confidentiality

1. All documents produced in the context of proceedings under this Protocol shall be kept confidential by the disputing parties, except for arbitration awards.

2. At the discretion of the National Section of each Party State's Common Market Group, and whenever necessary for the elaboration of positions to be presented to the governing body, said documents may be revealed exclusively to those sectors having an interest in the matter.

3. Notwithstanding the provisions of section 1, the Common Market Council shall regulate the method of disclosure of the pleadings and evidence presented in previously concluded disputes.

Article 47
Regulations

The Common Market Council shall approve the regulations of this Protocol within sixty (60) days from the date it enters into effect.

Article 48
Time Limits

1. All periods of time prescribed or allowed by this Protocol are absolute. Such time periods shall be computed by consecutive calendar days, beginning the day after the designated act or event. Notwithstanding the above, if the deadline for filing any document or completing any procedural step does not fall on a business day at the headquarters of the Mercosur Administrative Secretariat, the time period for the required act extends to the next business day immediately after that date.

2. Notwithstanding the provisions of the preceding section, all time limits set by this Protocol may be modified by mutual agreement of the Parties involved in the dispute. The time limits set for proceedings conducted before the Ad Hoc Arbitration Panel and the Permanent Appellate Tribunal may be modified by the applicable authority upon the request Parties involved in the dispute.

CHAPTER XIII
TRANSITIONAL PROVISIONS
Article 49
Initial Notice

The Party States shall make the initial appointments and give the initial notices set forth in Articles 11, 18 and 43.2 within thirty (30) days from this Protocol's effective date.

Article 50
Pending Disputes

Pending disputes, commenced under the Brasilia Protocol's scheme shall be governed exclusively by the Brasilia Protocol until their conclusion.

Article 51

Rules of Procedure

1. Within thirty (30) days of its formation, the Permanent Appellate Tribunal shall adopt its own Rules of Procedure which must meet the approval of the Common Market Council.

2. The Model Rules, to be approved by the Common Market Council, shall serve as the basis for the Ad Hoc Arbitral Panel's own Rules of Procedure.

3. The rules referred to in the preceding sections of this Article shall guarantee that each disputing party has ample opportunity to be heard and present its arguments and shall ensure that proceedings are conducted expeditiously.

CHAPTER XIV

FINAL PROVISIONS

Article 52

Effective Date and Filing

1. This Protocol, an integral part of the Treaty of Asunción, shall become effective the thirtieth day after filing of the fourth ratification instrument.

2. The Republic of Paraguay shall be the depository of this Protocol and of the ratification instruments, and shall notify the other Party States of the filing date of said instruments by sending a duly authenticated copy of this Protocol to the other Party States.

Article 53

Revision of the System

Before finalizing the agreement process regarding a common foreign tariff, the Party States shall revise the current dispute resolution system in order to adopt the Permanent Dispute Settlement System for the Common Market referred to in paragraph 3 of Appendix III of the Treaty of Asunción.

Article 54

Ipso Jure Accession or Denouncement

1. Accession to the Treaty of Asunción shall constitute *ipso jure* accession to this Protocol.

2. Denouncement of this Protocol shall constitute *ipso jure* denouncement of the Treaty of Asunción.

Article 55

Repeal

1. On the effective date of this Protocol, it repeals the Brasilia Protocol for the Settlement of Disputes, signed on the 17th day of December of 1991 and the Regulations of the Brasilia Protocol, Decision CMC 17/98.

2. Notwithstanding the above, until all disputes commenced under the Brasilia Protocol regime are totally concluded, and until such time as the procedures

set forth in Article 49 are completed, the Brasilia Protocol and its Regulations shall continue to apply when appropriate.

3. References to the Brasilia Protocol made in the Ouro Preto Protocol and its Appendix are deemed incorporated herein as applicable.

Article 56

Languages

Spanish and Portuguese shall be the official languages in all proceedings pursuant to this Protocol.

Entered into in the City of Olivos, Province of Buenos Aires, Argentine Republic, on the eighteenth day of the month of February of the year two thousand two with one original in Spanish and in Portuguese, both language texts being equally official.

FOR THE ARGENTINE REPUBLIC

EDUARDO DUHALDE   CARLOS RUCKAUF

FOR THE FEDERATIVE REPUBLIC OF BRAZIL

FERNANDO HENRIQUE CARDOSO   CELSO LAFER

FOR THE REPUBLIC OF PARAGUAY

LUIS GONZALEZ MACCHI   JOSE ANTONIO MORENO RUFFINELLI

FOR THE ORIENTAL REPUBLIC OF URUGUAY

JORGE BATLLE IBAÑEZ   DIDIER OPERTTI

Index